A Positively Final Appearance

ALEC GUINNESS

A Positively Final
Appearance

A JOURNAL 1996-98

VIKING

VIKING
Published by the Penguin Group
Penguin Putnam Inc., 375 Hudson Street,
New York, New York 10014, U.S.A.
Penguin Books Ltd, 27 Wrights Lane,
London W8 5TZ, England
Penguin Books Australia Ltd,
Ringwood, Victoria, Australia
Penguin Books Canada Ltd, 10 Alcorn Avenue,
Toronto, Ontario, Canada M4V 3B2
Penguin Books (N.Z.) Ltd, 182-190 Wairau Road,
Auckland 10, New Zealand

Penguin Books Ltd, Registered Offices:
Harmondsworth, Middlesex, England

First American edition
Published in 1999 by Viking Penguin,
a member of Penguin Putnam Inc.

1   3   5   7   9   10   8   6   4   2

Frontispiece: Portrait of Sir Alec Guinness by Derek Hill, reproduced courtesy of the
National Portrait Gallery, London.

LIBRARY OF CONGRESS CATALOGING-IN-PUBLICATION DATA
Guinness, Alec, 1914–
A positively final appearance : a journal 1996–98 / Alec Guinness
p.   cm.
ISBN 0-670-88800-1
1. Guinness, Alec, 1914–   .   2. Actors—Great Britain Anecdotes
I. Title
PN2598.G8A3   1999
792'.028'092—dc21   99–14264

This book is printed on acid-free paper.

Printed in the United States of America
Set in MT Bembo

For Merula, yet again

But one man loved the pilgrim soul in you,
And loved the sorrows of your changing face.

W. B. YEATS

Contents

Acknowledgements

The author and publishers acknowledge permission to reprint the following excerpts:

W. H. Auden: excerpt from 'The Riddle' in *Collected Poems*, edited by Edward Mendelson, copyright © The Estate of W. H. Auden, 1976, 1991, reprinted by permission of Faber and Faber Ltd.

Rudyard Kipling: excerpts from 'Dawn off the Foreland' and 'The Centurion's Song', reprinted by permission of A. P. Watt Ltd on behalf of The National Trust for Places of Historic Interest or Natural Beauty.

Cole Porter: excerpt from 'Kiss Me Kate', words and music by Cole Porter, copyright © Cole Porter, Buxton-Hill-Music Corp., Warner/Chappell Music Ltd, 1968, reproduced by permission of IMP Ltd.

R. S. Thomas: excerpt from 'Raptor' in *No Truce with the Furies*, copyright © R. S. Thomas, 1995, reprinted by permission of Bloodaxe Books.

Martin Woodhead: excerpt reprinted by permission of the *Spectator*.

W. B. Yeats: excerpt from 'When You are Old' in *The Poems of W. B. Yeats: A New Edition*, edited by Richard J. Finneran, copyright © Anne Yeats, 1983, reprinted by permission of Simon & Schuster and of A. P. Watt Ltd on behalf of Michael B. Yeats.

Every effort has been made to trace copyright holders. The publishers are willing to rectify any omissions in future editions of the book.

Preface

We live in an age of apologies. Apologies, false or true, are expected from the descendants of Empire builders, slave owners, persecutors of heretics, and from men who, in our eyes, just got it all wrong. So, with the age of eighty-five coming up shortly, I want to be in the swing of fashion and make an apology. It appears I must apologize for being male, white and European. I have never found much difficulty in apologizing to God or man for my wrong-doings; and yet, at the moment, I find it difficult to put into words the necessity for apologizing for this ramshackle book. It states it is a Journal and yet it doesn't quite aspire to that and it isn't a diary. Not many dates are to be found in it.

It is, I suppose, like a sort of sluggish river meandering hopefully towards the open sea but diverted by various eddies, pools or tangential tributaries. A straightforward diary would have been simpler; for with that at least you might have the daily excitement as to whether we would be heading shortly for Wolverhampton, a hilltop village in Italy or an English seaside watering-hole. A firm decision is rarely taken; and that about sums it up.

My gratitude must be expressed to the *Spectator* for permitting me to borrow a paragraph or two from articles I wrote for their Diary page a few years ago; and to various people for kindly allowing me to quote from poems or books under their control.

For the better part of a year I have grumbled daily at the task I had set myself, knowing that I was too often scraping the bottom of the barrel of memory. None of the above is likely to induce anyone to delve into his wallet or her purse – but then think what they would be missing! – a perfectly genuine swansong, however lame. (When Pavlova, towards the end of her career, was dancing her famous *Dying Swan* at Edinburgh two Scots ladies at a matinée nudged each other and one said, 'Just like Mrs Wishart.' And they fell about laughing.)

The photograph on the cover is of me as Dr Wicksteed in Alan Bennett's *Habeas Corpus*, in 1973. I had asked Alan, and Ronald Eyre, who directed the play, if I might have a little solo dance at the very end depicting rapid decline, stiffening joints, decrepitude and the fear of old age and death. It was simply and effectively choreographed by Phiz Fazan for someone with no terpsichorean talent at all. The title of the book I chose from the stickers frequently seen pasted across old theatrical posters in the provinces, which were usually meaningless, as the actors allegedly making their final appearances often bobbed up again within a year. This is mostly explained in a chapter called 'Mummers on the Road', taken from Rembrandt's sketch *Two Mummers on Horseback*, reproduced on the back of the book cover by kind permission of the Pierpont Morgan Library in New York.

My appreciative thanks must go to Christopher Sinclair-Stevenson and Tony Lacey, who put their heads together to cajole, bully and encourage me to continue with a task about which I have been very doubtful. If they shared my doubts they managed to conceal the fact successfully, helpfully and with charm.

I would also like to thank my dogs Japheth, Dido and Flora, who instinctively knew the right moments to interrupt me with their urgent demands for 'treats'. And also the birds outside my study window, who constantly reassured me that nothing is desperately important and the joy of life is just looking at it.

1. Men as Trees, Walking

The view from the small, spotless white room on the twelfth floor of the hospital was almost Wordsworthian: the Houses of Parliament glowing in summer afternoon sunlight, the mud-coloured Thames slowly eddying as the tide turned and a string of barges chugging towards Westminster Bridge. The river probably wasn't as brown as it looked; the outside of the hospital window was filthy. I wondered if it would all look clearer to me in two days' time or possibly dimmer; clever people were to operate on my left eye, which had been almost useless for ten years and virtually blind for the past twelve months.

A voice behind me said, 'I'm your sister.' I turned round rather sharply to be confronted by a stalwart young man fluttering sheets of paper. 'Would you please fill in these forms?' he said. 'And accounts would like a cheque. Oh, and the TV isn't working.' He disappeared and I studied the small print.

The forms, as far as I could make out, required my agreement to exonerate the hospital, staff, doctors and surgeons from all culpability should there be any mishap. In short, the operation was all my fault and no questions asked. Well, I had to sign; and then I wrote a surprisingly large cheque, unpacked my small suitcase and settled myself, as best I could, on a slippery chair by the window with the latest Patrick O'Brian novel unopened on my lap. The sister-chap reappeared to say they would like to do some tests on me on the ground floor and a thousand miles away.

Having successfully bypassed a starch-faced nurse who was suspicious of me wandering around in her area, I eventually found the team who were to operate on me the next day. They were housed in a vast ill-lit cavern but exuded confidence and charm. One of them ran a sort of magic pencil over my eyelid while the others discussed with enthusiasm the swirling pictures they saw on their little TV screen. I had the impression they were keen to take out my eye and give it a good scrub.

One of them said, 'We will now tell you what we intend doing.'

'I would rather not know,' I said.

'But you *have* to know,' he went on, 'it's the law.'

More signing, I thought. 'You fire ahead,' I told him, 'and I'll stop my ears.' And I signed something which said I thoroughly understood what they were going to do. To this day I don't know what they got up to.

A very attractive, sophisticated, Argentinian lady with dazzling fair hair and a shimmering smile introduced herself as the anaesthetist. She asked me in a whisper if all my teeth were my own. I assured her they were and she gave a nod of relief and approval. We encountered each other again the following morning when I was wheeled into the presence of the team, who were now all dressed as for a TV medical soap opera. 'Is the Princess of Wales here?' I asked facetiously. They smiled politely behind their gauze masks. The Argentinian lady took my hand. 'Just a little prick,' she said. 'And now another little prick. Now I think we are feeling sleepy, yes?'

An hour and a half later I sort of woke up in the recovery room.

'All is over, all has been well done,' said Argentina. I tried to say 'Good!' or 'Amen' but the words stuck in my throat, which was fiery and raw. Wherefore could I not say 'Amen'? 'You have small passage,' Argentina explained rather severely. It crossed my mind that she might have taken revenge for the sinking of the *Belgrano* in the Falklands war; but no, she was too good-natured for that. 'Soon you have some voice,' she reassured me. 'Tomorrow perhaps.' As they wheeled me back to my room, at a dizzying pace, I wondered if I could sue them all if my vocal chords had been destroyed. Then I remembered the small print. An emphatic No.

There was neither pain nor even discomfort under my plastic eyeshield, just the slightest irritation. With my good eye I looked towards Big Ben, which was striking ten o'clock. A sunny morning. I fell asleep.

Later in the day I croaked at a nurse that I would love some ice-cream. That proved a great comfort. The brilliant surgeon and Argentina looked in to see how I was and they were followed by a couple of jolly Scottish technicians who turned out to be *Star Wars* enthusiasts. They wanted me to write 'May the Force be with you' on scraps of paper.

No one mended the TV. I didn't see Sister again.

That was 14 August 1996.

The following morning I was told I could go home. As I didn't fancy the fifty-odd-mile car journey down to Petersfield after a general anaesthetic I booked myself a room at the Connaught. I got there at noon. It was another lovely day. As soon as I was by myself I took off the eyeshield. I was so astonished I burst into happy tears. The eye that had been operated on could see quite sharply and in full colour. The bedroom furniture was clearly defined, the bed-cover – which had a delicate, complicated pattern – looked brightly new and, at the window, I could see to the far side of Carlos Place. The only oddity was the bedroom door, which appeared decidedly crooked.

A week after the operation a slight deterioration set in. 'Just a little detritus,' the surgeon said. 'Give it a month or two. It'll get better and better.' I live in hope, of a sort. Hope has never been a virtue of mine. Gratitude I believe I do express, or certainly mean to. The operation has been more successful than expected. A useless eye can now see 'Men as trees, walking'; 'After that he put his hands again upon his eyes and made him look up; and he was restored, and saw every man clearly.' At least, when I look out of the back door with my good eye closed, I can tell whether it is my wife or the milkman.

This is not going to be the end of the eye saga. Cataracts are forming rapidly on both eyes. I was wondering if the national press had started to use grey printers' ink. Forty years ago I started complaining about the fuzzy printing of the London telephone directory (now nauseatingly called *The Phone Book*) but a pair of glasses rectified that. A few years ago I became exasperated by what I took to be the sloppy diction of a new generation of actors; a little machine in the ear assured me that their speech was fine, except for the slipshod accents they choose to use.

The humiliations of age are not always easy to accept.

2. A Dry Month

During the early part of March I spent a lot of time on medical jaunts, crossing, recrossing and criss-crossing the area bounded by Wimpole, Wigmore and Harley Streets. London provides intense specialist areas, whether in diamonds, bookshops, silver, painting, antiques or disease. It was the route of possible disease which I was following. It is not the consultations which are depressing but the awareness, as you trudge the empty pavements, that behind almost every façade are gloomy, high-ceilinged waiting-rooms with worn brocaded armchairs and polished tables covered with dog-eared, out-of-date copies of *Vogue*, *Country Life* and *The National Geographic*. In the corner of each room there is likely to be sitting, patiently resigned and sadly far from his palace or tent, a sheikh or eastern princeling; *Vanity Fair* will be of no interest to him and, probably, not even *Hello!*.

A trip to my doctor in Sloane Square – is valetudinarianism setting in? – led to the suggestion that there might just be a suspicion of cancer of the prostate; so off to Harley Street again.

A charming, very tall Australian chappie with a warm Sydney accent showed me into a small room which contained a high bed of sorts and a rather sinister little TV set. The TV was showing a static black and white image of what looked like a bunch of a few late chrysanthemums. The young man took my jacket and told me to lie on the bed. 'Doctor'll be here in a minute,' he said. 'Just undo the top of your pants. Doctor'll do the rest.' Catching my look of mild apprehension he sought to comfort me. 'They tell me you used to be quite somebody in the art world,' he said, with amazing admiration. I clicked a little snort of denial. 'No, truly,' he said. 'That's what the receptionist thinks.' He had a devastating smile, which could wipe away the slightest umbrage. I recalled the old, aristocratic actor Ernest Thesiger being stopped in Piccadilly by a woman who said, 'Didn't you used to be Ernest Thesiger?' 'Still am!' he hissed, and passed on. The Aussie dropped his smile and announced, 'Here comes Doctor. Ease your pants down a little, lie on your side and raise your knees. Comfy?'

The doctor, after asking a few questions, turned to his assistant and, without a trace of drama, said, 'Make me up a balloon.' A balloon? What the hell could they be thinking of? Bravely I determined to neither wince nor cry out. He probed me with some sonic device and I hardly felt a thing. His eye was kept on the TV and occasionally he gave a little grunt of satisfaction but whether that boded ill or well I couldn't decide. After ten minutes or so the doctor had finished and assured me that there wasn't any sign of cancer. Smiles all round. I asked him to repeat that; which he did with emphasis. As I left the room I threw a glance at the TV. The old clump of chrysanthemums was back on screen, bleakly indifferent. I was tempted to ask them, 'How was it for you?' but contented myself with a subdued but joyful wave of the hand.

Naturally I telephoned Merula, as soon as possible. When I had left for London in the morning she had suffered a sudden bout of inner-ear trouble which threw her off balance and caused nausea. As soon as she heard I was cancer-free her giddiness disappeared. Well, I suppose that has explicable reasons but I feel it is not far removed from the telepathic communications we sometimes experience, though these are usually about the most trivial everyday things.

Here we are in the midst of an ugly election campaign – but that is what they have always been – in spite of avowals from all parties that it will be a clean fight. The Lib Dems are the only people who, so far, have kept their heads; but then they haven't a hope of winning, so their warnings that they would put up income tax will not be put to the test. I don't know who our local candidates are. The only appeal for our votes has come from the Referendum Party, which pushed a video cassette through the letter-box. An extravagant gesture. We don't have a video so it was flipped into the waste-paper basket with a lot of German and American *Star Wars* fan mail. Like unsolicited, unwanted, trashy mail it can take its chance in some remote and receding galaxy.

The awe-inspiring events of the month have been the arrival of the comet Hale-Bopp and the descent from a clear sky of Mr President Bush. He was attached to what looked like a rainbow lilo. A perfect landing was greeted rapturously by Mrs Bush. For seventy-two he looked trim and trustworthy. Perhaps our politicians could be persuaded to follow suit by jumping all together from a plane. A free fall for all. It would certainly attract the media. The gleeful speculation and excitement for us at the grass roots would surpass the Grand National.

Hale-Bopp (I like the classy Home Counties hyphen) is an awesome sight, particularly when seen through binoculars, and makes all our current political activity no more than a tiny puff of dust. We are told it is made of ice and frozen gas and is the size of London, travelling at 100,000 m.p.h. From here in Petersfield, when the night skies are clear, we see it to the NW at about 30° over The Hangers. At first I thought its tail was shuddering with speed but it was the trembling of my hand holding the glasses, so impressed was I to be looking at something not seen even by Socrates, Christ or Shakespeare. The astronomers tell us that it hasn't been glimpsed by the human eye for around four thousand years and it will be another four thousand before it drops in again. We shall not be at home; none of us. Tony Blair, John Major, David Mellor, Princess Margaret, the latest hair-designer, all the pop groups, the City magnates, brave yachtsmen and mountaineers will have lain long and quiet in Melstock churchyard, together with Uncle Tom Cobley, Edith Sitwell and us of lower degree when Hale-Bopp next passes by.

By the year 6000 even our approaching second millennium will be seen to have been small beer.

March has slipped by with but a few lion-like winds and barely a drop of rain. Apparently it is the driest spring month for two hundred years so drought is predicted for the summer and already there are warnings about the use of garden hoses. Reservoirs are alarmingly low and rivers skimpy; we are told of millions of gallons of water just seeping away through water companies' broken pipes. In spite of dry ground this has been easily the best year for daffodils in our neck of the woods; but they haven't lasted as long as usual. The big plane tree which stands fifty yards from my study window and which was pollarded two years ago looks derelict − not the smallest green flick of a budding leaf. Last year it was vigorous; now it looks like a tree shelled in the 1914−18 war.

We have seen nothing in the theatre but took ourselves to three films − *Shine*, *Ridicule* and *The English Patient*. *Ridicule* was gripping, witty and beautifully acted. *Shine* involved us emotionally; not only is it marvellously done but among all the superb acting there is a truly great performance by Armin Mueller-Stahl, who plays the father. Marta Kaczmarek was particularly fine as the mother.

They say the book of *The English Patient* is very good but I'm afraid the film left us totally indifferent. I had the impression that the other customers, all four of them, in a six-hundred-seater cinema at an early evening performance, felt as blankly as we did. They groped their way out with unenthusiastic faces, muttering in monosyllables. Emerging into Shaftesbury Avenue, with its half a dozen glittering theatres, was like re-encountering a real world. We had been deceived by the hype and the razz-matazz of the Oscars. It was good to look at but too often suggested bits and pieces of David Lean classics. At least we were spared the Lara theme from *Dr Zhivago*. The next time I see the admirable Mr Ralph Fiennes I hope he will have sloughed off his latex face. It is always a mistake to let the make-up department have a field day. God knows I have submitted a few times to artistic endeavour but eventually I learned to do about three films without any make-up at all. Nowadays, of course, most actors look real and it is the newscasters and politicians who are painted an inch thick with artificial suntan, giving the impression that they have left their skis, momentarily, outside the studio.

A refurbished *Star Wars* is on somewhere or everywhere. I have no intention of revisiting any galaxy. I shrivel inside each time it is mentioned. Twenty years ago, when the film was first shown, it had a freshness, also a sense of moral good and fun. Then I began to be uneasy at the influence it might be having. The bad penny first dropped in San Francisco when a sweet-faced boy of twelve told me proudly that he had seen *Star Wars* over a hundred times. His elegant mother nodded with approval. Looking into the boy's eyes I thought I detected little star-shells of madness beginning to form and I guessed that one day they would explode.

'I would love you to do something for me,' I said.

'Anything! Anything!' the boy said rapturously.

'You won't like what I'm going to ask you to do,' I said.

'Anything, sir, anything!'

'Well,' I said, 'do you think you could promise never to see *Star Wars* again?'

He burst into tears. His mother drew herself up to an immense height. 'What a *dreadful* thing to say to a child!' she barked, and dragged the poor kid away. Maybe she was right but I just hope the lad, now in his thirties, is not living in a fantasy world of secondhand, childish banalities.

A couple of weeks ago, in a Chinese restaurant, the dapper little Chinese maître D bowed low as I left and, full of Chinese smiles, said, 'Sir Guin, now that *Star Wars* is being shown again you will be famous once more.' Oh, to be Ernest Thesiger.

The mornings, during the past few weeks, have started quite sharply and yet gently blurred in hazy sunshine. There is a very rounded cherry tree in the middle of the paddock, now in flower, but the haze softly obliterates the trunk of the tree, leaving the blossom looking as if it might be a small pinkish-white cloud that has settled with us. It spreads a feeling of calm like a blessing. I stand out of doors in my dressing-gown, gazing at it with gratitude, but know that all too soon there will be a thud of letters falling through the letter-box, including glossy photographs which no ordinary pen can sign. As often as not they have already been signed in a sprawling gilded signature by 'Darth Vader' from *Star Wars* – 'so-and-so IS Darth Vader'. Maybe – but it wasn't so-and-so's voice or face (when it was finally revealed) to the best of my remembrance. The 'IS', I suppose, is for reassurance, like clutching at something when waking from a bad dream.

Last Sunday, as Mass was finishing, a young man leaned over my shoulder and said, 'My pop is a great fan of *Star Wars*. Will you say hello to him as you leave the church?'

I asked where his father was.

'At the back in a wheelchair,' he said.

The priest gave his blessing and the ritual words, 'The Mass is over, go in peace.'

'Thanks be to God,' we chorused back, the young man adding, 'And can I have your autograph?'

'Not here,' I replied rather crossly.

At the back of the church, sitting in a wheelchair, was a large, middle-aged, genial-looking man. I went up to him all smiles, like a baby-kissing politician, and exuding the sweet benevolence of a hospital-visiting princess. I took him warmly by the hand and made one or two fatuous inquiries. He suddenly said the dreaded words – '*Star Wars!*'

'Ugh – hugh –uh –ha –hm,' I said, but I kept up my smile.

'Obi-Wan Kenobi,' he nodded at me and, for good measure, 'May the Force be with you.'

'And also with you,' I replied, to ecclesiastical merriment.

'*The Man in the White Suit*; that was you, wasn't it?'

'Yes, about forty-five years ago,' I replied, with a sense of relief that we might have reached saner ground; anyway terra firma. Then his face became grave and he said, 'Darth Vader.'

I backed away as quickly as possible, sketched him a valedictory wave of the hand and stumbled down the church steps into fresh air and morning sunlight. The young man pursued me. 'The autograph,' he said, quite politely. But that was suddenly too much for me. 'Not in front of the parishioners,' I said. Then I disappeared.

A second later I was deeply ashamed but the damage had been done. No excuse. Just sudden bloody-mindedness and panic. It's no good saying to myself, 'Watch out in these declining years, things could turn nasty.' Donkey's years ago I remember seeing an elderly man in Harrods screaming and screaming at a shop assistant because she was buffing her nails. I felt sad contempt for him and it never occurred to me to mutter, 'There, but for the Grace of God, go I some day in the future.'

The evening news announced that dust bowls have formed on the dry farmlands of Cornwall. Cornwall, of all places, where there used to be so many hedges.

We all need hedges, I thought. They don't have to be prickly though, like mine.

3. The Cruellest Month

At six this morning I rejoiced to see dark, rain-laden clouds shifting up from the south-west. Rain at last for the parched land – or so I surmised. I was wrong; the clouds have thinned out to a pale grey blanket and not a raindrop has fallen. The wind is bitter, tearing the camellia to shreds, and the daffodils are like twists of brown paper: but then we have always known in this country that April is untrustworthy.

'Untrustworthy' is the keyword in the election campaign the nation is currently suffering. Each side accuses the other of duplicity or worse – at any rate the Tories and New Labour do – while the Lib Dems are virtually ignored. Two weeks to the election and the squabbles on radio and TV are getting more raucous. 'Trust us,' they all shout, but trust them to do what? Just to behave themselves in the House of Commons would be something. I suppose, come 1 May, I should vote New Labour, except that locally they haven't a chance. At the last election Labour clocked up about five thousand votes against something approaching thirty thousand for these blue remembered hills. I couldn't bring myself to vote for the sitting Tory candidate, even if I was in sympathy with the cabinet or its rebellious backbenchers. So, in spite of the Lib Dem leader's furrowed brow and the fact that I barely know the names or faces of any of his colleagues (which have been a well-kept secret) I shall endeavour to find out the name of the local yellow candidate and, on the day, place my mark against it. It won't make any difference. If only one party had a bold, enthusiastic, pro-European line I would be genuinely behind it. Without Europe I have a gut feeling we are lost.

Of course, one of the troubles with the Lib Dems is that they have a very poor record on the abortion issue and I fear, given the chance, they would recommend euthanasia all round. Painful as it would be I confess I like their honest, gloomy insistence on putting up taxes to pay for education, etc. Instinctively I am a Whiggamore but I find aristocratic Whigs snobbish and most of the others smug.

It might have been sensible, during these fraught, political, April days to have reread Trollope's *The Prime Minister*. (I was never convinced by reports of Mr Major's appreciation of it.) Instead I settled for *The Way We Live Now*; the third time of reading. First published in serial form in 1874, its picture of 'sleaze' in England at that time is either dispiriting, if you take the view that we are still in the same moral trough of greed and deception, or slightly encouraging, in a cynical way, if you shrug it all off with the observation, 'So the Victorians were sleazy before us.' *Plus ça change*, etc. In any case *The Way We Live Now* is a great book and I suppose we shouldn't be surprised that it made but little appeal when it first appeared. There is no character to root for in a big way – Roger Carbury is upright and admirable but stiff in manner and snobbish; his cousin Felix Carbury is an unspeakable shit and his sister, Hetta Carbury, although pleasing in many ways, is a remote sort of heroine. All the characters are spot on and might have been caught today on concealed video cameras. When my eye falls on full-page advertisements for menswear – handsome young men posed in sharp suits, leering sulkily and sexlessly – I shall mutter to myself, 'Good casting for Sir Felix Carbury.'

One of the constant minor joys of reading Trollope is coming across descriptions of little gestures which reveal character in much the same way as a good actor does, either deliberately or half-consciously. There is an example early on in *The Way We Live Now* in his description of Father John Barham, a young, overenthusiastic, gentlemanly Catholic priest. 'He had thick dark brown hair, which was cut short . . . but which he so constantly ruffled by the action of his hands, that, although short, it seemed to be wild and uncombed . . . In discussions he would constantly push back his hair, and then sit with his hand fixed on the top of his head.' I have seen many highly strung intellectuals do the same thing. The pleasure lies in recognizing, today, habits which were to be found among us a hundred and twenty years ago however much the mores and manners have changed; and a hundred years before that, and before that as well. The sense of continuity, going both backwards and forwards, I find endlessly rewarding.

Shakespeare's birthday, 23 April; he would be four hundred and thirty-three today so I greeted him by going to the Odeon, Marble Arch, to see Baz Luhrmann's film *William Shakespeare's Romeo and Juliet*. I enjoyed it a lot and I find my mind keeps returning to its images and ideas, but I regret the title. 'Rom and Jule' or 'Eo and let' or 'Cut him out in little stars' or 'A word and a blow' or 'Peppered for this world' would all be extravagant but possible titles, and more justifiable.

The story comes over strong and very excitingly, in much the same way as it did in *West Side Story*. But the plots of Shakespeare's plays are nearly all good and remain gripping in spite of familiarity. I never understand why drama critics are so dismissive of most of the stories. This film has everything going for it except the greatest ingredient, the verse. For the verse there is substituted powerful visual imagery. Needless to say that, set in modern times in some Verona in Mexico, the verse is cut to shreds and minimalized; speech is often inaudible because it is either whispered or shouted or mumbled through lips munching at other lips – such as we are boringly used to in sex dramas. But somehow Shakespeare survives. There are reasonably well-sustained passages; thought and feelings are always present; and what a relief it is to listen to American accents dealing with Shakespeare. They sound much more authentic than our own overrefined or suburban efforts. The Prince, played by a black

actor as a chief-of-police, speaks admirably and some of the
others throw in a well-spoken line – and that is about all they
have the chance to do, so far as speech is concerned.

A young black actor, wearing corkscrewed dreadlocks, cross-
dressed into a silver lamé miniskirt and tottering on great wedge
shoes, plays Mercutio – a performance about as far away from
Olivier's macho, vulgar, rumbustious Mercutio in 1935 as you
could get. I thought I would quickly weary of the black campery
but then came the Queen Mab speech and I was thrilled by its
sinister drug-induced quality. The speech has always seemed to
me tiresome (all that talk about fairy coachmakers and wagon
spokes made of daddy-long-legs' legs is almost as wearisome as
Rossetti's 'Goblin Market') and downright embarrassing when
delivered by a bluff actor trying to be cute. The speech is
decimated in the film but nevertheless is a revelation, demanding
a new look at all hackneyed set pieces. What was intriguing
about this Mercutio was the way in which, when he substituted
blue jeans and T-shirt for the glittering drag, his performance
deepened. The wit was still there but a dimension of impending
doom was added.

TYBALT: . . . a word with one of you.
MERCUTIO: And but *one* word with *one* of us? *Couple* it with something,
  make it a word and a *blow*.

The light emphasis on 'blow' was outrageous but funny. I had
feared it was all going to be American brat-pack stuff but it
quickly rose above that. Miriam Margolyes did wonders with
what was left to her of the Nurse and caused me to shed a tear;
a modest, perceptive performance, never striving for laughs and
always totally believable. I did *not* believe in Friar Laurence giving
a botanical or chemistry lesson to two small boys while delivering
his opening speech about 'baleful weeds and precious-juiced
flowers'. And I always suspend belief, whatever the film, when
a camera glides us around a Catholic church; there is always a

blaze of limb-sized candles, vast blue and white statues of the BVM and never a sign of the Tabernacle or anyone at their devotions. But I did believe this boy and the girl were in love, even when Shakespeare's balcony scene was played by them up to their necks in water in Mr Capulet's swimming-pool.

The worst Romeo ever to disgrace our boards was given by none other than me, *moi-même*. It was to be seen, a bird of ill omen, in Perth during the summer of 1939. I wore a reddish wig (I can't think why), a droopy moustache (a big mistake) and Larry Olivier's cast-offs from the Gielgud production of four years earlier. Pamela Stanley, who had recently made a success in the West End as Queen Victoria, played Juliet and brought to the part all sorts of pretty little Victorian manners; in fact everything except a German accent.

The first night was memorable. I leapt the garden wall for the balcony scene – 'He jests at scars that never felt a wound' – whereupon the wall fell flat. With professional sang-froid I ignored the whole thing and struck a romantic pose of extreme yearning.

> But soft, what light through yonder window breaks?
> It is the east and Juliet is the sun.

At which moment the balcony fell off, to reveal, gasping with astonishment, Miss Stanley in her nightie. Another foot forward and she would have tumbled to her eternal rest. The curtain was lowered. After ten minutes of hammering we started again, to tumultuous applause. The audience was thoroughly enjoying the mishaps, as they always do, but they also wanted, I think, to show their admiration for Miss Stanley not succumbing to the vapours. A few nights later we got successfully as far as 'It is the east and Juliet is the sun' when – no, not so, there was no Juliet. Distant cries for help were heard; she was locked in the lavatory. The curtain was lowered once more while the stage carpenter was sent to release her. It should never have risen again but we persevered. On the last night my ginger moustache got stuck to the phial of poison and after much spluttering with Romeo's last line, 'Thus with a kiss I die', it managed to transfer itself to Miss Stanley's lips. She was not amused.

A day before the dress rehearsal of Romeo I had done a wicked thing, of a sort that I had never done before and never, I hasten to add, since. I would be too scared. There were costume fittings in the theatre wardrobe in the afternoon to be followed by a run-through of the play in the evening. Motley had designed the beautiful and simple costumes which Olivier had worn in 1935 and which now came my way. They fitted perfectly. However, the lady in charge of the wardrobe for this production, a Mrs Lewis, had decided they needed prettifying. Without my knowledge, she had glittering sequins spangled all over my dark red velvet doublet. I blew my top, said they must all be ripped out or I wouldn't wear it, and stumped off back to my digs in high dudgeon. Merula was in the kitchen preparing some haddock for my meal while I kept up a wildly indignant account of the wardrobe department's tastelessness through the open door to the sitting-room. Suddenly I noticed on the mantelpiece a small lump of grey Plasticine, presumably left there by a child of the previous occupants of our rooms. I picked it up and started to model it into a crude little figurine, at the same time calling out to Merula, half laughingly, what I was doing.

'*You* are Mrs Lewis,' I said, 'and I have found a needle and I'm going to stick it into you.'

Merula screamed from the kitchen, 'You're not to *do* that! It's very wicked.'

'I'm only joking,' I called back. 'I won't stick the needle into her middle, I'll just prick her left foot.' So I added a little foot and stuck the needle in it. Then I forgot all about it and enjoyed my haddock, bread-'n-butter and tea. An hour or so later I was back at the theatre. At the stage door I was greeted by ashen faces.

'Isn't it terrible what happened to Mrs Lewis?' one of them said.

'What happened?'

'The ambulance has only just taken her away,' said another. 'She dropped a red-hot iron on her foot.'

'Which foot?'

'The left. She was in terrible agony. I hope they don't have to amputate it.'

They didn't. I have remained conscience-stricken and chastened ever since.

Recalling that spookiness of fifty-eight years ago puts me in mind of a very different, but also slightly spooky, incident on 22 April this year. I woke in the morning wondering if it would be acceptable or not to write a short note to Martin Bell to wish him good luck in the election campaign, in which he is standing as an Independent in Cheshire. I barely know him – we met only once, and chatted for a minute or two at a crowded party not long after he had been nastily wounded in Bosnia. I liked him. On this Tuesday morning I decided at 11 a.m. that I would drop him a line. I wrote: 'Dear Mr Bell, This is just a note to wish you well on 1 May.' I was about to continue, the ink was scarcely dry at the full stop, when the telephone rang. It was my agent in London saying, 'We have just had a fax from Mr Martin Bell's campaign manager asking, should you happen to be sympathetic to his election effort, if you would be prepared to send him a line of encouragement.' Naturally I immediately finished my brief letter and posted it. It was the exactness of the timing which startled me.

Lady Windermere is up and down the country leaving her fan on various seats. There has been such a flutter of Wilde in recent years that I begin to wonder if he has come to represent the soul of the nation. Two nights ago I had intended to go to see Alec McCowen and Michael Gambon in *Tom and Clem* or *Clem and Tom*, the new play about Attlee and Driberg, but at the last minute decided I would go mad if I had to listen to any more political talk during all this electioneering, so went instead to see Simon Callow in *The Importance of Being Oscar* at the Savoy.

Clem and Tom, or vice versa, shall have my custom when Mr Blair has settled in as Prime Minister.

Simon has enormous energy and conviction. He had done a matinée before the performance I saw and when I went round to see him afterwards I felt he would be quite prepared to start all over again. Apart from anything else it is a prodigious feat of memory – two hours' solid high-powered talking at each performance. The audience was rather sparse and pretty peculiar but hadn't thrown him in the least. A pasty-faced young woman sat next to me accompanied by the mother of all popcorn paper bags. She shovelled the stuff in at enormous speed, crunched away and then rattled the bag as if she was conducting a game of bingo. I shifted my seat and found myself in front of two large white-haired women who had a lot to whisper to each other. I shifted again. This time I was about four seats away from a surly-looking youth who produced a bottle of beer from his anorak pocket, opened it with a Swiss Army knife, and glugged from the neck of the bottle. This time I removed to the very back of the dress circle, where I was alone.

Simon's recitation of 'Reading Gaol' was very impressive but he used so much voice at one moment that I think he put paid to my hearing-aid. And I mean paid; about £700. I haven't dared test it since. The drama critics, for the most part, seem to have preferred the second, more serious, part of the entertainment, but I think I preferred the light-heartedness of the first. Without the horrors and ignominy of the trial – which is assumed to have taken place in the interval – the full pathos and drama is missing; a touch of sentimentality rears its pretty head. Well, Wilde now has his little place in the Abbey (a small lozenge in a stained-glass window) and society has paid him its debt. I wish he could rest in peace.

New Labour is in with a vast majority and the Lib Dems have doubled their number of seats. There have been some enjoyable falls from grace of faces and attitudes we have got sick of. In five years' time we shall probably be sick of the new lot, but with their powerful numbers they will be hard to shift. Mr Major conceded defeat with dignity, calm and a sad charm; obviously a good man. Mr Blair paid him, properly, a courteous and kindly tribute, which was only marred by some feeble booing from a few undesirables in the crowd in Downing Street.

Martin Bell, to my great relief, got in as an Independent with a healthy majority of eleven thousand. He looked somewhat bemused. I do hope that when he enters Parliament he will abandon that crumpled white suit which he has made his logo. It would be amusing to see him in a navy-blue double-breasted pinstripe, but wearing sneakers.

The ugliest little scene on TV was the hissing spat on the Putney electoral platform when the local results were announced, between Mellor and a slow-hand-clapping Goldsmith. It was as edifying as a snake pit. As both candidates failed to win the seat the petty rumpus will be swiftly forgotten in the dust of contemporary history.

There is no doubt that the nation feels it has taken a gulp of fresh air. People's eyes look more hopeful and their voices sound more confident. It was much the same when the Queen came to the throne in 1952; we talked with excitement of a new Elizabethan Age and rejoiced in the infectious smile of an attractive young monarch. The Beatles, the dismissal of the censor, *Hair*, the royal infidelities and divorces, and the actual shaking of the dynasty lay in the future and were not discerned in our bright blue crystal ball. Now we live in determined expectation that well-stuffed brown envelopes are a thing of the past. The new Prime Minister has broadened his smile, if that is possible. On his return from Buckingham Palace after his appointment as the Queen's chief minister, he spoke well, warmly and with controlled emotion. And yet, for my taste, it was a little too similar to an Oscar acceptance speech. Everyone was meticulously remembered and genuinely thanked, including his mother, who is no longer alive.

Mr Major spent the afternoon watching cricket at Lords. He

wore dark glasses. It was a day of blazing sunshine. The six-week campaign must have been gruelling for them all; it certainly was for us, the wearied spectators. One wonders if for the next week or so they will have the energy to govern or the opposition the will to oppose.

The last days of April were warm with glorious sunshine; May started hot and bright. Now some much-needed rain has come in fits and starts, driven by strong cold winds. Flowers have flowered abnormally early and died before their time. There is snow, we are told, on the high ground and making its way south. This afternoon there has been sleet mixed with sunshine.

Mr Blair faces 'his May of youth'. We keep our fingers crossed that it won't be much ado about nothing.

4. Matter for a May Morning

Only twice in my life have I sidled through the glossy black door of Number 10. The first occasion was during the premiership of Major Attlee, when I was bidden to a bunfight which must have been attended by about sixty elderly ladies in velour hats and coupon clothing. I cannot remember what the event was in aid of but I have a clear memory of leaning against an open door in a large room while balancing a teacup and saucer. There was a little shuddering or resistance from behind the door and perhaps a muffled protest. I eased the door a bit and a rather squashed, disgruntled Prime Minister emerged from behind it. He had probably been hiding from the more serious ladies among his guests who had calculating eyes on him. I mumbled apologies and escaped.

The second time I squeezed into Number 10, some years ago, was with a great flurry of showbiz and media folk, all of us invited to a pre-dinner drinks bash given by Mrs Thatcher. Our names were announced in stentorian tones as we were propelled towards our hostess. I had never seen her in the flesh before and I was astonished, indeed captivated, by her splendid appearance; it wouldn't surprise me to be told I had genuflected. Well, when in Rome, etc.

Mrs Thatcher was most elegantly dressed from top to toe in some glittering, form-friendly gown which appeared to be made of minute metallic tiles; black, dark green and midnight blue. Perhaps it was bullet-proof. But it was the Eyes that had it; they were amazingly and totally mesmeric. I couldn't help feeling that she might single me out and whisper, 'There is a tree in the midst of the garden of Number 10, with a magnificent apple on it. Come with me and you shall have a bite.' But the announcing gentleman was booming out other names and Mrs Thatcher's eyes swivelled and focused elsewhere. David Lean kept plucking at my sleeve in a state of high excitement, hissing between clenched teeth, 'She is all woman, all woman, all woman!' And heavens, with his experience, he would have known.

I slipped away as soon as I could do so with decency. Besides, Sir Richard (as was) Attenborough, or maybe it was Sir Dirk (as is) Bogarde, was receiving a *lot* of attention and I suddenly felt like a discarded shoe.

The new Prime Minister has announced his intention of living with his family in 11 Downing Street and Mr Gordon Brown, the new C of E, single as yet, will occupy the flat at Number 10. That all sounds like sensible good housekeeping. The little spotless kitchen in the flat, glimpsed from time to time on TV when Mrs Thatcher was preparing her Marmite sandwiches, would be much too small for a young family.

Today we hear that the new Chancellor has upped the interest rate by a fraction and liberated the Bank of England from much government control. I simply don't understand such things but the speedy moves and decisiveness must surely impress everyone. Meanwhile, I am sorry to say, the Tories are already crying '*Et tu, Brute!*' at each other and fumbling with their daggers.

Oh, I must be careful, even in my most rambling, feeble thoughts. Yesterday evening, opening Sir Thomas Browne's *Religio Medici* at random, I came across, 'The cause of truth might suffer in the weakness of my patronage.' That gave me a salutary pause.

The manners and mores of the civilized world have changed much in the past forty years, sometimes recognizably for the better; or so it seems to these old tortoise eyes when I stretch my neck out of my carapace.

The ten-year-old daughter of a friend of mine brought me in 1960 an unexpected birthday present. She was a quaint, bright child, very Victorian in appearance. 'Many happy returns,' she said, handing me an envelope which obviously contained a paperback book. 'I bought it with my own money; it didn't cost much,' she added. I took out the book and thanked her warmly. She looked at it, I thought, with a touch of envy. 'It's the book all grown-ups want to read,' she explained. It was, of course, *Lady Chatterley's Lover*, recently made available in all the High Streets of the country. Housewives were popping it in their shopping bags with groceries in keen anticipation of a good afternoon's read. I didn't let on that I had read it in 1933, when I was working as a copywriter in an advertising agency.

The copy which I read – plain paper cover in those censored days – had been smuggled from France by one of the staff and was doing the rounds of the office. It was probably a month before it reached my humble desk. It had not been greatly appreciated as literature, I felt, as many of the pages had been barely turned; but a dozen or so were grey, greasy and dog-eared. Somewhere at the back of my mind I see a couple of typists removing the slides from their hair and letting it go loose while at the same time casting strange glances at the office Mellors. The office Mellors, for his part, kept up his usual phallic chit-chat and continued to shuffle through his collection of semi-pornographic snapshots. D. H. Lawrence, Penguin Books and obscenity laws would never mean anything to him – life would go on in the same suggestive way it always had.

Watching an episode of the TV *Lady Chatterley* some time ago and wanting more volume I accidentally pressed the wrong button. For a second or two I didn't realize what I had done. Things looked much the same – a vast baronial hall, candlelight. 'But wait a moment,' I thought. 'Why is Mellors dressed as a butler? And Sir Clifford is being highly mobile without his wheelchair.' Then the penny dropped; Fry and Laurie as Jeeves and Wooster. The dialogue seemed just as funny as D. H. Lawrence's, so I stayed with Channel 4.

Sometime in 1993 the *Spectator* set a competition which required the retelling of a well-known piece of literature in the metre of 'Hiawatha'. Mr Martin Woodhead was the winner with his version of *Lady Chatterley's Lover.*

> You shall hear how Lady Constance,
> Tiring of her wounded husband
> (Poor Sir Clifford, high war-hero,
> Inconvenienced by shrapnel),
> Found a gamekeeper called Mellors
> Who could teach her in his lunch hour
> (And in language frank and fearless
> Such as wives and servants blush at)
> To admire the lower orders.
> While the hapless Bart, Sir Clifford
> (Let us waste no pity on him,
> For the man was paraplegic),
> In his new electric wheelchair
> Tried to drive it up a tussock –
> Tried and tried, and couldn't make it.

At the Lady Chatterley obscenity trial, if I remember correctly, the prosecution was pretty feeble and the defence called a cloud of distinguished witnesses with devastating success. In any case they had a simple, almost unanswerable question ready to put to everyone, 'Do you consider you have been corrupted by reading this book?' Who would stand up in a lawcourt and admit to corruption? Certainly no one in the public eye; and if they did do so, what rich pickings this would give for a lip-smacking press. The truthful answer for some should have been, 'No, it never corrupted me. I was corrupted before I read it.'

Great play was made in the press of E. M. Forster's shabby appearance in the witness-box contrasting with his calm, purse-lipped, amusing championship of Lady Chatterley as one of the great works in English literature. (A school exam book for the future.) Forster was, I think, one of the chief contributors to the success of the defence. The chattering classes of the time were well satisfied, nodding their heads with knowing smiles. Personally I have never quite made up my mind, having seen the faces of my fellow office workers while reading it; and I'm sure my own was just as lasciviously drop-jawed when it came to my turn. – Ah, here comes *The Last Train to Brooklyn*, crowded with hot ladies in jodhpurs or ripped bodices, clasping to themselves their fetid works.

I think I spy, travelling on the footboard of a similar but earlier train, but refusing to be associated with these gals or their camp followers, the lonely genius of James Joyce. Now, *there* is a pornographer worthy of the name; a true artist from his head to his crotch.

Yesterday evening dark sausage-shaped clouds, looking like *boudins noirs*, grumbled their way across a pale blue sky. It being the eve of Ascension Day we took ourselves to Mass. A small oddity struck me. In the account in the Acts of the Apostles of Christ's disappearance into a cloud on the hilltop two men appear in white garments and say to the gathered disciples, 'Why stand ye gazing up into heaven?' Were they the same angelic couple, 'in shining garments', who were on duty at the empty tomb a few weeks earlier and said to the distressed visitors, 'Why seek ye the living among the dead?'. Returning to *Religio Medici* I find, 'In Eternity there is no distinction of tenses.' So I try to unravel whether those events were in the past or will be in the future or are eternally now.

Mathematics has eluded me, beyond adding two and two; algebra has been a firmly closed book since the age of eighteen and never appealed; and logarithms (although briefly re-encountered, with sines and co-sines, during naval cadet days) never meant more to me than 'dot and carry ten'; philosophy has been hardly glimpsed through a glass darkly as it passed rapidly by; but religion, in its various aspects, I have always found absorbing, but with no good recognizable results. Knowledge has always been at a pathetically low level and yet I remain fascinated and deeply puzzled by TIME.

My trouble is that, although absorbed by the mystery of time, and perhaps fearful of it, I am acutely aware of the time of chronometers. Ask me the time and more often than not I would give an answer within five minutes of the time on an unseen clock. Routine and habit, the body's clock, may account for much of this awareness; and yet I can easily get wrong the day, the date and even the month.

For most of our major poets time has been a dominant theme; Shakespeare's speculations, from the terrors of the Scottish Play to the cynicism of Ulysses' great speech in *Troilus* which begins –

> Time hath, my lord, a wallet at his back
> Wherein he puts alms for oblivion,
> A great-sized monster of ingratitudes . . .

– are so numerous that we almost pass them by as clichés.

There is much rejoicing that Betty Boothroyd is again to be Madam Speaker. Her strong smile, jolly hairdo and shapely legs hearten us all no end as well, of course, as her fair-mindedness and the firm grip she keeps on the wheel when the ship of state is lashed by squalls. This time, I imagine, with a course clearly set to port, she will probably have a smoother ride. I hope the ship doesn't take on too great a list. Perhaps the Lib Dems can run from side to side to balance things. The Speaker's difficulty is going to be getting to know the names and constituencies of all those new girls, in their first flush of power. I do hope it is not going to be all Christian names, such as the Prime Minister has suggested to his cabinet. *That*, I fear, will make all recorded proceedings sound like the daily synopses we read for TV soap operas. 'Samantha has a surprise for Trevor which he doesn't much like. Alice keeps her own counsel, while Ted and Lil exchange looks.'

Alex Jennings has received good notices for his *Hamlet*, which has just opened at Stratford-upon-Avon in a production by Matthew Warchus, who directed so brilliantly the admirable *Art* last year. It sounds marvellously offbeat and at the same time refreshingly true. Years ago I said I never wanted to see another *Hamlet* – I felt I had had a bellyful of them and I was too familiar with the changes which could be rung – but this one attracts me. So an opportunity must be found to get to Middle England.

In 1938 Tyrone Guthrie directed a full-length *Hamlet* in modern dress at the Old Vic. Malcolm Keen played the Ghost, Andrew Cruickshank and Veronica Turleigh the King and Queen, Anthony Quayle Laertes with his then wife Hermione Hannen as Ophelia. I brought up the rearguard, at the age of twenty-four, as a fairly negative Prince. My only concession to an unhinged mind was a loosened necktie, such as is now the fashion with middle-aged actors to show they are 'with it'. Guthrie should have encouraged me to drop my trousers when confronting Ophelia. The modern dress was non-aggressive. Contrary to those critics who panned the smoking of cigarettes and drinking of cocktails (obviously they had not seen the performance, since there were no such activities) the whole production was almost severely classical. All these decades later I wish we had been much more daring. The most memorable visual effect in the production was the use of umbrellas in the graveyard scene, which caused adverse comment from those who had never experienced the melancholy of a damp funeral. Now I think that in a production presented in contemporary clothes there could be justification for the insertion of a line or two of current English when the need was felt. I would enjoy a very slight addition to the following dialogue between Hamlet and Polonius:

HAM: Do you see yonder cloud that's almost in shape of a camel?
POL: By th' mass and 'tis like a camel indeed.
HAM: Methinks it is like a weasel.
POL: It is backed like a weasel.
HAM: Or like a whale?
POL: Very like a whale.
HAM: Perchance it is a UFO.
POL: My Lord, it *is* a UFO.

The thing that worries me about cleverly fooling around with Shakespeare is the false impression likely to be made on the young seeing the plays for the first time. That they should look on the plays as modern is one thing, and no doubt admirable – and we all know the strength of visual impact – but if they are faced with *As You Like It* dressed up as Jane (BBC) Austen or *Macbeth* as Victorian melodrama, then they are lost on all counts; not only are the plays being presented out of historical or modern focus but damage is being done to appreciation of the rhythms and styles of speech of earlier centuries. Consequently language goes for nothing. Shakespeare can take care of himself, however jaggedly spoken, but I have doubts about the lesser great. Congreve and Sheridan have their own appeal but to put *The Tempest* into powdered wigs and fluttering fans would be a disservice all round.

It looks like bare-knuckle fisticuffs being prepared for our delight, distress or embarrassment in the Westminster gym: Widdecombe v. Howard. On our right God's Girl Widdecombe socking it to the Evasive Basher, also on our extreme right. It won't be a pretty sight, with Ann smashing the ex-Home Secretary's reading spectacles and Mike trying to find a belt below which to hit. Step forward as referee our one and only Independent, Martin. Madam Speaker will be too busy shooing away the IRA to pay too much attention, and after the first bloody round or two I anticipate the fairground spectators will drift away to see what is on offer in other sideshows. God's Girl may lose her political career but I'll bet she has the grip of a badger. I wouldn't like to be wearing Howard's torn pants.

But this isn't the end of this shocking affair,
All along, down along, out along lee,
Nor, though they be dead, of the horrid career
Of – well, all who take part in Widdicombe Fair.

The barren-looking plane tree has suddenly sprouted some little green leaves. The great horse chestnut which stands magnificently, about seventy feet high, on its small triangle of grass in our village of Sheet, is now a flowering candelabra. Passing by it yesterday so rejoiced my heart that I went on to local nurseries and pet shop to buy fish to replenish the pond. A heron, I suspect, has been foraging. I got three smallish koi carp, six very small but brilliant koi and – holding my breath – a sturgeon about a foot long. The sturgeon disappeared immediately to the bottom but the koi all look like sparks as they flash through the water. Weather is grey and damp but there is a recognizable summery smell in the air. It is still only May.

The sturgeon looks rather like our dog Flora – long, thin and sharp-nosed – except for colour, he being dark grey and she a light chestnut; but there is also, of course, the matter of no legs and long legs. We have had Flora for six months; she is now a year old and has settled firmly in our hearts, and also in the heart of Dido our Border terrier, who adores her. Even Michaelmas the cat, not a great dog fancier, is content to curl down at her side. God knows what breed she is. A sort of lurcher, I suppose, as her mother was a Border collie and dad, we surmise, was probably a whippet. She looks very whippet-like, has a tremendous turn of speed and is set to win all high-jump trophies. She is also very elegant, with a black fichu and errant ears. It is rash at our age to have such a wildly active creature streaking between us, rummaging in waste-paper baskets, stealing hairbrushes, making off with the Andrex in a puppyish way, but it is proving healthy, I think, to be looking after something so excitingly young, so full of curiosity and life. I am afraid we cast sentimental or forgiving eyes at her each hour of the day. She has brought also a new lease of life to Dido, now ten years old, but has added, I fear, a year or so to Japheth (Labrador type) who is eleven. He is almost saintly but has reached the age of quietly grumbling at the younger generation. In the past year, since his mother died, he has taken to coming to my bedside at 7.15 each morning to sing me a little song, which is exactly what she did in her last year. He doesn't sing as prettily as she did – she was remarkably tuneful – but the feeling behind his efforts is very moving.

Not having played it for a few years, this evening the mood came to me to put on a CD of Ravi Shankar at his sitar. It is beautiful, indeed thrilling, for five minutes and then, I am ashamed to admit, my dull ears are deadened by Indian monotony and I get images of a wireworm drilling its way through a stick of celery. I opened up the breakfast-room door which leads to the lawn and drank in the evening mistiness and the gentle smells of May. Kipling almost said it all in 'The Roman Centurion's Song':

> Will you e'er forget
> The scent of hawthorn in the sun, or bracken in the wet?

5. June's Long-lighted Days

The long-lighted days that Kipling wrote of are not quite with us yet but the month promises well. In a week's time Merula has a few paintings and stitchwork pictures in an exhibition in Cork Street of her family's artwork – oils by her brother Mikey, pottery by her sister Jill and various oddments. Ten days later we set off for Baden-Baden where we shall sip the waters, which must surely be preferable to Bath water, and maybe we shall brave a mud bath to relieve our aches and creaks. I pray to God I may be given the strength to resist the apfelstrudel.

I have no German to brush up but today I unearthed from a shelf of jumbled maps and guidebooks a pocket-sized phrase book which I thought might prove useful. Now I have my doubts, being dismayed by a page of 'Colloquial Expressions'. They range from the German equivalents of 'ouch!' and 'yum-yum!' to 'barmy, bastard, boozer, nutter, pissed, twit, shut up! I'm absolutely knackered! don't make me laugh! struth! get on with it! learn to drive!' And there is not a lot else by way of colloquial chit-chat. If that is the language our tourists are encouraged to bawl out when visiting a foreign land I don't see much hope for the unification of Europe.

The Island Race can have nothing to complain about this late-spring-bank-holiday weekend. There are no strikes to interfere with air or rail travel; it is true the roads are over-crowded and will witness much road rage, but the sun shines brightly from a clear sky and the air smells fresh. To be perfect it should be five degrees warmer but it is agreeable as it is. Give it another hour to make it almost sleepy weather and I shall cast myself on to a ship's deckchair and gaze at slowly moving sheep against their background of green field and newly leaved trees.

In July 1993, in a brief article for the *Spectator*, I reminisced about the joys of crossing the Atlantic in either the *Queen Mary* or *Mauretania* in the 1950s. I said the great morning luxury was to have beef tea brought to one by a charming steward while lounging, wrapped in a rug, on the sun-deck. There was always a wind of course, intensified by the speed of the ship, and the sea was nearly always a deep blue with sparkling broken water. A week after the piece in the *Spectator* was published there appeared in the correspondence column a sour little squib of a letter, signed with an English-sounding name from an address in, I believe, East Berlin. The gist of the letter was that the crew of the *Queen Mary* didn't get elevenses brought them by charming stewards and how would I like to give up my first-class luxury to share a wretched little cabin with five others. At the time I was tempted to reply but, thinking that might flatter the writer, I resisted. Time has passed and I find the ignorance, chilliness and smugness shown in the letter still irritates, even if it doesn't exactly rankle. So I reply now, four years later.

(1) I was travelling first class – and delighted to be doing so – because the theatre company for which I was working paid my fare. I couldn't have afforded it out of my own pocket.

(2) I wonder if the curmudgeonly letter-writer had any experience of service at sea during the 1939–45 war. Did he ever have to sleep (well, spend the night) in the Chatham naval barracks bomb-shelter tunnel, which housed up to seven thousand sailors? Perhaps he was too young to know about such things. Hammocks were slung about three deep and you had to pick your way in semi-darkness through puddles of urine and lumps of vomit. The air was fetid and it took about half an hour to get in or out of the place. Once slung in your hammock a fitful sleep was ripped apart by nightmare cries, resounding farts and endless cursing. Food, in the overcrowded messes, had almost to be fought for – something I refused to do. Often a kind mate would barge his

way through the crowd and bring a meal for us both. That embarrassed me so I took to spending a few pennies on chocolate and biscuits at the local store instead of being waited on. At all times you had to listen carefully to the Tannoy system in case your number was called out, summoning you to a ship. That was something we partly dreaded, as it would mean leaving England and family and really facing up to the war; but a ship – even an old, rusty, greasy merchantman with one feeble gun – would mean escape from this nineteen-fortyish version of Dante's *Inferno*.

That was my experience; I assume it can't have been the experience of the ex-*Queen Mary* crewman who complained so bitterly at being one of six in a cabin. We grumbled at conditions, I know, but I never heard anyone whingeing about the 'superior accommodation' of admirals or captains. Also during the war, after being commissioned, I sailed in the *Queen Mary* from the Clyde to New York; on that trip eight of us were squeezed into a cabin designed for two – just a bit more uncomfortable than the Berlin letter-writer's cabin. When I looked at his letter I heard his voice; the whine of that perennial, unpleasant plant, 'the barrack-room lawyer'.

No one to bring me beef tea these days, or come to that for more than forty years, so I must get my own Bovril.

The tourists are with us; a mixed blessing. I can't remember them before the war – I suppose they were individual visitors and not in long crocodiles or anacondas. Years ago *The Times* set a competition for the unkindest piece of advice to give a visitor to this land. The winning entry was 'It is customary, when using public transport, to shake hands with other passengers before disembarking and to thank them for having shared the journey.' Contributor's name forgotten. At least the tourists don't jabber on mobile phones or ride us down on the pavements with silent bicycles. Window-shopping in the West End has become a major hazard of London life.

The opening of the Salaman exhibition in Cork Street looked a fair success; Merula's stitchwork pictures were much admired and a satisfactory number of red dots soon appeared. James Huntington-Whiteley had arranged everything beautifully; pictures were displayed with a good space around them and thoughtfully juxtaposed. There were too many people – over a hundred – squashed noisily together on a warm evening. Apart from a few friends spotted over other people's shoulders there were clusters of M.'s relatives and our great-grandchildren at our feet looking bewildered. There were a lot of half-recognized faces to which no names could be attached. How wise the Americans are to wear name tags at gatherings or to announce loudly who they are. After twenty minutes I sought air and comparative quiet in the street, down which the evening sun was slanting. Marius Goring gripped me so emotionally I wondered for a moment if I had been manacled. He knew all M.'s family well and the warmth he expressed for them was touching.

A lady followed me into the street and, with her head on one side, smiling sweetly, said, 'You don't remember me?'

'Er – er – help me,' I suggested.

'Remember *The Card*?'

'Yes, well,' I said. The film of *The Card* was made forty-five years ago.

'I was one of the crowd artistes for a few days. Then I gave up acting,' she said.

'Ah! So! Well!'

'During a lunch break you spoke to me.'

I shook my head with amazement at my feeble memory but I don't think that quite satisfied her. I struggled back into the inferno of the gallery to rescue M., who was dealing charmingly with embraces and congratulations. We gathered Mark and Marigold Kingston and walked – M. and I rather slowly with the aid of our sticks – to a posh new restaurant where Alan Bennett was to join us. The food was superb but noise was still with us, echoing off the wooden floor and bouncing off walls and ceiling. The clientele appeared mostly to be well-turned-out yuppies being entertained by not-so-young yuppies. Each looked rich enough to stroll up the street between courses – and they would have had plenty of time – to Jack Barclay's showroom and buy a Rolls-Royce or two. We grimaced at each other but could make little headway with hearing. As far as I could make out Mark was being very insistent on the benefits of overripe bananas and Marigold on the skills required to catch shoplifters in Richmond. Alan had come from a lecture at the National Gallery but I couldn't make out by whom or about what. All rather frustrating; but I expect the yuppies did their deals successfully.

When we left Alan collected his white helmet from the hat-check girl and flashed off on his bicycle, somehow suggesting a tall pedalling toadstool. The rest of us returned to the Connaught for coffee and a chit-chat in quiet. The Kingstons had brought me from Paris, at my request, three tins of Grains d'Arabica, the world's finest chocolate-coated coffee beans, from the chocolate shop in rue des Saints-Pères. Lauren Bacall is my usual supplier of this most insidious drug. We parted company at midnight.

The following day was Corpus Christi – now called something unwieldy – and we went to the twelve o'clock Mass at Farm Street. It was refreshing to hear a priest speaking with proper emphasis on the right words and so avoiding the ubiquitous thumping of personal pronouns; it also meant that everything said was easier to follow. On leaving the church we were caught up by Piers Paul Read. Curiously enough I had decided that morning to start reading his new novel, *Knights of the Cross*. In the late afternoon we took ourselves to the *Romeo and Juliet* film. It was the second time for me and I found it even more enjoyable than the first. Merula, I was relieved to find, shared my enthusiasm; particularly for Mercutio.

Back at the hotel we had a late cold supper. Unless my eyes deceived me outrageously it was Mr Michael Howard at a table opposite us. It wasn't so much the looks but the body gestures, with which we had become so very familiar when he was on the front bench. Was he aware, I wonder, that a little further down the room, at a large round table, sat eight stalwart Americans and – wait for it – yes, surely, the new Home Secretary, Mr Jack Straw? Sometime around ten thirty the Americans received a message and they rose as a man, bade farewell to the two ladies present and accompanied Mr Straw – if it was Mr Straw – from the room. I had the feeling they were President Clinton's aides. The President was dining with the Prime Minister somewhere down river. The ladies looked forlorn and bereft. It reminded me of an incident at Malta in Easter 1939. The Old Vic Company was playing at the Opera House (later bombed by the Italians) and halfway through a performance of *Henry V* a naval officer marched on to the stage and addressed the audience. All naval personnel were to report to their ships immediately and the military to return to barracks. Ladies were requested to remain in the theatre. We continued to act, in an apprehensive way.

> ... behold
> Upon the hempen tackle ship-boys climbing;
> Hear the shrill whistle which doth order give
> To sounds confus'd ...

Those were lines I was to say. It felt odd to be saying them to a half-empty house of women, whose thoughts must have been a mile away at the Grand Harbour, where liberty boats were ferrying their husbands and boyfriends back to their destroyers and great warships.

It transpired that Italian submarines had concealed themselves below the waters just outside the harbour entrance. The destroyers skimmed out, dropping depth charges, and the subs shot to the surface protesting loudly. The Navy's response was, 'So sorry, didn't know you were there.' The Italians withdrew but Mussolini invaded Albania that weekend.

Although we all knew that war was inevitable sooner or later we somehow managed to kid ourselves that, by some miracle, it might pass us by. We certainly had no confidence in Chamberlain's 'Peace in our time'. It would have astonished me profoundly if, looking into the make-up mirror in my dressing-room at Valletta's Opera House, I had caught a shadowy image of myself returning to Malta in four years' time. In that mirror I would have seen myself, darkly, as a sub-lieutenant in charge of an LC1(L) with a crew of twenty, on the eve of the invasion of Sicily. The Opera House was, by then, a heap of rubble. The great battleships, with their vast gleaming guns, highly polished brass and ranks of sailors in immaculate white, had left for distant seas in either the Far East or north Atlantic and some, tragically, to the bottom of the ocean. Submarines, the odd frigate, the lovely mine-layer, HMS *Manxman*, or battered rusty merchantmen were the only ships to be seen, apart from the invasion craft. Walking past the remains of the theatre I tried to work out where my dressing-room had been; an airless box of a room, as I remembered it, with a faded wallpaper of climbing roses. I gave up. That, indeed, seemed at the time to have been a Positively Final Appearance.

This week I picked up on TV a happy Chinese sound-bite. An ever-so-smiling Chinaman (but not like Hamlet's villainous uncle) replied to a political question about the handing over of Hong Kong with the words 'The poof is in the pudding.'

Before leaving for our eight-day holiday with our friend Marriott White in Baden-Baden (jokey pc from Alan Bennett wishing us a gooden-gooden time) I got very fussed about what to take to read. A little pile was made of Herodotus, Elmore Leonard's thriller *Out of Sight*, Shakespeare's *Henry VIII* and Piers Paul Read's new novel, *Knights of the Cross*. Unfortunately, having looked into the Read book I couldn't put it down, so that was finished before we even started. Iris Origo's *The Last Attachment*, her account of the loving and exasperated relationship between Byron and Teresa Guiccioli in Ravenna, was substituted for the finished Read. Origo only came my way this year, when

I was given a copy of *War in Val d'Orcia*, which must be one of the finest books to have been inspired by the 1939–45 war. That led me to seek out her *San Bernadino*. Herodotus was abandoned to its English Patient and *Pericles* swapped for *Henry VIII*. All rather pointless as I read very little while in Germany, preferring, for the most part, to doze and gaze.

Turgenev is said to have met up daily, when he lived in Baden-Baden, with Russian emigré chums under a particular tree in the parkland of the Lichtentaler Allee, where our hotel is situated. I pictured myself lolling in dappled sunlight while reading Origo's elegant prose. It didn't occur to me that rain falls in Baden-Baden. An appreciative glance at the rich green of trees and grass should have warned me. One vast weeping beech, re-rooting itself from its dipping boughs over a wide area, is one of the most magnificent trees I have ever seen. Most of its great branches are wrapped around in hospital-like bandages; it has stood there for over a hundred years. A tree to venerate; I like to think it is the one that attracted Turgenev.

Here, on the edge of the Black Forest, the days have been mostly sunny and hot, sometimes wearily humid and only occasionally plain wet. The mother of all thunderstorms struck one night, threatened to return the following evening but it only grumbled and withdrew, leaving the air fresh and lively – which cannot be said for most of our fellow residents. Nearly all are approaching our age and, like us, use a walking-stick for a third leg. Couples in bathrobes can be seen shuffling, arm in arm, along wide, richly carpeted corridors to various silent, glossy therapy departments where they will be either hosed down, manipulated, acupunctured or subjected to shiatsu massage or encouraged to take part in hatha yoga exercises or, most popular of all, I suspect, to dance in water to gentle music from the thirties.

Merula and I avoided all that but we did experiment – boldly, we thought – with 'pack' treatment. Somehow we had assumed this would involve us in being caked with mud and we rather liked the idea. It wasn't mud at all. We went our separate ways and sat, bare bottomed, on flat, scorchingly hot cushions, which made us gasp as if scalded, and then we lay on them for twenty minutes wrapped up in towels and blankets. After a short time it seemed quite a comfortable way of life. Would a medieval Hell be like this? The sweat poured off. For a good hour after we had been released it was almost impossible not to fall asleep. Merula went for the treatment three times and there is no doubt it has done her good, even if only temporarily. She is walking much more freely and has sometimes forgotten to arm herself with a stick. She would rightly deny that she speaks any German but a few words slip around in her memory from schoolday lessons. She decided to ask the jolly *Frau* who dealt with her what the packs contained. (The packs were hardish, about 3 × 2 ft.) She returned to announce triumphantly that they were stuffed with petroleum jelly and yellow mushrooms. It now turns out that her German is *very* shaky: the packs contain a brew of paraffin and volcanic debris.

Our driver, Herr Hubert, had met us at Stuttgart airport and made himself available throughout our stay. He was a small, slightly rotund, middle-aged man, very friendly, informative and full of laughter. When I asked him where he had learned to speak such excellent English he said he had never been taught, but he had picked it up from reading English books and carefully listening to people. He took us, on a rainy afternoon, for a drive through a part of the Black Forest and miles of vineyards. The few villages we passed all looked very prosperous, the houses beautifully painted, their gardens and window-boxes blazing with colour. Herr Hubert would point to a rustic restaurant, saying, 'Here Mr Yeltsin had dinner with Chancellor Kohl a few weeks ago.' Or, 'In this place General de Gaulle met Dr Adenauer in 1962.' During our stay we must have driven much more than two hundred miles over excellently surfaced roads and I think we only spotted roadworks once – of a very minor sort which didn't interfere with traffic. At home one is lucky to get more than ten miles without a hold up.

St Josef's church at Baden-Baden is a modern circular building set back from a fairly busy road among strips of grass and spindly trees. I guess that it could hold a congregation of about six hundred but at the eleven o'clock Mass on Sunday it looked barely half full. Probably only twenty of those present were under fifty and I saw only one small child. The women wore smart but sensible hats and the men were in very bespoke summery tweeds. They all looked hugely respectable, grave and kindly. The apse, which is a broad, gentle curve, is constructed of dark grey-blue bricks and supports a large dark crucifix, which is difficult to see. The sides of the church are made of tall, narrow slits of stained-glass depicting nothing in particular. They made me feel I was in a child's kaleidoscope, the colour patterns changing as the sun shone or shifted or went behind a cloud. We had hopes of the singing, being in Germany, but it wasn't remarkable. There were six girl servers, brisk, solemn and very regimented; *Mädchens* in surplices. The organist, who was loud, sat at his instrument on a sort of flying saucer or a vast McDonald's Big Mac (painted grey) about fifteen feet in the air with no visible means of support or protection from falling. As we left the parishioners greeted each other charmingly, like good Catholics, and eased their comfortable bodies into terribly expensive cars. Shining Mercedes stood nose to tail around the church grounds. For a moment I couldn't think where I had seen it all before; then I recollected a church in Hollywood where, of course, the cars were Cadillacs instead of Mercedes. We got into Herr Hubert's Mercedes, drove the short distance to the hotel and so on to lunch at a very good open-air restaurant supervised by a Ruby Wax clone with her jolly waiters. The restaurant was totally empty and remained so.

During our last night at B.-B. nature summoned me in the early hours with one of her imperious and too frequent commands; after she was satisfied I groped my way through the dark of the sitting-room, opened the door to the balcony and stepped out into the moonlight. A gibbous moon rode high and the trees of the park looked almost black and much closer, like a jungle wall. It looked like the end of the first act in Barrie's *Dear Brutus*, when the curtains to the French windows are drawn open. It is Midsummer Eve and the trees in the garden have advanced on the house like an invading army. Below me I could just make out some lavender bushes which, when we arrived, had appeared as bunches of dry grey stalks; now they were in flower. There were neither scents nor sounds. For a second I thought I heard an owl but dismissed it as an illusion – just a sound in my head. Which is what it was. A few days earlier Marriott had shown me a copy of R. S. Thomas's slim book of poems *No Truce with the Furies* and I had copied out 'Raptor' with the intention of learning it. Small hope, with my fading memory. Standing on the balcony in my nightshirt the opening lines did come back to me, however.

> You have made God small,
> setting him astride
> a pipette or a retort
> studying the bubbles,

then it all escaped me. Looking it up I find Thomas's poem goes on, later –

> I think of him rather
> as an enormous owl
> abroad in the shadows,
> brushing me sometimes
> with his wing so the blood
> in my vein freezes . . .

So that is where my owl sound had come from and why I suddenly felt chilled.

I returned indoors, switched on a light on the desk to check the poem only to find it wasn't there. But I picked up a tiny notebook and found I had scribbled in it a line from *Religio Medici*: 'We behold him but asquint upon reflex or shadow.' Well done, Sir Thomas Browne. I slept happily until 07.30 when breakfast was brought with its daily fading yellow rose. Then the casual process of packing began, interspersed with fumbling through my Deutschmarks, verifying and re-verifying air tickets and patting the pocket where our passports were. I'm a fussy traveller. We were in Stuttgart by late afternoon and at awful Heathrow in the early evening.

6. Tuesday's Bells

On Tuesday evenings the church in the scattered village of Steep has its bell-ringing practice. One of our pleasures, when the weather is warm and we sit down to dinner out of doors, is to hear the gentle peal of its six bells wafted towards us over the fields. In recent years the noise of traffic from the new A3 London-to-Portsmouth road has spoilt it — aggressively so at weekends — but on Tuesdays, if the wind is not too southerly, a measure of quiet seems to descend and the bell-ringers provide balm to our ears.

All Saints, Steep, which has existed since the twelfth century (with alterations, of course), gazes down from its fairly high position on the pretty surrounding countryside and towards the low hills of the Hangers, which are close by to the north. It has seen Spaniards bargaining over wool in the area called the Spain; it has undergone the Reformation; it could have glimpsed a part of Cromwell's army, on its way to Winchester, camped on my little patch of land; it probably welcomed William of Orange (or if not him then his rather fine equestrian statue erected in the Square in Petersfield); and it has been and still is the spiritual refuge for many retired Royal Navy personnel who live in the district. Bedales, the co-ed public school with advanced liberal attitudes, is within a stone's throw or two. The church's spiky wooden spire, unusual and elegant, is a landmark, but was added only in late Victorian times.

The interior is solemnly quiet and probably prayerful. It boasts two wonderfully evocative plain glass windows engraved by Laurence Whistler of the poet Edward Thomas. Thomas roamed these hills and fields and lanes, writing of them with delicate feeling and a deep love of nature. When he was killed in Flanders during the Great War someone (Walter de la Mare?) wrote of his death, 'A mirror of England was shattered.' The church also has a remarkable collection of about a hundred and fifty hand-stitched hassocks, probably the finest in the country. Each hassock depicts something – bee, flower, butterfly, fruit – in a very English way. When I took an American friend to see them she exclaimed, 'My! And they haven't been stolen! In the States they wouldn't have lasted a week.' Long may it so continue, but the number of nightly thefts round and about make me uneasy about that. Still, the hassocks would look so conspicuous in a car-boot sale I think they might make potential thieves wary.

Bells have signalled much in life, from hand-rung school bells summoning us back into classrooms and the sharp information of ships' bells – dog watches, eight bells and so on – to the victorious jangle to be heard throughout the land on VE Day. Goat bells in Greece, cow bells in Switzerland, the rasping sound from the tower of some remote continental church, and temple bells in the jungle of Sri Lanka have always delighted.

The most beautiful sound of bells I have ever heard was when, a year before being reconciled to Rome, I attended a dawn Mass at Mount St Bernard Abbey (which is a Trappist foundation) in Leicestershire. The great doors of the church were wide open to the red disc of the rising sun. From a dozen side-altars came the discreet unsynchronized tinkle of sanctus bells, like the chirping of birds or the whirring of insects. It was as if all country life, and indeed life itself, was starting to rejoice at another day. A few years later, filming in France, I attended Mass at the Benedictine Abbey at Solesmes, the home, so to speak, of Gregorian chant. There the famous bells stun the air and shake the ground with their tremendous peals. On a second visit to Solesmes the service coincided with an apocalyptic storm. My driver had said he would be interested to accompany me. No sooner were we seated, our ears still throbbing from the sound of the bells, when there was an almighty crack of thunder, the lights fused and although it was mid-morning it was as black as night. Lightning forked outside the windows, the singing of the monks was drowned and my driver went into a dead faint.

In the theatre bells have been constantly heard or imagined. Macbeth says to a servant,

Go, bid thy mistress, when my drink is ready,
She strike upon the bell. Get thee to bed.

It is a simple, practical instruction, as if he had said, 'Tell Mrs Macbeth I'd like a glass of hot milk and to give me a buzz when it's ready.' Also, 'Get thee to bed', sounds like the kindly advice of a considerate master. But, 'when my drink is ready', for all its ordinariness, carries a terrifying image – a chalice of the king's hot golden blood. Then, a little later, Lady Macbeth quietly rings the bell; perhaps just a scarcely audible sound but enough to make us jump. And Macbeth, after all his procrastination, hears it and obeys: 'I go, and it is done: the bell invites me.'

Henry Irving's performance in *The Bells* made tiptop theatrical history in the 1870s and subsequently. The sleigh-bells of his murdered victim were always ringing in his head. Sir John Martin-Harvey, as a boy, was with Irving in a later production and for many years was greatly under his influence. After Irving's death he did his own production of the play and acted the same part, of Mathias, as Irving had done. It was said that he copied every move, gesture and inflection with which he had become so familiar. It must have been about 1930 when I saw him in *The Bells*. He was an impressive actor and yet, with the crossness and resentment of a teenager, I remember feeling cheated that I wasn't seeing the Governor himself. I was chilled rather than scared. In the late sixties I did a play in the West End called *Wise Child* and John Gielgud, who was temporarily in the USA, suggested I should ask his old dresser, Mac, to assist me, which I was happy to do. Mac was a dear, very professional and very un-gossipy. He had also been Martin-Harvey's dresser over a long period. One day, when I managed to get him chatting, he told me that Martin-Harvey had never got over the nightly terror of seeing Irving's face on his first entrance in *The Bells*. He had been a lad of about sixteen, walking on in the first scene, and the vision of hell in that gaunt face haunted him to the end – and was an excuse for a tipple.

As a child I didn't take much pleasure in Peter Pan's fairy Tinkerbell although I loved, in a shuddering way, Mr Darling being beastly and pouring his horrid medicine into Nana the nursery dog's dinner bowl. (There was, incidentally, a scandalous tale of a production of *Peter Pan* in the thirties in which it was said that Nana contracted syphilis from an affair with Smee. Those were the innocent days before AIDS.) And in my mid-teens I had reservations about Sybil Thorndike's famous St Joan hearing voices in the bells. It was an aria that moved or astonished more experienced heads than mine; but for me it was like beautifying a salvo of naval guns. That couldn't be said of Celia Johnson's Joan; I fear she only heard a little tinkle, like that of a silver bell on a cat's collar. Eileen Atkins, who played the embarrassingly impossible first scene better than anyone, gave the impression she had never heard the bells at all, let alone any with voices attached.

In the past few weeks there have been suggested all sorts of new schemes for quickly getting rid of unwanted babies in the womb. In my head I hear a snatch of office chatter.

'Free for lunch today?'

'Awfully sorry, no. I thought I'd just slip out and have an abortion.'

If the human race survives to the third millennium will our age be given a thought? Will we be hailed as the pioneers of cloning or dismissed as a trashy slip-up after the centuries of recognizable values? Most likely the future will be ignorant of the fact that we even existed.

A couple of nights ago we watched an hour-long TV

programme called *Heaven's Gate*, about the San Diego 'suicides'
in January this year. I had marked it down as something I wanted
to see; it was admirably done but very disturbing. All those eager
young faces with their sickly sweet smiles, expecting to board a
spacecraft following the tail of Hale-Bopp as it approached earth
and to experience a 'Level above Humanity', but only experiencing death by poison. Thirty-eight of them and their insane guru
and murderer, Marshall Applewhite, known to his chums as
'Do', – well, he committed suicide it appears – a sort of happy
euthanasia for a group who were fed up with the rest of us and
our wicked ways. Noah's family, I assume, as they climbed into
the Ark, only expected to float around for a few weeks and then
be lowered back on to a decently cleansed terra firma. (American
lady, stepping ashore after crossing the Atlantic for the first time,
'At last I've got my feet on terracotta.') Do looked and sounded
so bizarre on the box I cannot imagine how his followers gave
him any credence, let alone devotion. Perhaps all great spiritual
leaders have looked odd, from gap-toothed Semites, anorexic
saints and Gandhi to Rama Krishna (who was king to all the
monkeys and greatly revered by Christopher Isherwood) but the
look in Do's eye is horribly familiar. Perhaps he had charm, like
so many villains. After all, a sophisticated, worldly-wise hausfrau
like Marlene Dietrich could convince herself that each New
Year's Eve she had an assignment in the Californian desert with
a well-set-up gentleman from outer space. Or so she assured me.
She went into the desert by car, got out and walked to where
his flying saucer had landed. There was no physical contact, she
said, just a mutual recognition on a very high level. When I
asked what he looked like she replied, 'Handsome, my dear, and
dressed all in silver.' I forgot to ask what she was wearing, but
in my mind's eye it must have been a gold lamé evening dress
dripping with white fox. She wasn't trying to have me on I'm
sure, because her sense of humour was somewhat limited. But
she could tell you the best way to roast a chicken, how to remove
a coffee stain and – above all – the right pill to take to jerk you

awake in the morning ready for a day's filming. She sent me a vast pink pill, after I had listened to her for hours late into the night, which activated me for two solid days and robbed me of all sleep for the remainder of the week. I liked her in spite of her vanity and her dismissal of Garbo – 'My dear, she has bad skin.' But I wouldn't trust her desert dreams.

Oh, the millennium is to be dreaded for what madness it may disclose among our friends or, indeed, about ourselves. The Pope is keen about it as a birthday celebration, which is fine, but perhaps the real two thousandth birthday is this year, 1997, or was last year or may not be until 2001.

Perhaps the Millennium Dome to be erected at Greenwich should be, basically, a place of contrasting darkness and illumination; an appraisal of the great achievements of the past two thousand years placed side by side by the misuse so often made of them. Next to Caxton's printing press could be displayed a contemporary pornographic magazine; a magnificent eighteenth-century sailing-ship revealing its hold to be crammed with negro slaves; a 1914–18 machine-gun at the foot of the statue of the beautiful young man at Hyde Park Corner with its terrifying engraved message 'Saul hath slain his thousands, and David his ten thousands'; there could be photographs of happy groups of Barnardo boys and the latest figures for convicted paedophiles; a painting of Faraday and his electrical experiments alongside the most up-to-date electric chair; various aircraft for transport and medical use alongside photographs of the bombing of Dresden. And, of course, a model of the first atomic bomb – with no comment.

After stumbling about in our semi-darkness we might emerge to see dawn breaking over the Thames estuary, and hear welcoming bells from all the City churches, with St Paul's and Westminster Abbey. Not until the year 2622 will the minarets summon us to prayer in celebration of the second millennium of the hegira.

There was a small group of well-heeled people in

Knightsbridge, about twenty years ago, who had worked out a comfortable future for themselves when the world ends. A very mystic lady had informed them over the teacups that 1 January 1980 was the date to watch out for. She advised two safe havens – a wee hotel in the Hebrides or a handsome villa near Venice. From both those places they would be able to watch the horrors engulfing the rest of us. Needless to say she could make all the financial arrangements. So as soon as possible after Christmas the group moved to a villa in the Veneto. Later the mystic lady admitted she had got her tea-leaves wrong for 1980 but she managed to persuade them to try again in 1981; and a few subsequent years. I don't know if any of them are still alive but if they are I bet they are confidently putting money on the year 2000. Sitting round the bridge table and hearing the first rumble of doom they will nod complacently to each other and whisper, 'Told you so!'

The bells ringing from Steep church last Tuesday, 19 August, as we sat down to dinner on a hazy evening, were comforting and reassuring. I wouldn't admit it at the time but I was rather apprehensive and melancholic. On Wednesday I took myself to London to be ready, bright and early on the Thursday, to report to King Edward VII's hospital ('Sister Aggies' – founded in 1899).

They operated on me at two-thirty in the afternoon, removing the cataract in my right eye and implanting a new lens. God knows what material was used; anything, I imagine, from an industrial diamond to a piece of perspex or plastic. Anyway, it was a miracle of surgical engineering and the world is brighter than I have known it for about forty years. Leaves on trees fifty yards away are sharply defined and even the veins on leaves twelve feet away. The *Daily Telegraph* and the *Independent* have been much better printed since last Friday; they appear to be using a more solid black ink and white paper. For the first time in about twenty-five years I can shave without having to wear glasses. The only disadvantage is that I can see my own face only too clearly; and some other faces have aged somewhat during the week. I am astonished at how much detail I have been missing. Flora, our fairly new and beloved bitch, has a light coat and mahogany ears. Not until I got home from hospital did I realize how colourful, varied and striped her coat is.

The whole experience turned out to be unexpectedly pleasant from the moment of walking into the very un-hospital-like hospital and being greeted by the charming nursing staff and shown to my smart, spotless room (with clean windows). There was an atmosphere of unfussed quiet.

Nurses came at increasingly short intervals to put drops in my eye; and the only thing I objected to (but obeyed instructions) was when I was given a flimsy, skimpy pair of disposable knickers. Talk about getting knickers in a twist; you might as well try to get into underwear made of cling film. Having demolished one pair I had to ask for another. I could imagine a whole morning being wasted in the effort and blood pressure rising steadily. They might be suitable for some TV games show or an up-to-the-minute version of *The Full Monty* film.

Reassuring consultants visited me an hour before the operation and told me what to expect. A local anaesthetic had been decided on and I was pleased about that; I don't want tubes down my throat again. 'Don't think we have blinded you,' one of the consultants said cheerily, 'but as the anaesthetic takes effect you will lose your sight for some minutes. Everything will appear dark grey. Then you will have a sense of bright lights and colour.' Which is exactly what happened. There was no sense of pain or irritation, just this remarkable impression of being in a tropical forest with brilliant butterflies fluttering around, all the colours of the spectrum but greatly intensified. When it was over I felt a sense of disappointment that such a beautiful vision had been withdrawn. I was wheeled back to my room and told to keep the eye shut for a few hours.

When the eye was opened, cautiously, the world it saw was

very light, white and bluish. By the morning I realized I was in a new world of sharp definition and rich colour. If only my lousy left eye could be dealt with in the same way I would be doubly happy but they say it can't. It is doomed to extinction and no surgical skill can save it. *Tant pis.* I am more than thrilled with what has been done for me. Gratitude all round.

Merula presented me, when I got home, with a stitchwork picture she had been working on in secret. It is of Flora, back view, sitting very upright and alert on a strip of terrace, flanked by pots of geraniums, watching with suspicious interest a magpie on the lawn and some sheep beyond. The whole picture conveys the essence of Flora – and of my wife.

7. Summer Solstice

The summer solstice has come and gone. It may have been the longest day yesterday but it was certainly one of the darkest; rain and black clouds most of the time and an unpleasant cold wind. Today is the fifty-ninth anniversary of Merula's and my wedding in 1938 and also Japheth's twelfth birthday. Our marriage was registered in a very agnostic way at the Reigate office for such things. It was a lovely sunny day, my mother-in-law kept interrupting the proceedings by announcing she had to go to the loo and I dropped my trilby hat half a dozen times from nerves. We flew, from Croydon airport I think, to Dublin where we spent the night at the Gresham Hotel. The bar at the hotel I can still see, propped up by a dozen or so priests drinking their usquebaugh and dragging on crumpled cigarettes. The place was thick with smoke, raucous laughter and betting talk. We felt lost. The next morning we took the train north to County Monaghan to stay a happy week with Tony and Judy Guthrie at Annaghmakerrig, Tony's mother's large ramshackle house standing by a lake on a Chekovian estate. From there we set off for Donegal where, with rucksacks on our backs, we trudged and trudged along the marvellous coastline, curtained in perpetual rain, spending our nights in any house or pub where we could find a bed.

On what turned out to be, unexpectedly, our last day in Donegal we spotted a lonely, shabby, small house about three hundred yards across derelict land from a single-track railway. There were no other dwellings around so we went there. A bony, black-haired woman, who resembled a pike in broken-down bedroom slippers, came to the open door. I asked if she had a room to let for the night. She was immediately joined by a small, unsmiling group, probably her sisters and brothers. They eyed us suspiciously, muttered among themselves and the woman finally said, 'Yes. Five shillings.' She showed us upstairs to a square room at the front of the house and left us. There was a squashy bed in a corner, a hand basin on a table, a pock-marked mirror and a couple of rush-bottomed chairs. Merula cautiously pulled back the top sheet on the bed. It made a crackly, retching sound. The sheets were stuck together with old sweat and grease and were grey. My foot accidentally kicked something under the bed; I pulled out a chamber-pot, filled to the brim, with, horror of horrors, floating on top a pink swansdown powder-puff. We pondered what to do; the whole atmosphere was sleazy in the extreme and sinister. We knew we had to get out. We opened the window and there, a mile away, a little single-coach train was approaching. I plonked five shillings by the wash-basin; we walked gingerly downstairs with our rucksacks and, once free of the house, ran and stumbled our way to the rail track. The train stopped at our frantic signals and we clambered aboard. Turning to look at the house we saw the same group staring at us, rigid and menacing. Within fifteen minutes we were over the border and by the afternoon in Belfast. We were young and inexperienced. Today I like to think we wouldn't behave with such panic – but now, of course, we wouldn't have the energy or capacity to run.

Now we are back from Germany, it still being June 1997, we find pleasant things have happened in our short absence; also bad things and indifferent things. One of the good things has been the announcement of a knighthood for Donald Sinden; at last. Not only is he a tiptop comedian but he is also a kindly, genial man of great generosity and quietly given to doing good works. He must be just about the last repository of theatrical memories and memorabilia. When I saw him a few months ago he asked if I would leave him my (very ordinary) walking-stick in my will. 'Not if you want it very badly,' I said, 'because then, in your impatience, you would have me bumped off.' It's funny the way we so often decide other people are likely to die before ourselves. A few years ago John Gielgud kindly gave me a huge, richly bound Italian edition of *Hamlet* with incomprehensible coloured illustrations by Henry Moore.

'I was going to leave it to you in my will,' he said, 'but as I seem to be still going strong you may as well have it now.'

'Who would you like me to leave it to in my will?' I asked. 'The Garrick Club?'

'I rather hoped you might leave it to Paul Scofield. That would be killing two birds with one stone. He's a lot younger than you.'

True: eight years. But Paul wouldn't kill for any possession.

One of the bad things we read about when we got home was the continued sectarian killings in Northern Ireland. Now is the start of the marching season. A clockwork Orangeman explained on TV, 'The marches are part of our culture.' I saw him as a Cultured Man, wound up to march throughout the summer, beating a drum.

One of the indifferent things, to me at any rate, is the national excitement expressed at Mr William Hague taking over the leadership of the Conservative Party. It has been made to sound like the Second Coming, albeit a small one. The Second Adventists have always believed the Second Coming would precede the millennium; and for the millennium, Mr Blair assures us, the eyes of the world will be focused on a covered arena or dome at Greenwich, not Jerusalem or any holy place, it would seem. So it could all tie in.

It probably isn't 100 per cent true but a schoolmaster is reported to have said that when William Hague was aged fifteen he could recite the names and constituencies of all the members of the House of Commons. Or was it only the names of Tory MPs? Even if only 10 per cent true I find it dispiriting. A great feat of memory admittedly and yet how much more cheering it would be to know that he could name the country's great cricketers, tennis players, the kings and queens of England and a variety of wild flowers. That sort of information was inhaled by boys of my generation from the precious cigarette cards we collected and swapped. Cigarette packets in those days carried no Government Health Warnings but they were an encyclopedia of general knowledge. Not many of us, I am sure, could have named any politicians beyond Lloyd George, Stanley Baldwin or Ramsay MacDonald and we would have been doubtful about what they stood for.

At election time then we were presented with little Union Jack buttons which we wore on the lapels of our jackets, to show we were small conservatives. And how. It was very much a cry of 'My country, right or wrong'. I pray God we shall never be beguiled again into ghastly xenophobia.

Dear Anthony Trollope, one of the most English of great Englishmen, wrote in a letter to Kate Field in 1862, 'One's country has no right to demand everything. There is much that is higher and better and grander than one's own country. One is patriotic only because one is too small and weak to be cosmopolitan.' Eurosceptics, please note.

I shall miss seeing Mr Kenneth Clarke's relaxed figure and saucer eyes on the front bench but no doubt his good-blokeish commonsense bark will be heard wherever he sits, championing our European heritage. I have been a fan of Mr Clarke's from a day or two after he assumed office as Chancellor of the Exchequer. It was dinner time, and there were only about four members sitting at the long table in the Garrick when Mr Clarke entered the dining-room and sat himself beside me. 'I know who you are,' he said, 'and I expect you know who I am.' He was so easy and amiable that I took courage and put a question to him which he could have considered impertinent. In any case I had a genuine human interest in what the answer might be.

'We may never meet again,' I said, 'but I would like to put a question to you, so long as you don't feel it is too personal.'

'Fire away,' he said; and maybe a shadow of apprehension crossed his face.

'Would you, could you, tell me,' I asked, 'how you spent this last weekend, knowing as you did that you were to be Chancellor within twenty-four hours?'

'Easily,' he said, with some relief. 'I'll tell you exactly what I did. I did what I do so often at the weekend. I took myself to Norfolk, bird-watching.'

I am no twitcher myself but my heart warmed immediately to a man who was clearly unaffected, trustworthy, and with interests outside himself.

The heavy June rainfall we are experiencing is disastrous; the worst, they say, for fifteen years. Farmland inundated, crops flattened, Wimbledon a wash-out and days of 'Rain stops play' at many cricket grounds. Depressing shots on TV of great tarpaulins being dragged out to protect pitches and tennis-courts while disconsolate spectators sit crouched under dripping umbrellas, looking like highly coloured poisonous toadstools.

The pond is giving trouble in spite of these sunless days. The water is a gloomy green, the fish just discernible below the surface. Five koi carp have died in the past three weeks and since I put in a careful dose of something to destroy algae and blanket-weed a lot of the oxygenating and other pond plants have withered. It is a sorry sight but what I dread is the amount of bewildering and contradictory advice I shall receive from well-meaning and knowledgeable friends.

Yesterday, when I turned on the fountain, which throws up a vigorous jet about fifteen feet high, I noticed it was slightly off the perpendicular. Taking a pole I gave the fountain head a gentle push, which seemed to do the trick, but the moment I took the pressure off the water lashed back and soaked me.

While I changed I thought again of *Pericles, Prince of Tyre*. 'Enter Pericles, wet.' That is a nice, specific stage direction which makes me think that Shakespeare's theatre paid more attention to realistic detail than we give it credit for. Did some stage manager, just out of sight of the audience, pour a bucket of water over the leading actor's head a moment before he made his entrance? Did the actor catch cold? It would be some time before he could take off his wet shirt and dry himself. Did the actor demand compensation money, as his modern equivalent might? The shipwrecked grandees in *The Tempest* don't have to face such inconvenience: they arrive on Prospero's island, straight out of a strong sea, with their clothes perfectly intact, as if they had been returned from the dry-cleaners. Gonzalo, 'an honest old Counsellor', bores his companions with saying:

– the rarity of it is, which is indeed almost beyond credit, – That our garments, being, as they were, drenched in the sea, hold, notwithstanding, their freshness and glosses, being rather new-dyed than stained with salt water.

Again I think that possibly points to the fact that an audience at the Globe would have expected the actors to have arrived wet from the sea, until the idea of the magic of the island took over from their down-to-earth realism.

The best first scene in *The Tempest* I have ever seen was in the production by Billy Harcourt Williams at the Old Vic in 1933; it was also the most simple. There were the usual noises off – thunder-sheets clanging, rolls of drums, cracks of lightning and so on. The stage was completely bare and dark, except for a storm lantern, hung high up, which swung slowly in a great arc from one side to another. The actors, huddled together for support and crouched against an invisible wind, staggered across the stage under the lantern, creating the impression that the ship was rolling perilously under the impact of great waves. At the cry of 'We split, we split, we split,' the lantern went out, there was the sound of wood breaking, and in the silence and dark which followed could be heard Gonzalo's plaintive voice, 'Now would I give a thousand furlongs of sea for an acre of barren ground, long heath, brown furze, anything.' In the blackness you didn't know if you were up to your neck in water or clutching desperately at rocks on shore.

When Pericles is wrecked and his crew drowned he manages somehow to gain a strip of beach on the Grecian coast, where he collapses. Three fishermen, who have seen the ship go down, enter discussing the storm and lamenting the loss of life, but fail for a few minutes to spot the hapless Pericles. They are probably good parts to act (I have never seen the play) – similar to the gravediggers in *Hamlet*. Something about their personalities – the young simpleton and the foreman, a Mr Know-all – suggests the same two actors may have been a team, cast in both plays and possibly a dozen others. We have seen the same thing in more recent times. Few British films of the thirties could do without Basil Radford and Naunton Wayne, for instance, the Aldwych farces without Ralph Lynn and Tom Walls would have been unthinkable and today, on TV, we have the always enjoyable David Jason and Nicholas Lyndhurst.

Here is a slither of dialogue between two of the fishermen from Act II of *Pericles*:

2ND FISHERMAN: Nay, Master, said not I as much when I saw the porpoise, how he bounc'd and tumbled? They say they're half fish, half flesh . . . Master, I marvel how the fishes live in the sea.

1ST FISHERMAN: Why, as men do on land: the great ones eat up the little ones. I can compare our rich misers to nothing so fitly as to a whale; a' plays and tumbles, driving the poor fry before him, and at last devours them all at a mouthful. Such whales have I heard on o' th' land, who never leave gaping till they swallow'd the whole parish, church steeple, bells, and all.

After some friendly dialogue with Pericles the fishermen have difficulty dragging their net ashore and believe they have caught a great fish. It turns out to be a suit of dented, rusty armour. It belongs, of course, to Pericles. (It must have rusted very quickly.) Since being wrecked he has been slopping around I imagine in little more than a wet shirt. The scene lasts about six minutes. Did the actor complain during rehearsals? Perhaps Shakespeare, or whoever was in charge, might have said, 'It's only for a few minutes and then you can get dried off and change into your armour and then, four minutes later, I have arranged for you to do a Greek dance. That'll warm you up. You'll be one of a chorus. [Grim looks from actor.] But you'll stand out – as the best dancer – naturally.' (Smiles and reconciliation.) As the actors dance, in their armour, wearing perhaps those white ballet skirts Greek ceremonial guards flaunt, with their arms round each other's shoulders, shuffling backwards, forwards and sideways, dipping to the ground, making barbaric cries, I think I hear the haunting, whining, reedy but invigorating sound of bouzouki. I'll leave Pericles to warm himself up. He's a nice enough fellow.

There is a Greek taverna in Beak Street, Soho – or there certainly was in 1971 when I frequented it after performances of John Mortimer's *A Voyage round My Father* at the Haymarket. After I had visited it once, casing the joint, I often persuaded members of the cast to join me there for ouzo, retsina, a meal of sorts and an effort at Greek dancing. I fondly imagined that one day I would pick up the steps accurately; I never did. It was a small place, looked authentic with its walls covered with graffiti, but there was not much room between its two lines of tables for flamboyant footwork. Some nights it would remain quiet and boring; on others it took off spectacularly. The two bouzouki players pitched up the adrenalin and soon people were kicking off their shoes and, if feeling very confident, would dance solo on the tables. For most of us it was staggering in to some sort of line and, after a brief demonstration from the patron, we would exhaust ourselves dipping up and down travelling the length of the room and back. On one hot summer night we chained our way out into Beak Street and down as far as Regent Street. Stockings were laddered and socks had to be abandoned. Never a sign of police but faces in passing buses were amazed. Then back to the taverna for a long cold beer.

Touring Europe and Egypt with the Old Vic Company in the spring of 1939 provided Merula and me with our first visit to Greece. At that time tourists were a rarity; you could stroll almost alone round the Parthenon, butterflies were everywhere and the air was unpolluted. There was no barbed wire and no charges. We found Athens marvellously cheap; it was almost difficult to pay more than a shilling for a rather greasy lunch. A taxi, hired for the day to take us to Sunion and back cost about seven shillings. The temple at Sunion, standing on the very edge of an idyllic beach lapped by a pale blue sea, we had entirely to ourselves. Apart from the sound of water all was quiet, except for a shepherd playing on his pipes. A short way inland were fields of asphodel – or so we assumed the plants to be. That was our only, very minor, disappointment. We didn't think that 'Resting weary limbs at last on beds of asphodel', as Tennyson suggested, would be all that comfortable.

On our way back to Athens the taxi coughed and spluttered its way along a rough country road. Suddenly, racing towards us was a smart open car and only last-minute violent swerving, nearly throwing us in the ditch, avoided a disastrous accident. The car, apart from the uniformed driver, had four occupants. Two of the faces were familiar from photographs: Goebbels and Goering. Both men were in uniform. It's not likely that all our deaths would have prevented the Second World War, but it might have postponed it.

King George of the Hellenes came to the theatre almost every evening and, during an interval, would provide hospitality to some of the cast in the anteroom to the Royal Box. The attraction for him was our leading lady, the distinguished Cathleen Nesbitt, with whom I had become good friends. She told me the King had been smitten by her in the twenties and on one occasion, in the early hours of the morning, had chased her round and round the rotunda which used to grace the Midland Hotel, Manchester. On one occasion at the theatre in Athens he had with him a tall, fair-haired youth of about seventeen. The poor chap was desperately bored by our theatrical offerings and could hardly disguise it. I didn't catch his name when introduced: I think I was supposed to know it. He asked me, shyly, 'Got a yacht?' I said I hadn't. That was the end of our conversation. He was Prince Philip.

In late March 1974 we rented for a month a small, damp, uncomfortable but not altogether unpleasing cottage at Galaxidion, a ramshackle, much broken-down port some miles south of Delphi – where oracles come from, like nuts from Brazil, as well as superb olives and a lovely runny honey. (I have never found out why honey, once the jar is opened, gets everywhere.) For the first fortnight we were joined by our friend Marriott White and for the second by Margaret Harris (Percy), of the theatrical designers, Motley. Some early mornings we taxied up to Delphi before the coaches arrived from Athens (a three-hour journey for them) and could soak up its pregnant atmosphere undisturbed; in the afternoon we would often walk through the woods and rough fields to the sea. Once or twice we adventured much farther afield, to Corinth or Epidaurus (the best theatre in the world). It was amusing to watch our guests' outdoor habits; Marriott, who has an interest in wild flowers, always walked through the woods with her eyes on the ground while Percy, who has a passionate interest in birds, strode along, her head held high, trying to spot what might be on the wing. Merula adapted herself happily to each of their enthusiasms, while I warily stamped about to discourage any snakes, which we had been told abounded. We saw none. I have only to hear that there are snakes about and a walk becomes an apprehensive experience.

John le Carré asked me in 1980 if we would like to take over a large bungalow he had rented at Nikiti, not all that far from Thessalonika, for the last three weeks of September. We jumped at it and invited Anne and Irving Kaufman Schneider to join us from New York, together with Jill Balcon and the military historian Antony Brett-James from Petersfield. Nikiti is a very small town on the western shore of the Sithonia peninsula, the central of the three fingers that jut dramatically into the Aegean and which are so recognizable on any map. The bungalow, well-planned and attractive, had a garden which sloped down to a narrow sandy beach and a sea which was very shallow for the first hundred yards, the colour of aquamarine. It was lovely for sloppy bathing about four times a day, except when rather disgusting brown jellyfish showed up. Weather was perfect, fruit abundant and there was nothing to do, apart from lazing, except to walk a mile along the beach to the local store (for lavatory paper, wine, cheese and straw hats). Nikiti, eight miles away, boasted a quite good restaurant, built partly over the sea, and there we had our lunch as often as not. It was all highly satisfactory. But there was no Greek dancing. Neither did we see any when we were guests on Honor Svedjar's yacht, *Cloncilla*, for a six-week cruise of the islands some years earlier. I begin to suspect that it is only seen and enjoyed in Beak Street or the odd Hollywood film. Oh, come to think of it, there is a rather jolly subterranean spot in Nottingham where they indulge in a lot of plate breaking, while dancing. It is perhaps a little hazardous and the plates (neatly stacked for the purpose) add considerably to the bill.

Beak Street runs its narrow and busy way west to where it joins the expensive clamour of Regent Street. Halfway along, on the right-hand side, is the famous shopping precinct called Carnaby Street, where the young merrily jostle each other for what look like highly coloured cast-offs and Muzak screeches out of every little shop. Its popularity seems as permanent as *The Mouse Trap* and has the same tourist appeal. But Beak Street wasn't always like that. In the mid thirties it was quiet and dingy but at No. 14 – a real touch of glamour – Diaghilev had had his ballet rehearsal rooms. Did Nijinsky do his bar practice there, I wonder, and try out a leap or two as the ghost of a rose?

No. 14 was for a short time important in my life as a young actor. Gielgud had invited Michel St-Denis (of the brilliant

Compagnie des Quinze) to direct him in André Obey's *Noah*. That was in the summer of 1935 and the production was at the New Theatre, now the Albery. Michel, with his charm, dedication and insight, soon became a very strong influence; but many actors were divided in their opinions. There was more than a touch of Stanislavsky in his approach and he aimed, eventually, at total theatre. An endearing, robust elderly actor called Frederick Lloyd once asked Tony Guthrie what it would be like working with St-Denis. '*Very* interesting,' Tony said, 'very pleasant – so long as you don't object to rehearsing for three months in a chicken-run in preparation for the *Ghost Train*.' Some middle-aged actresses were scandalized when Michel suggested it would be much better if they abandoned high-heeled shoes and cartwheel hats when they came to rehearsals. We had got used to the vagaries of Theodore Komisarjevsky (reliable with Chekhov of course but wayward with Shakespeare) but this was something new, a facing up to reality – which was not in great demand on the West End stage – and a stimulus to the imagination.

Gielgud, Peggy Ashcroft, George Devine, Glen Byam Shaw and the Motley girls quickly succumbed to his enthusiasm and ideas. A school for aspiring actors was proposed and Michel, George and Glen formed what became known as the LTS (London Theatre School). The first premises they had was the top floor of 14 Beak Street. Michel used to smoke a rather chunky curved pipe. George and Glen (very much a cigarette man) followed suit and I maintained that for a time they all spoke with French accents.

The school was divided into two sections; the first and major part was for the full-time training of would-be performers and the second for young actors who were already earning some sort of living in the theatre. I joined the latter group, paying £1 a week. We met in a room at No. 14 five mornings a week and for an odd afternoon or two. When, after a few months, the triumvirate moved to their proper premises and small attractive theatre in Islington the pound-a-weekers were dropped and handsome fees were paid by the younger lot.

The days always seemed sunny but they can't have been. Those autumn and winter weeks passed swiftly. Although I was far too frivolous to give in to the intense atmosphere, which sometimes prevailed, and too often couldn't resist sending up the more serious exercises in mime (ten girls pretending to bake cakes without any props could be hysterical as well as confusing), I somehow knew in my heart that a door had been opened for me. It dawned on me that acting could have an affinity with the arts. I think I can pinpoint the moment when this first occurred.

It was in the middle of an afternoon rehearsal (purely an exercise, not for performance; what would now be called a workshop) of the opening scene of *The Cherry Orchard*, with Michel St-Denis directing. Epihodov, the clumsy, wrong-footed clerk on the Ranyevsky estate, was being played by Marius Goring; he had reached the moment when he complains to anyone who will listen about the squeaking of his boots. After a moment or two Michel said, 'Marius, I don't hear the squeak in your boots.' Marius replied, 'Of course not. I'm wearing gym shoes with rubber soles.' Michel persisted, 'But I should hear the squeak.' He got up to demonstrate what he meant. (His own shoes, of course, were squeak free.) With great concentration and concern, his head on one side, he listened to a shoe as he bent his instep up and down. I could swear we all heard a squeak, though naturally it was only in our imagination. From then on I was in love with the idea of trying to exercise a touch of magic on an audience, of persuading people to see and hear what wasn't there. Beak Street was my road to Damascus even if there was no blinding light and the voice I heard was muffled by my own egotism. The results have not been exactly world-shattering; indeed I cheerfully concede that they have been humdrum; but the hope of realizing a sort of magical moment has remained with me from 1935 until my present retirement. A fond but foolish hope, it now seems.

The trouble with Michel was his secret conviction that he could break down young personalities, as if a psychiatrist, and built them up again in an image suitable for the Compagnie des Quinze. He didn't attempt it with older actors, set in their ways, and he failed singularly with Peter Ustinov, James Donald and myself, all of us choosing to go our merry, separate ways. If the truth be known, I suspect we each resented the onslaught on our integrity – a sort of rape of unformed talent – while admiring the man. He was undoubtedly, when in his heyday, a great theatrical guru.

Summer has come back to us after monumental rain, and lunch and dinner can be eaten out of doors again. Great sleepy flies settle on everything and by late afternoon the dogs are flaked out.

8. Glittering Eye

The hotel is usually very quiet at night so I was astonished and angry to be jumped awake at five on Saturday morning by the radio from the next-door room being switched on monstrously loud. The news was being thundered out and I could hear almost every word. At that hour I certainly wasn't remotely interested in the affairs of the world or its scandals. I thumped on the wall; no effect. I telephoned the night porter. 'It will be seen to immediately, sir.' Nothing. After ten minutes I telephoned again. 'The gentleman has been informed, sir.' No results. I put on a dressing-gown, went out into the passage and banged on the door of room 261.

'What is it?' came a quavery male voice.

'Please turn down your radio,' I called.

'Hold on,' came the voice. Then the door was opened. Before me stood a long-white-bearded gnome-like gentleman, roughly sixty inches high, wearing classic underwear and a baseball cap.

'Please turn down your radio,' I repeated.

'I'm listening to the news,' said the little old person.

'We don't all want to hear it,' I said, 'and certainly not at five in the morning.'

'I'm ninety-one,' said the baseball cap by way of explanation.

'Then you've known it all and seen it all; and you're only four years older than me.' (Why do we so often lie or exaggerate when we are angered? I'm only eighty-three.) 'I don't care,' I called out while striding back to my room, 'if the news is even about Princess Diana.' A few minutes later the radio was turned down or off. For half an hour I lay exasperated, with my mind racing through the stinging remarks about antisocial behaviour

I should have made. Then I overslept by an hour. So the day began badly.

Downstairs, later in the morning, the manager kindly asked after my eye. 'Fine,' I said, 'but glittering a bit after a disturbed night. You may not know it but you have a gentleman guest in the room next to mine who is a radio ham who trots around in his underwear wearing a baseball cap. He is ninety-one.'

'Oh, he's a bit more than that,' said the manager. 'I noticed on his passport that he is ninety-nine.'

Oh, well; at that age maybe you should be encouraged to play the radio at whatever volume suits you and wear in bed what hats you fancy. But in future I hope to keep my distance.

I wrote about the above silly incident on Saturday afternoon, when I had got home. This Sunday morning I heard the appalling news of the death in Paris of the Princess of Wales, Mr Dodi Fayed and their driver. One forgets how much she has entered our national consciousness. For sixteen years the media have kept us aware of her daily; and even now, when the poor woman's life has been snatched away, I doubt they will let her die. For the present generation she will continue to live – I pray she will not become iconized like Elvis Presley – but for her sons her death will always be a tragedy to be somehow overcome one day. In the meantime I fear we are likely to be exposed to ghastly tea mugs, plastic figurines and images from the silver shop of Demetrius in Ephesus (Acts xix, 24).

Although Diana's death far outstrips, emotionally, many others it seems to have a similarity to the fate of film stars like Grace Kelly and James Dean; though neither of them were being pursued by paparazzi when they crashed their cars.

From the moment she walked up the aisle of St Paul's Cathedral on her father's arm, a truly modern beauty – her head slightly and shyly bent forward, her lips sweetly smiling – we were aware that the superb eyes knew intuitively where the lights and cameras were placed. Watching on TV we were suddenly faced with a big, big, glamorous international star. That should have made us apprehensive, through observation of the world and its ways, of the possibility of shipwreck ahead. Yet no one could have foreseen the hell of death in a Paris underpass pursued by a camera-flashing press. Did she, I wonder, and Dodi Fayed, and their chauffeur and bodyguard think that they were winning over the hounds at their heels because they were travelling at 100 m.p.h.?

Apart from deep sympathy for the Princess's sons and her immediate family I find my next most sorrowful feelings go out to the elder Mr Fayed. He begins to emerge as a truly tragic figure whom the Fates have tricked.

Recent reading has been mostly confined to the sea, although there has been some happy foraging into James Lees-Milne's diaries and Anthony Powell's journals, together with a rather prolonged but interesting journey through a crumbling Levant with William Dalrymple in *From the Holy Mountain*. My friend Anne Kaufman Schneider brought me from New York *The Perfect Storm* by Sebastian Junger, knowing that any account of hurricanes and hundred-foot waves is going to pulverize me into slack-jawed silence. Which *The Perfect Storm*, with its factual account of the meeting of three hurricanes off the coast of Nova Scotia in 1992, certainly did; but I got a little impatient with its over-meticulous detail; also I longed for some haven in which to find a laugh or an exhausted, wintery smile. The sea often does something biblical to serious prose, as does the desert. Charles Doughty set the over-rich example in *Arabia Deserta* with his Old Testament Authorized Version rhythms; and T. E. Lawrence caught something of the habit when camel-riding in *The Seven Pillars*. Perhaps it has to do with wide skies, far horizons and the suddenness of storms, of sand or sea.

When I had finished the Junger book I immediately picked up *In Hazard* by Richard Hughes, last read over forty years ago; I wanted to compare a scientifically factual account of a hurricane with that in a novel. *In Hazard* stands up to the passage of time as sturdily as the well-constructed cargo ship at the centre of its story. The stricken *Archimedes*, its funnel having been swept away, its engines without steam, listing heavily in gigantic seas, reaches for a few hours the comparative lull found in the eye of every hurricane. It is then, I think, that Hughes is at his best. The ship becomes a sanctuary for bedraggled, exhausted and doomed bird life of every description, clinging desperately to the twisted rails on the sloping decks, and even hummingbirds from tropical islands, fixing their tiny pin-like toes into human heads. There are funny bits as well, and the observation of characters under stress is always gripping. The novelist wins.

Wednesday, 10 September. The atmosphere of the past ten days has been the most extraordinary I can remember and I can't shake it off. Not even the Abdication, the Munich crisis in 1938 or the declaration of war in 1939 can quite compare. Munich (with its shameful sense of relief) and war with Germany (with its attendant fears and determination) were clear-cut issues that united the nation; I have a nasty feeling that the tragic death of the Princess of Wales has divided it. The sorrow is universal but the national reaction has disclosed, I believe, a deep rift among us, almost a fragmentation. It is no use the great ones saying that the tragedy has united us – we were pretty well united before it happened, or so we thought; but now, quite clearly, we are not. The majority showed its love and sorrow with mountains and acres of cut flowers in Cellophane, cuddly woolly toys (some of which were quickly stolen) and much weeping on shoulders. A few had strokes when they heard the news and promptly died. The British 'stiff upper lip' is now frowned upon or treated with contempt.

On our TV screens cameras seem to have sought out the most unpleasant people they could find (women mostly, and ugly ones) whose self-righteous petulance has been expressed with downright vindictiveness towards the royal family while at the same time spitting out words like love and compassion. Had they lived in the reigns of Henry VIII or Elizabeth I they would have quickly suffered the big chop for high treason. There were moments when I thought a grandstand might soon be erected outside Buckingham Palace for the comfortable viewing of many a latter-day Madame Defarge spitefully knitting while waiting to see the humiliation of the Queen. For me the most exasperating statement made by one or two of these harridans, and picked up by the press, was how cruel it was of the Royals to *force* the young princes to go to church within hours of hearing of their mother's death. Who knows they were *forced*? Certainly not the know-all interviewees. It could well have been the boys' own choice, without even gentle persuasion by their father or grandmother. It is, of course, people of no religion who grumble about the consolation others find in their faith; in the same way as people who never step inside an Anglican church hold forth on the current debasement of the Book of Common Prayer. When I heard a friend voice these opinions my blood ran cold; I knew it must be, undramatically, the Parting of Friends.

Other friends have expressed the same feelings of inertia and depression that M. and I have been experiencing. It isn't just sorrow for the loss of a remarkable personality, who gave generously so much of herself to sad causes, but a sense of malaise throughout the country. I, for one, feel for the first time in my life out of step with the nation as a whole. But now I also know that I am not the only one. Maybe it has to do with age and its discontent. Oh, I hope so, as then, in time, I shall be able to laugh at it. All is happening so quickly – a wobbly throne, devolution all round, subtle dictatorship of our lives from America and before long, I suppose, a disunited kingdom. Or not even a kingdom.

So far I have been unable to put the images behind me – the brilliant precision of the funeral cortège (even the horses pulling the gun-carriage barely winced as flowers were carelessly thrown at them), the strict regimentation of the Abbey service, the vast crowds sitting in Hyde Park in the sunshine to watch it all on giant T V screens, the spontaneous clapping at the close of Lord

Spencer's eulogy of his sister (with its forthright and unpleasantly sharp and impertinent comments) were all moving or fascinating to watch and hear. Perhaps Elton John's guttering candle in the wind was a verse too long but he did it brilliantly. The Archbishop of Canterbury was his usual self, unappealing. I have heard praise all round for the reading by the People's Prime Minister of the well-worn passage from Corinthians about faith, hope, charity (or love), but to my mind it would take a world genius to read that nowadays without straining to find any new emphasis. It calls for total simplicity, not theatrical know-how.

As on so many state occasions Dimbleby was to the fore on the box, giving us confidence that what he said was what, and where was where. Once inside the Abbey we were submerged in Tom Fleming's particular brand of ripe and hushed commentary. With the exception of the Duchess of York, who wore a frothily built-up black confection on her head, like a chocolate box in mourning, most of the ladies present sported large black cartwheels, which were troublesome in the breeze outside. They all had pearl necklaces.

Mid-September is proving fresh and glorious in Hampshire. Trees are still green – although a large ornamental cherry is looking tired and weary of life – and a few geraniums continue to dazzle in their pots. The outside of the house has been repainted during the past month, making it look cared for and presentable. Inside is another matter, but that must wait for next year. A week ago I changed my sleeping arrangements, moving from the small room I have occupied since Merula had an operation on her leg a few years ago to the more spacious spare room, which looks out to the north-west. Recently it had new windows put in, including a large handsome affair which goes to the ground and slides completely open. The balcony outside is big enough to stroll about on and has marvellous views over farmland to the Hangers and Steep church. To wake up to such a view at 7 a.m. raises my spirits. These September days mist is in the hollows, sunlight on the treetops and I begin to throw off the jaded feelings of the past fortnight. All, perhaps, is well with the world – or could be. God is more or less in his heaven.

Then the postman delivers the mail, and I take a step backwards. There is a long invitation from a group in the USA, faxed to my agent, to go to California this evening and 'talk to us about your beloved Princess Diana'. Too short notice, I am happy to say.

9. Indian Summer

In my abysmal ignorance I have always assumed that an Indian summer referred to agreeable, gently warm weather in the sub-continent during autumn, at some place like Simla, to which Europeans liked to escape from the oppressive Indian heat. Today I looked it up in the incomparable Brewer to find, to my surprise, that it is an American expression for the mild and misty weather enjoyed by the Indian lands of the Midwest during the fall. Here we are in late September and, with the exception of one chilly day of drizzle and one of boring grey, we have had fourteen glorious days of powder-blue skies, gentle breezes and a smell almost of spring rather than autumn. The dogs lie outdoors contentedly sunning themselves or having an occasional exuberant roll, wriggling with their legs in the air – something which looks as if it would be fun to be able to do.

One day last week it was so warm we decided to lunch in the kitchen arbour which we haven't used all this summer, largely because builders and decorators have had their ladders, trestles and buckets there; also the vine has got hopelessly tangled, making the spot feel impenetrable. So I pruned off a few tiresome branches and chucked them down near by, together with some fruitless bits of the fig tree. They made a pile about two feet high and about five feet across which I intended to clear away after we had had our meal. While carrying plates back to the kitchen I noticed that beloved Flora, our beautiful small lurcher, was stretched out on the grass facing the pile, approaching it cautiously then withdrawing before approaching again and making odd little sounds of curiosity. I couldn't think what was fascinating her and for some moments I couldn't see because the leaves were too dense. Perhaps there was a toad there, a mole, a squirrel, a bird or, most likely, her vivid imagination at play. Maybe she saw it as a wigwam with braves and squaws. No smoke signals emerged so I accompanied her on one of her approaches, praying it wasn't an adder she had spotted. Peering into the dark green tangle I saw two large familiar eyes – Michaelmas the cat. He stared us out of countenance until Flora did an acrobatic leap of joy at which he slowly emerged, sat for a moment to sort out his enormous Maxim Gorky moustache and then walked sedately by us, hissing 'Fools!'

Flora was about seven months old when she came to us. She was as thin as a wire coat-hanger when she arrived; now she has filled out in a muscular and elegant way. Her beauty is such that when she is around I can hardly take my eyes off her. All our dogs have been loved for their individual personalities and treated as unique beings. All have been affectionate but with very different temperaments; some comic, some serious and some self-consciously beautiful. At least two of them have understood simple English, more or less, or at any rate have put on an intelligent expression when spoken to. (I remember using the same trick as a schoolboy when interrupted in my daydreams.) Flora is going to follow suit; she cocks her head to one side, fixes one with her luminous almond eyes, furrows her brow into puzzlement and seems to say, 'I would understand you thoroughly if you could speak more clearly. And, incidentally, have you got a biscuit on you?'

Merula, having been brought up in the country, dealing efficiently with hounds and horses all her young life, always owned a dog until she married me. Working in the theatre and living in a small London flat ruled out the idea of any dog but we felt the need of some sort of pet, something which could be left alone during our long working hours and could arrange its own meals as it wished. We hit on the idea of a dormouse. We had just been reading *David Copperfield*, so he was called Trotwood and occupied a small but elaborate duplex made of plywood. Poor Trotwood's brief life was adventurous and finally tragic. His first major escapade was when he escaped up the chimney and came down a ball of soot. This was followed by M. cleaning out his house into a lavatory bowl, thinking he was safe in the top storey. Suddenly she saw a snout, tiny eyes and scrabbling paws amidst the detritus floating on the water. Shades of the mouse swimming in the vast pool of Alice's tears in Wonderland come to mind. Trotwood was rescued, dried and spent a quiet month in his bedroom before being taken to my in-laws' home in Surrey, which we thought would be a safe place while we went on a three-month tour of Europe and Egypt with the Old Vic Company. He was left in the charge of my eldest sister-in-law. She had the idea he would like a warm spot for the winter and placed his duplex on a radiator in the hall; a radiator which got very hot. When we returned from abroad we found Trotwood was only a thimbleful of dust.

In 1946 we rented a house in St Peter's Square, Hammersmith, which had a small garden, so we decided we could have a dog at last. Dingo was a collie, bought from the Battersea Dogs' Home. He was pleasant, boisterous and a great raper of local bitches. More worryingly, it became apparent that he had belonged to someone in the army, for whenever he spotted a man in a trench coat he made straight for him, leaping up for recognition. In those immediately postwar days there were innumerable ex-soldiers on the streets. It was infinitely sad to see him always rebuffed and returning to us as second-best. It was this constant seeking for his former master that led to his death. M. and I returned from a short holiday on the morning he escaped from the guardianship of my youngest sister-in-law, dashed into the road, having spotted an army coat on the far side and was instantly killed by oncoming traffic. Trotwood and Dingo were both ill-fated but all the others have had long and happy lives.

That is not quite true, as Zossima, a beautiful Siamese kitten I got from Harrods, developed some beastly disease after eighteen months and had to be put down. He was very charming and loving but had bad breath. One day he disappeared and of course we couldn't tell if he was lost or stolen. Notices were placed on lampposts and in newspaper shops but never a response. It so happened that I was filming at night not far from St Peter's Square and if there was a sufficiently long break would return home about midnight for a coffee. Zossima had been missing for five days and all hope of his return abandoned when, at about 2 a.m. when I was having a drink I heard his voice, very faint, at the front door. We rushed to let him in. He was thin, bedraggled and his claws were worn down to stumps, presumably from trying to scratch his way out of wherever he had been trapped. We took him straight to the kitchen where saucers of food and milk were put down for him. He kept up an ecstatic purr, looked at the saucers without touching them and then dashed to the top of the house where our son Matthew was sleeping. After a few minutes with Matthew, dizzy with purrs, he returned to the kitchen and sat down soberly to eat his meal. We, of course, were mopping our eyes at his return and the love he had expressed. His priorities in life were surprising.

In those first winters after the war food shortages were still with us. (Rationing continued until 1954.) The wartime sumptuary laws were tiresome but understandable. Black-market eggs, butter and even the odd loin of pork were offered by people seeking to ingratiate themselves, and as often as not were shame-facedly but eagerly received. On one occasion I remember being asked by my father-in-law to receive a parcel, at Victoria Station, from a butcher whose wife worked for him in the country. The war was still on and the parcel, well wrapped up, was a joint of beef. 'He's a nice man, Mr Salaman,' said the butcher, 'even if he is a Jew.' My instinct was to throw the beef on the platform but I knew my father-in-law was desperate for food to feed a large, fluctuating household, some of whom were likely to be without ration cards, so I knuckled under the flagrant anti-Semitism.

Merula used to keep an eye well open when passing through the Hammersmith markets in 1946 and one evening triumphantly produced from her shopping bag what she said was a duck. It had been plucked and didn't look much like a duck but that is what the marketman claimed it to be. The cooking smell wasn't too pleasant and it was completely inedible – as you would expect from a seagull.

On another dusky evening, when passing a grubby little butcher shop, she noticed in the window a skinny little puppy, flat out, flies buzzing round it and obviously dying. She was furious at the sight, stomped into the shop, chucked down a ten shilling note and scooped up the little thing into her basket. It was possibly a minute runt Alsatian and we named her Tilly. For the first few nights with us she lived inside one of my socks to keep her from shivering and M. sat up all night feeding her driblets of brandy and raw egg. The vet, to whom she was taken the next day, said there wasn't the remotest hope of her survival but M. wasn't having any of that sort of talk, so back to St Peter's Square she came and the brandy and egg regime was continued. After three weeks her ears were well pricked up, her eyes bright and she settled down to being our happy companion for nineteen years.

Tilly had two major obsessions, chocolate and matchsticks. Chocolates she would trace across the house however carefully hidden. Any matchstick she found she would place carefully on one's knee and invite one to throw it. You can't throw a matchstick very far so within seconds it had been retrieved and placed again on the knee. The matchstick might just as well have been a boomerang. It was an exhausting and exasperating game and she was very hurt when it had to come to an end. I associate her mostly with summer holidays either in the Lake District or by the sea – which she adored – with my socks, missing slabs of Cadbury's chocolate and the intensity of her games. While rationing was still on John Gielgud kindly sent us from New York, via airmail, a couple of dozen eggs – a rich and thrilling rarity. They should not have been left on the kitchen floor; Tilly wolfed the lot. It put her off eggs.

(Montaigne, 'On Sumptuary Laws': 'The law ought to state that purple and goldsmithery are forbidden to all ranks of society except whores and travelling players.' Walking down Old Bond Street yesterday and passing an overclipped poodle wearing a collar studded with what looked like rubies and nuggets of gold, led by a teetering female skeleton, I sympathized with Montaigne's view – but then I nearly always do.)

It is hard to resist going on about our dogs and I find myself weakening as I gaze blankly at the foolscap before me, conjuring up their images. Apart from Japheth, Dido and Flora, who are still very much with us (though the first two are getting on in years), there have been Vesta (Tilly's illegitimate daughter by a lover in the hedge), Shem, a black and white shih-tzu who had a will of his own and whose greatest pleasure was to visit London, straining at his lead to examine every lamppost; also Dorcas, a beautiful but rather alarming Belgian shepherd. Children loved her in spite of her farouche manner.

The first Belgian shepherd I knew belonged to Iris Tree and went with her everywhere in Europe, except of course in the UK, because of our absurd and cruel quarantine restrictions. He was called Alguri and was a dog of remarkable intelligence. I met him and Iris one morning in the hall of the Alfonso XIII hotel in Seville. She was at the reception desk, inquiring if there was a room available and Alguri, large and formidable, sat at her side. There was no room and she turned to the dog, shook her head and said, 'No good.' Alguri immediately made for the swing doors, pushed them open, crossed the street and sat next to Iris's car. On another occasion, in Rome, Iris, Merula, Jenny Crosse, Alguri and I went to dinner at a large, popular restaurant in Trastevere. The head waiter refused Alguri admission. Iris pleaded, 'But you know him. He'll sit quietly under our table and no one will be aware of him.' The waiter was adamant. Iris turned to the dog and said, 'The fools won't let you in. Sit outside and – [with great emphasis] – *see to it.*' Which is just what Alguri did. He sat outside on the pavement and prevented all would-be customers from entering the restaurant. The last years of his life were spent in France, mostly in Rothschild's kitchen, which he had made his own and where he stuffed himself to death.

It was Alguri's intelligence and formidable character that made me decide I wanted a Belgian shepherd. Eventually I found a breeder in north London and bought Dorcas. At about the same time I persuaded Albert Finney to have a dog, which was a mistake. Dorcas proved highly strung and erratic but her brother, Albert's dog, was an hysteric who had to be dosed regularly with tranquillizers. Dorcas was named after the lady, recorded in the Acts of the Apostles, who lived in Joppa and made children's clothes, and whom St Peter pulled back from death. (Incidentally there is a first-class fish restaurant in Joppa, a somewhat scruffy small town washed by the eastern Mediterranean. When we lunched there a few years ago they brought to the table a huge grilled fish, rather similar to a sea bass, into which had been inserted, 'like quills, upon the fretful porpentine', a number of sparkling indoor fireworks. It was a surprising but pretty sight and oddly enough the sharp smell of gunpowder went very well with the fish.) There were innumerable Dorcas Societies early in the century consisting of kindly ladies who did caring work for the very young and the old; we assumed our black farouche animal would follow suit, which in a way she did.

She behaved oddly one night when our grandson, aged about eight months, was staying with us. Matthew, his wife, Merula and I were at dinner while Samuel was asleep upstairs. All doors were open so we could listen for any sound he might make. Halfway through the meal I realized Dorcas wasn't in the room and I immediately thought she had padded up to his room, smothered him or possibly eaten him in her silent way. She had a mesmeric way of quietly taking birds out of a hedge and swallowing them. In a panic I rushed upstairs. The boy was sound asleep in his cot and there was no sign of Dorcas. Wanting a handkerchief I crept into our bedroom, switched on the light and there was Dorcas, lying in the middle of the room, contentedly banging her tail. She was curled up on a pile of Samuel's clothes, which she had stolen from the next-door room. Was it jealousy, love or instinctive shepherding?

The Indian summer has finally drifted away, leaving a morning frost on the grass, sharp air to stiffen the nostrils and conjure up the blood, and marvellous wide blue skies. Very few trees have turned but leaves are beginning to fall.

Japheth and Flora have developed a 'kennel cough', which is rife in the district and Dido looks uncomfortable about something.

Yesterday afternoon Merula went to Chichester for her cataract operation. When I telephoned at nine o'clock last night she sounded chirpy, had had a meal and was sitting up in bed drinking coffee and smoking a cigarette. It sounds a very easy-going hospital; they even allow patients to be visited by their pets, which seems to me admirable, particularly for the emotionally deprived. When I telephoned this morning she said she had had an uncomfortable night and a certain amount of pain. I go to collect her at lunchtime, after the surgeon has seen her.

(Later) All is well. She was a little off balance and felt as if under water for a few hours but now is fine and observing familiar things with a certain wonder. She was astonished to discover that our very upright Restoration chair is covered in bottle-green velvet and not grey, as she had supposed. No doubt she will experience the same visual delight as I have had in the past few weeks.

The lovely October has passed. The great leaves on the plane tree outside my study fell with a clatter overnight. The Spanish scarlet oak has gone brown instead of red; busy groups of chaffinches are quickly picking their way through the grass; and an unwelcome magpie, very smart in his black and white, is monopolizing the bird table. The Guy Fawkes fireworks, now seemingly extended over five days, have made each evening a misery for the dogs. Christmas is weeks away but the shops and advertisers are putting pressure on us all, jumping the gun as usual. And a tatty Union Jack with a hole in it fluttered upside-down from the mast of the Ministry of Defence on Remembrance Sunday. The Prime Minister is said to have been appalled. His children watched the ceremony from a balcony in extremely casual clothes. All this followed the bonding in Brighton of the Conservative Party, tieless and in hideous knitwear.

A few days ago, rummaging in a drawer of batteries, film spools, etc., I spotted a sixty-minute cassette tape I must have recorded ten years or more ago of various poems or speeches I had wished to learn. Playing it I found that, although I could remember a few lines in sequence here and there, I couldn't quote one piece in its entirety. The tape included 'The Love Song of J. Alfred Prufrock', Ulysses' great cynical speech from *Troilus*, beginning 'Time hath, my lord, a wallet at his back', the nineteenth psalm, poems by Robert Graves, R. S. Thomas, Vaughan and Herbert, and the Duke of Burgundy's marvellous evocation of the French countryside in his championship of peace towards the end of *Henry V*. The last came back to me new minted; I remembered with happiness listening to Leo Genn speaking it night after night in Guthrie's production at the Old Vic in 1937 – great heaven, sixty years ago – with Olivier as the king.

> The even mead, that erst brought sweetly forth
> The freckled cowslip, burnet, and green clover,
> Wanting the scythe, all uncorrected, rank,
> Conceives by idleness, and nothing teems
> But hateful docks, rough thistles, kecksies, burrs,
> Losing both beauty and utility.

That's not very far in imagery from Cordelia's description of the
mad Lear –

> Crown'd with rank fumiter and furrow weeds,
> With burdocks, hemlock, nettles, cuckoo-flowers,
> Darnel, and all the idle weeds that grow
> In our sustaining corn.

Why do some names, in the right circumstances, come to us
charged with almost uncontrollable emotion? Leaving the Burgundy speech I looked up the lists of names presented by the
herald to King Henry after the battle of Agincourt. And there it
was again, the most insignificant and yet, thanks to Shakespeare's
alchemy, truly great name recorded among the handful of English
dead. The first list the King reads is a roll-call of the flower of
French nobility, all high sounding and grandiloquent. The last
names are 'Grandpré and Roussi, Faulconbridge and Foix,/
Beaumont and Marle, Vaudemont and Lestrale.'

Henry then says, 'Here was a royal fellowship of death!/Where
is the number of our English dead?' He reads the only names
given him. 'Edward the Duke of York, the Earl of Suffolk,/Sir
Richard Ketley' – and, yes, here it comes – 'Davy Gam, Esquire.'

'What's in a name?' Juliet asked. Pretty well everything.

Kipling is a great one for springing surprise tears. For me, and
I cannot account for it, the names of his five minesweepers in
the poem which begins 'Dawn off the Foreland' nearly always
make me put a knuckle to my eye.

> Dusk off the Foreland – the last light going
> And the traffic crowding through,
> And five damned trawlers with their syreens blowing
> Heading the whole review!
> 'Sweep completed in the fairway,
> No more mines remain.
> 'Sent back *Unity, Claribel, Assyrian, Stormcock,* and *Golden Gain.*'

Philip Sparrow and Little Musgrave are other names that compel my attention, but with smiles rather than tears.

It sounded like the telephone ringing but I knew that could not be so. A starling, probably; yet the starlings round here took off for warmer climes a week ago. They sat shoulder to shoulder all along the arms of the television aerials, waiting for some unseen, unheard signal. Suddenly they scrambled like Spitfire pilots and wheeled away in perfect formation, circling the house a couple of times before heading south. Then I spotted one starling left behind. Not up to the journey, I suppose.

The daily offering of ghastly media news – murders, muggings, abductions, rapes, kidnappings and suicides – has been broken, for one day at least, by a heart-warming account of a Frenchman leading a dozen barnacle geese across four hundred miles of hostile territory in his microlight aircraft. Photographs show the young geese flying under the safety of his wings, as if he were their mother. He cruised at 35 m.p.h. and each time he landed to take a rest the geese bathed with him in a lake or clustered round him while he took a nap. His object was to escort them past French game hunters. He left them in some cherished spot in Brittany, where it is hoped they will escape Christmas festivities. 'Winter's not gone yet, if the wild-geese fly that way.' But winter is hardly upon us. Mid-December, heavy skies and unseasonably mild.

10. The Moths of Ithaca

You would be another Penelope; yet they say, all the yarn she span in Ulysses' absence did but fill Ithaca full of moths.

Those lines are spoken by the Roman Lady Valeria in the first act of *Coriolanus* when she calls on Virgilia – 'wife to Coriolanus' – in an effort to persuade her to go out for a jolly afternoon in Rome, shopping and visiting the sick. You can hear the affected, overbred lisping in 'Ulysses' absence', 'Ithaca' and 'moths'. It is the moths that intrigue me. I saw none when visiting the island, donkey's years ago, but I well remember the 'Valley of Butterflies' on Rhodes, which is many miles from Ithaca, but perhaps Greek moths travel to and fro between the Ionian Sea and the Dodecanese. There, in central Rhodes, we walked for two or three hundred yards up an undistinguished gorge thickly planted on either side with slender, droopy trees; not a butterfly in sight. The guide halted us and loudly clapped his hands, and the whole place turned into a fluttering black and white turmoil. After a couple of minutes the millions of butterflies returned to their green leaves, folded their wings and became, once more, invisible.

That little experience came back to me when listening to a marvellous tape of Miriam Rothschild being interviewed for BBC radio. The tape was made for me by a friend, while we were in Baden-Baden, who knew of my reverence for Miriam Rothschild and knew that I would be unaware of the broadcast.

As a result of that tape I wrote to La Rothschild (who when at home is the Hon. Mrs Lane) with one or two childish queries, particularly about her claim – she is a super scientist so I had no doubt about her facts – that certain caterpillars and moths exude a chemical which, if sniffed, boosts our memory. (I'd like to order a bushel of caterpillars right away, together with a jar full of fluttering moths, and take a good deep breath.) In reply to my letter she writes, 'These caterpillars are memorable beasts. The defensive volatile (chemical jargon calls it "pyrazine") which they exude does in fact improve recall in *us* if we sniff it again – which brings back vividly some event which occurred at the time we first smelled it. In other words it improves the memory of something you learned previously. If you wanted to learn "Friends, Romans, countrymen" it would help to sniff pyrazine at the time, but *again* when you were about to say "lend me your ears". The rest would follow easily. In nature presumably this smell reminds predators of nasty experiences in the past and so the caterpillar is protected. The moths and caterpillars have the same memory booster.' Miriam Rothschild goes on to comment that pyrazine is now used commercially to boost the flavours of tinned foods.

One other thing: Miriam Rothschild's caterpillars wave away aircraft that have the temerity to fly overhead, while at the same time they let off little puffs of gas. Obviously the caterpillars look on the aircraft as giant predatory wasps. As the aircraft never attack them the caterpillars probably congratulate themselves on being so well equipped for dealing with such foes. There is a moral there, somewhere, but I can't figure it out. No moth could resurrect my schoolday chemistry lessons or sharpen my wits on ethical problems.

Peter Raby, in his enjoyable biography of Samuel Butler, goes into some detail about Butler's obsession, in later life, with the idea that Trapani, on the extreme western coast of Sicily, was really the Ithaca of Odysseus and that the epic had been written by a woman. A long time ago I sailed past Trapani but I was ignorant of its possible – but unlikely – importance in world literature. Much as I would like to go there now, to follow Butler's footsteps and ideas, I know I lack the energy. Besides, it would be a fool's errand to follow someone else's fantasy.

With the exception of *The Way of All Flesh*, which I could never get on with, I have had a lifelong fondness and admiration for Samuel Butler – or at any rate since *The Notebooks* and *Erewhon* came my way when I was about twenty. Who could not love and respect a man who could write: 'The three most important things a man has are, briefly, his private parts, his money, and his religious opinions?' (I am tempted to add, 'The first two diminish with age and only the last is rigid.') He also informed the Victorians that the marble angels in their graveyards, to be physiologically correct, should have chests four feet deep to house the muscles for their enormous wings; something very pleasing to a young man's sense of the ridiculous.

In 1990 I read for the first time *Alps and Sanctuaries* as well as *Ex Voto*. His enthusiasm for the clusters of little sixteenth- and seventeenth-century chapels, perched on various Sacro Monte sites in NW Italy, prompted us to go to Orta San Giulio the following spring. Lake Orta is the smallest and most westerly of the Italian Lakes and its Sacro Monte is a half-hour walk uphill behind the small town. The 'chapels', nearly side by side, dating from about 1500, are mostly not much larger than a sitting-room and are more than half taken up by tableaux – one vivid scene to each little house. There are twenty or more at Sacro Monte d'Orta, nearly all depicting incidents from the life of St Francis of Assisi. The figures are of painted plaster, full of expression and realistic gesture. In some cases you feel they have suffered neglect – dust is lodged in the folds of a gown, a beard has come loose here and a hand has fallen off there – but nothing that a little washing with Flash or a tube of Secotine couldn't remedy. The view over the lake is fine, the smells are country smells, there is no noise and there is hardly a soul to be seen.

It is almost as quiet at Varallo, where the Sacro Monte is a much larger affair, more sophisticated, well cared for, and the chapels – in this case depicting the life of Christ – were built over a period of about two hundred years. If moths are serving my memory at all then I think there were about seventy scenes, some not much larger than peepshows, others immense. The earlier and simpler ones often have a figure by Tabachetti and your eye quickly settles on the work of an undoubtedly great artist. At the extravagant end of the scale, in the eighteenth century, is a Last Supper (or was it the Wedding Feast in Cana?), which is clearly taking place in the Ritz. Innumerable waiters are hovering, the Maître D is in a frenzy, fruit is piled high and the disciples or guests are dressed in the height of gaudy fashion by a long-forgotten Versace.

A big happy surprise at the Varallo Sacro Monte was to come across, in a sort of wide open-air passageway, a handsome bas-relief stone carving of Samuel Butler with an appreciative tribute to the Great English Writer who had helped revive Varallo. Stupidly I didn't copy down the exact words but I know my heart rejoiced for a man too much neglected by his own country.

At the gates of the Sacro Monte, just by a shed-like shop selling postcards, ice-cream, fizzy drinks and other tourist entrapments, there stands, unaccountably, a smart, red, English telephone box. As we were leaving the grounds we noticed it was occupied by a large German nun in distress. She was stuck inside and couldn't turn round. Her wimple and coif were awry. Her muffled guttural shouts and grimaces drew the attention of some Italian passers-by who quickly went to her assistance; they managed to drag the poor soul out backwards. Collapse of Stout Party. She was led off to the fizzy drinks but I think she could have done with a bracing *grappa*.

A week ago I went to London to do various chores – bank, doctor, haircut – and also to take an old friend to lunch. I waited in the restaurant forty minutes before ordering. She never turned up. A bottle of moths with a perforated lid to facilitate sniffing must be sent to Mu Richardson.

In the evening I thought I would take myself to the Gielgud Theatre to see *Shopping and F***ing*, which had received interesting notices and now its last three weeks has been announced. Stupidly I imagined I would be able to walk in without booking. There was not a seat to be had; such is the pull of a title. What *can* the asterisks stand for? Jill Balcon suggested 'Shopping and Feuding' as a possibility. 'Shopping and Feeding'? 'Shopping and Farting'? – but that is getting a bit near the knuckle. As I am told the play contains an explicit scene of buggery on a sofa (something not dreamed of by Dodie Smith, John Van Druten or Esther McCracken in the polite drawing-room vehicles of the thirties) I suppose the asterisks mean what they usually mean. It was a hot humid evening and I was rather glad I couldn't get in. Struggling away from crowds besieging the theatre I walked slowly down to Leicester Square where it was difficult to put a foot to the ground without disturbing squatting youth. They were all very genial, drinking from cans, biting at buns and having animated conversations, but somehow it wasn't even the Leicester Square I have known recently, let alone what it was like before the war. Farewell Leicester Square.

The glossy black slab of the Odeon Cinema stands on the hallowed ground where the Alhambra Theatre once stood. The Alhambra had a sort of Moorish look and offered not only superior music-hall entertainment but now and then classy things like the Monte Carlo Ballet with Lifar and others high off the ground. The theatre, at the back of the dress circle, had a wide, soft-carpeted promenade, shielded from the auditorium proper by a very fancy glass partition. Up and down the promenade gentlemen with large cigars paraded, stopping now and then when something on the stage caught their eye. It was, I suspect, a pick-up place for the well-to-do.

Standing as firmly as I could against the tide of tourists I stopped to look around. On which side of the square had Robert Louis Stevenson described a smoking divan – a long dark room in Turkish style into which a man might saunter for a quiet sit down, an enjoyable smoke and perhaps a small cup of bitter coffee? There at least he would be safe from encountering any lady he might know, which in the street would obligate him to throw away his newly lighted cigar. Before my time of course. The excellent chemist's shop, close to where the Empire now is, was the most popular place for West End actors to get their make-up and, almost opposite, a marvellously good classical gramophone shop: both gone. Also long gone and much lamented, closer to Piccadilly, was the vast, glamorous Lyon's Corner House. This was a godsend for actors. Not only was its food first-class and cheap but a large section stayed open all night. We would gather there after a first night to wait for the early-morning editions of the papers. When the papers arrived they were grabbed, and noisy, anxious tables fell silent. Heads disappeared into folds of *The Times*, the *Daily Telegraph*, the *Manchester Guardian*, the *Morning Post* or the *News Chronicle*. After a few moments there would emerge a moan, or a yelp of delight or a scoffing laugh. Then comments would come thick and fast. The livelihood for the immediate future of the readers was in the balance. 'That bastard is complaining again that no one can be heard. Also he says the lighting is too dim. Well, he's deaf and blind.' A loud grumble from behind the *Manchester Guardian*, 'They've spelt my name wrong.' 'Well, you're lucky to be mentioned.' 'I don't think poor old Jack will consider himself lucky to be mentioned – miscast and in two minds about what to say next.' We would all nod our heads wisely. 'True enough. And he's as old as the hills. Over sixty if he's a day.'

On this hot and crowded evening in Leicester Square there were three large circles of young people, about four deep, watching either a guitarist, a contortionist or a trickster. All the young men wore the uniform of blue jeans and from most of their back pockets protruded combs or documents; easy pickings for petty thieves.

JAQUES (in *As You Like It*): Ducdame, ducdame, ducdame . . .
AMIENS: What's that 'ducdame'?

JAQUES: 'Tis a Greek invocation, to call fools into a circle. – I'll go
   sleep if I can; if I cannot, I'll rail against all the first-born of Egypt.

A film I would like to have seen didn't start for over an hour so
I decided to return to my hotel, have a sandwich and beer,
perhaps watch some TV and then follow Jaques to bed and
sleep. In any case William Dalrymple's new book, *From the
Holy Mountain* was at my bedside and from the little I had
read of it I knew I had a treat in store. Slowly I made my way
from the overheated crowd to the Haymarket, where I found a
taxi. The taxi driver was a very pretty black girl with an Afro
hairdo, who looked as if dressed by Versace when in sober
mood.

Now I'll never know how they managed the sofa scene at the
Gielgud without arousing Mrs Mary Whitehouse.

At the end of last week we had two family visits. The first was
from our great-grandson, Otis, aged nearly two years; the second
was from his Aunt Bethany, just ten months old. Otis is the son
of our granddaughter Sally; Bethany is the late offspring of
Matthew and his wife Joanne.

Otis, who has Barbadian blood and boasts several other names
including Marlon and Simeon, looks like a very appetizing
milk chocolate éclair. Aunt Bethany is also just plain Angelica
Henrietta. Otis stomped around the place indefatigably, quietly
murmuring observations to himself. He seems to have a quite
extensive vocabulary. His eyes light on everything: knobs on
drawers to be pulled, switches on the electric stove to be twisted,
grapes to be grabbed and pictures to be pointed at. He has a
winning shy smile and his only sign of distress was when faced
with gentle Japheth, a dog at least twice his size.

Bethany, with cheeks as round and stuffed as a hamster's, is
the colour of cream at the top of a milk bottle. She is a great
thumper of tables and drums on the floor with sturdy legs. Any
day the crawling will start and parents and all of us will be off

on mad rescue expeditions. She has a gorgeous, rich, cackling laugh. The previous time I saw her was when the weather was cold; she came dressed as the Dalai Lama with a variety of Tibetan hats and bright, multicoloured robes; this time it was almost virginal – white-on-white just off the shoulder. Her arrival was something; to such a degree that I wondered why she hadn't got a police escort. There she was, sedate in her car, smiling sleepily at her subjects, and followed at the proper distance by a Japanese van full of her clothes: elaborate see-through cot, push-car, machine for heating things which looks like a newfangled laboratory, ditto for cooling, provisions for a long expedition to some remote part of the world, blankets, clothes and alarm systems. Merula and I stood amazed as our house filled up. We were joyful to have her of course, and her proud parents, but it took our minds back to the very different circumstances of travelling with a baby in wartime.

We pushed poor Matthew into a basket too small for him, loaded him with gas masks, phoney orange drinks and nappies. This we carried between us with the free hand dragging a suitcase. We sat around in the dark on grimy, sooty stations which had no lights, waiting for the train – always an hour late because of air-raid warnings – to take us to the darkness of Glasgow, Newcastle, London or Liverpool. When the train did finally pull in, with a shower of sparks, it was dimly lit by a few low-wattage blue bulbs which just enabled us to see that every carriage was full and the corridors jammed to suffocation with soldiers and their kitbags. Somehow we managed to get aboard, somehow someone found a bit of space for us to squeeze in. It was always a sympathetic, kind and often jolly atmosphere. The end of each journey seemed an eternity away and when we did reach it there would be an exhausting wait for an already full taxi (sharing taxis was essential) or the scarce public transport. No two cars or escort ready for us. Oh, lucky Bethany, living in the quiet Welsh countryside with a couple of cats for companions, a handful of hens, a duck or two and a small pond.

I swear I haven't been sniffing at the pyrazine but straight into the vision of my memory came –

> Four ducks on a pond,
> A green bank beyond,
> A blue sky of spring,
> White clouds on the wing –
> What a little thing
> To remember for years –
> To remember with tears!

I can't have read that in the last sixty-five years or so except to verify the lines just now. – What a pity William ('Up the airy mountain') Allingham felt he had to put a Victorian exclamation mark at the end of something so simple.

11. From Year to Year

The days, they say, are drawing out. All that strikes me is that in spite of the slowing up of time the weeks gallop apace; Sunday comes sharp on the heel of Sunday.

Male striptease has become the current nude fashion. On 23 December the BBC offered *Brazen Hussies*, 'a comedy drama about a landlady who teams up with a former schoolfriend to stage male strip shows'. And on Christmas Day *The Bare Necessities* was shown on ITV – 'a comedy drama about redundant Yorkshire miners standing in for a group of male strippers'. Somewhere in the line-up stands the touching and funny *The Full Monty*. Which was the chicken and which the egg? The world looked more recognizable last night with the showing of the 1950s film *The Man Who Never Was*, exciting, interesting, beautifully scripted and directed. Everything about it was good except for Clifton Webb as an RNVR Lieutenant-Commander in an itty-bitty little moustache and goatee beard. All the gold braid on naval officers' uniforms was Christmas-tree bright, not a sign of tarnish or service at sea. Fair enough perhaps but that, combined with a glossy-looking wartime London, suspended belief from time to time; and of course I was distracted by seeing the faces of old friends and acquaintances now dead.

Clifton Webb had never been a friend but he had been kind and hospitable to me when I first worked in Hollywood, making *The Swan* for MGM, which starred Grace Kelly and Louis Jourdan. Saturday nights in Los Angeles were always partying nights and people were marvellously generous with their invitations, among them Clifton Webb. The palatial venues changed from week to week but the guests were nearly always the same bunch with slight – or sometimes considerable – variations. Substitute Norma Shearer for Audrey Hepburn one week, or David Niven for Laurence Harvey, Fred Astaire for Gary Cooper, Zsa-Zsa Gabor for Aldous Huxley or, a very rare bird, Stravinsky. Apart from relieving the loneliness of being thousands of miles away from home, the parties were always worth going to just to gawp.

Clifton Webb gave a glamorous party for his birthday while I was there. He had, I suppose, about sixty guests, including Humphrey Bogart, Betty Bacall, Noël Coward, Grace Kelly, some smooth agents with well-padded shoulders and some re-faced female beauties of indeterminate age and some blond young men who had been working hard at their pectoral muscles. One of the latter trapped me on a sofa as he wanted to talk about the Method, something about which I know nothing. I pleaded my ignorance but he kept at it. On entering the vast drawing-room I had noticed a grand piano but because of the enthusiastic, dull, young man I failed to notice Noël Coward approach it. Suddenly I received a sharp rap across the shoulder. It was from Humphrey Bogart. 'Shut up, you!' he said. I shut up, although it was really the tedious young man who was doing the talking. All was silent in the room except for Noël's light vocalization of 'London Pride'. He looked across the piano at me with a sweetly pained smile. There was no doubt I had blotted my copybook. Noël kept up his unexpected entertainment for an hour. He had started at midnight and everyone felt privileged; and ready for another drink when he had finished.

The following Saturday night an almost identical group was gathered in some other, very similar Hollywood palace. Noël was there (and, of course, an inviting grand piano). Towards midnight I kept my eyes skinned and didn't miss a trick. Sure enough, I saw Noël modestly approach the piano, unnoticed by others, and run a light hand over a few notes. 'London Pride', etc., etc. Or possibly it was 'Mad Dogs and Englishmen' that floated towards us. Before he had got out half a dozen bars Bogey strode over to the piano, swiped him across the shoulder and said, 'Shut up, you! We had enough of you last week.'

The other night we watched a TV showing of the 1950s film about the sinking of the *Titanic, A Night to Remember*. It was in black and white and beautifully scripted by Eric Ambler. What good stories were told in the cinema in those days, swiftly, directly and without affectation. And how blessedly short they were when compared to the three-hour marathons that we are now expected to sit through, with aching bums, fatigued eyes and numbed ears. *A Night to Remember* was admirably directed – give or take a cliché or two – and there were some beautiful moments. My favourite shot was of an old scholarly-looking man, who rather resembled Thomas Carlyle, sitting alone in the vast smoking-room of the ship, totally absorbed in a small classical book. The ship was beginning to list and on deck all was hurry and distress, but drowning in icy waters was not going to disturb that gallant old scholar. He would die, I think, with a line from Euripides on his lips.

> Just when we're safest, there's a sunset-touch,
> A fancy from a flower-bell, someone's death,
> A chorus-ending from Euripides. (Browning)

Yesterday morning, 11 January, Teresa Wells telephoned to say John had died in the early hours. Cancer. Ten years ago he had a bout followed by a happy recession, but for the past year or more he fought bravely against its recurrence. He submitted cheerfully, and with hope, to chemotherapy; was funny about the wig he had made as his hair began to fall out and was always a model of gentlemanly courtesy and patience. When I saw him last, a few weeks ago, his face had become almost Churchillian. His hair was growing again but was still short, which enabled one to appreciate the nobility of the shape of his head. He had difficulty standing but his manners insisted on the attempt. His handshake was firm and his eyes remained bright and benevolent.

We met for the first time in a little restaurant I greatly liked, La Sorbonne, in Oxford. Alan Bennett and some of the cast of his play *Habeas Corpus* were lunching with me. John came to the table, wearing a raincoat and carrying an umbrella, and joined us for ten minutes. There was a very pretty, sweet-natured girl in our party and when John spotted how extraordinarily well-endowed she was he stamped the umbrella on the floor exclaiming a lot of, 'Aghs! Ha-haghs!' like some overexcited Blimpish colonel. It was absurdly funny but somehow not the least bit rude, let alone coarse. I never got to know him intimately but in recent years our paths often crossed; we talked quite a lot on the telephone and we met several times over a dinner table. He exuded goodness and high spirits. Merula fell in love with his voice and was always happy when he called.

John is the second friend to have died in the past three weeks. That doesn't augur well for 1998. I pray it is not going to be the Year of the Reaper.

Merula has put on my desk a little bunch of snowdrops, winter forsythia and wilting, pale mauve crocuses. The crocuses are unlikely to survive the night. Outside, on this grey afternoon, all is dank and quiet. It would be cheerless except for the news that the Christmas tree outside Norwich town hall is not to be taken down for some weeks because a blackbird is nesting in it. A foolish blackbird to be setting up house so early in the year, but the goodwill of humankind can be touching when it is allowed to be shown. Two long-tailed tits have suddenly shown up around the bird table. We are much relieved, as they should have put in an appearance weeks ago, and we were fearful that they might have left us and the district for ever.

Two months ago I bought for the house a white, plastic, electric kettle. Yesterday I threw it away. It was quite a handsome instrument and to begin with I was full of praise for its perform-ance. Water boiled quickly and the gauge, with a little red ball showing how full the kettle was, was also a satisfactory feature. The water we used was always filtered and the kettle descaled (not that there was any sign of scaling) a couple of times. Then, a fortnight ago, it began to foam up thin white blobs of scum, a greasy substance which disintegrated in one's fingers but would form again on the surface of a cup of tea. So we decided to go back to a metal kettle. An easy decision but not all that easy to realize. It took two days to find a decent solid one which you didn't have to plug or unplug, which wouldn't whistle at you and didn't have a tiresome fidgety lid. Having despaired locally I telephoned an admirable shop in Chichester. 'Yes, we have a variety of kettles. No, none of them are metal. The demand these days is for plastic. You might try So-and-So's.' So I tried So-and-So's. Same story. Then another place – 'We do have a whistling kettle, but it's not electric.' It seems you have to be sick for plastic or wildly old hat. I almost longed for a big, iron, sooty kettle which you could stand on an open range; a sort of Dickensian kettle. Finally we tracked down the last and only presentable electric job in Petersfield. At a price. So now we are boiling happily away and drinking too much tea.

For the past three weeks I have been happily reading *The Pickwick Papers*. Although I have never read it all the way through (which I shall do now) because the melodramatic or facetious stories which occasionally interrupt its flow irritate me, I have been fairly familiar with large sections. Last night I was carefully looking at the Phiz illustrations, with joy and amusement, when my eye caught something in the background of one of them which I had never spotted before. And it startled me.

In Chapter 33 there is an etching of Mr Weller Senior, standing expansively in front of a fire in the Blue Boar tavern in Leadenhall Market, London, smoking a long clay pipe, while his son, the glorious Sam Weller, is at a table trying to write a Valentine letter. It is a marvellously detailed, funny picture and, as always, Phiz fills out Dickens's description with great accuracy and makes his own atmospheric contribution. On the wall above the fireplace are lightly sketched in a few sporting prints; propped up on the mantelpiece are a couple of framed advertisements. One reads CIDER and the other GUINES'S DUBLIN STOUT. Being so familiar with the misspelling of my surname I immediately felt at home. And yet it may have been a deliberate little joke on Phiz's part, as the D in Dublin is in reverse.

Knowing nothing about Phiz other than the fact the name was a pseudonym and he and Dickens collaborated happily in their young days, I looked him up in the *Dictionary of National Biography*. His real name was Hablot Knight Browne, the youngest son of a family of nine which stemmed from Norfolk but lived in Surrey. He was born, significantly, on 15 June 1815. Hablot, as a Christian name, seemed odd. It turns out that his eldest sister was engaged to a young French officer named Hablot who was killed at the battle of Waterloo, 15 June 1815. Phiz had a successful career as an illustrator but later in life, it appears, he and his professional partner found it increasingly hard to make ends meet because they wasted so much time laughing. I like the whole story.

Here is Dickens on Sam Weller laboriously writing the letter:

[He] sat himself down in a box near the stove, and pulled out the sheet of gilt-edged letter-paper, and the hard-nibbed pen. Then looking carefully at the pen to see that there were no hairs in it, and dusting down the table, so that there might be no crumbs of bread under the paper, Sam tucked up the cuffs of his coat, squared his elbows, and composed himself to write. To ladies and gentlemen not in the habit of devoting themselves practically to the science of penmanship, writing a letter is no very easy task; it being always considered necessary in such cases for the writer to recline his head on his left arm, so as to place his eyes as nearly as possible on a level with the paper, while glancing sideways at the letters he is constructing, to form with his tongue imaginary characters to correspond. These motions, although unquestionably of the greatest assistance to original composition, retard in some degree the progress of the writer.

Sam's letter-writing brings to mind Ruth Gordon as Mrs Margery Pinchwife in *The Country Wife*, which she acted at the Old Vic in 1936. In writing the quite long letter towards the end of the play Miss Gordon went through every contortion known to man or woman, including, I seem to remember, climbing on to the table at which she was writing, or at any rate getting a leg over it. She was hilarious and in that one scene almost challenged Bea Lillie as a clown. Thinking about it today I wonder if Tony Guthrie, who directed the play, and who was deeply versed in Dickens, may have drawn her attention to Sam Weller's effort.

The funeral of John Wells was held last Saturday, 17 January, at the little village church which adjoins his and his wife's lovely manor-house home at East Chillington in Sussex. It was a bright sunny morning and remained so until after the burial, when dark clouds gathered and a chill wind got up. Everything looked lovely, from the marvellous surrounding countryside to the great pots of syringa scenting the pathway to the church, and the sheaves and posies of wild flowers and grasses from the fields. The fragility of the bunches on his coffin and catching the sunlight in the windows was fitting and moving. There was even a vagrant wasp – extraordinary for this time of year. Somehow it seemed appropriate; not that John was ever remotely waspish, although his wit could be penetrating. He had chosen his own hymns – 'The day Thou gavest, Lord, is ended', 'Dear Lord and Father of mankind': 'Abide with me, fast falls the eventide'. Whether he chose the reading from Ecclesiastes iii I don't know but I would guess it was very much his taste. It is the passage which begins, 'To every thing there is a season . . . a time to be born, and a time to die.' The verse that most intrigues me is, 'A time to cast away stones, and a time to gather stones together; a time to embrace, and a time to refrain from embracing.'

As I said goodbye to Teresa Wells I decided it was a time to refrain from embracing. I pray that my instinct was correct.

★

In the past three days two people have telephoned to inform me that *The Times*, the *Guardian* and the *Independent* have carried prominent articles listing the alleged salaries received by highly paid British actors during the past year. Apparently I am third on the list, after Rowan Atkinson and Richard Attenborough. Naturally, being gullible, I am inclined to believe the figures given for other performers; but the four and a half million pounds which is supposed to have come my way would be hilarious if not so irritating. This figure cannot have been provided by the Inland Revenue, or my accountant or my agent, so how the hell is such a piece of nonsense arrived at? I have no intention of divulging, except to the proper authority, what I have earned professionally, as that is my personal business, but I will go so far as this: if the four and a half million was divided by thirty – repeat, thirty – and the result cut in half to accommodate US Federal Tax, Californian State Tax, British VAT, etc., it would be nearer the mark, and still be my concern only. None of it greatly matters, except that I know from experience that the next week or so will provide a sackful of begging letters and pleas from struggling theatre companies for financial assistance I'm not in a position to give. I rather wonder if the people who so carelessly concoct such way-out articles have families, or dependants or commitments or interests to satisfy. Roll on death and the publication of my will, when it will be revealed, to an astonished small part of the world, that I have little more to leave than Anne Hathaway's second-best bed.

The jolliest thing that has happened in the past week has been the escape of two pigs – boars actually – from an abattoir. They dug their way out, swam a swollen river and made a successful getaway. The might of the law was summoned and was led a merry dance. Sadly, the pigs were eventually captured. They have become national heroes. Given time there will be figurines of them and board games – 'Chase the Pig'. Maybe they will be set up in their own private, well-appointed zoo. There must be money in it somewhere – other than bacon.

★

Last Sunday, being twenty minutes too early for a luncheon date in Salisbury, I spent the time wandering in the cathedral grounds. I had seen the Elizabeth Frink sculpture of the Virgin Mary shortly after it was erected some years ago and, in my mind's eye, it had appeared a large, rather forbidding piece of work. In fact it is quite small, perhaps standing not much more than four feet high. Also, in my mind's inaccurate eye, I had thought of it as a woman in a billowing gown striding purposefully to market; now I see it as a thinly clothed lady taking a tentative step forward. And where was the shopping basket I could have sworn she carried? It is all very fine, but I was dismayed at how my memory had played me false. It took a lot of very good wine during lunch to relax me. Possibly all our memories are subjective and become false with exaggeration; but does that matter? The very intensity of the falseness may contain the essential truth. (What the hell that means I have no idea.) Pontius Pilate has always come in for a lot of unfair stick, it seems to me, for asking a perfectly proper and very modern question. It was his misfortune, historically, to put the question to the very wrong – or very right – person. I see Pilate as a cynical, disappointed, career diplomat. He has been demonized down the ages. Was his sending for water to symbolically wash his hands in Shakespeare's mind when he gave Lady Macbeth the line, 'A little water clears us of this deed' after the death of the King?

'Of course I hope I am wasting your time,' I said to the dermatologist, 'but I think I may have skin cancer.' 'Let's have a look,' he said, without a trace of concern. I bowed my head towards him. 'Yes, there's a touch of something there,' he said, 'but I can clear that up for you before you leave the room.' Which he proceeded to do, freezing bits of my scalp with gas at −200°C. It felt hot but not painful. He suggested I should go to see him again in three years time, well into the millennium, but I doubt if I shall care by then whether I have skin cancer or not.

Light of heart, and my head thawing out, I walked down

Sloane Street, bought a couple of miraculous garlic presses and then taxied on to South Audley Street to order some nice-looking Wedgwood dinner plates. (Michaelmas the cat got behind our diminished number of Spode plates on the draining-board a day or two ago, and did a Greek plate-breaking dance with spectacular results; chips with everything.)

Daffodils stand six to eight inches high, the clumps of snow-drops are in vigorous flower and ice on the pond is as thin as a stretched sheet of polythene cling film.

12. A Coffee-spoon Life

Merula and I decided we might enjoy a cruise up the Norwegian fjords in late May or early June, in spite of her dislike of being on water. We reckoned those long arms of sea stretching inland off the coast of Norway must surely be glassy still; in photographs they look like mirrors. Anyway, she was prepared to take the risk, probably just to please me. We both knew we didn't want to be on a large cruise liner with its attendant horrors of organized jollity, one-armed bandits and evening entertainment, so I sent for the brochure of a small ship which plies the Scandinavian coast. It arrived this morning and quite put us off breakfast. The illustrations showed us staterooms and cabins all draped and swagged with silk-like curtains in rich floral designs. Even the king-sized bed was canopied. A slight sea and I can imagine the whole decorative scheme swaying nauseatingly. Apart from that all looked pleasant enough until I spotted that the promenade deck, 'where you might like to take a stroll under the stars before turning in for the night', sported city street lamps, looking very like Belisha beacons. I prefer a ship to look like a ship and not a zebra crossing; and I enjoy the creaking of a ship when at sea; the give and take of stress is reassuring and I don't want it muffled by fabric. So that is that, I fear, so far as a northern summer holiday is concerned.

There are several places we could cheerfully revisit and there are many others we could explore for the first time, but they nearly all involve starting from the dreaded Heathrow or, well on its way to equal awfulness, Gatwick. Everyone says Stansted is lovely but I haven't sampled that yet. The Euro-tunnel is likely to be stuffed with soccer fans. Maybe a nice health farm in Suffolk is the answer, but I do long to face and smell the sea.

Friday, 30 January: there is a lot of 1998 to come. A chilly misty morning but my heart was quickly cheered by seeing two wagtails strutting and dipping their way past my study window. They are the first I have seen for quite a long time and, like all wagtails, I look on them as clones of Fred Astaire; their white tie and black tails are the height of unobtrusive elegance. The robins stood stolidly, beady-eyed, as the wagtails pranced around, the blue tits didn't care a hoot and the beastly magpies, seeing my reflection in the window, kept their distance and refrained from marauding. 'And small birds fly in, and out of the world of man' (W. H. Auden, 'The Riddle'). Much of yesterday I spent reading, and rereading 'The Scholar Gipsy'. This I do almost every year and it always reduces me to melancholic tears. Last week I was asked by a newspaper to answer questions about my literary tastes. One of them was, 'What do you consider the most exciting line in English poetry?' I replied, in a slapdash way, quoting (inaccurately I now think) a line written by an obscure poet who was killed in the trenches in 1917. It is an invocation to an ancient Greek hero to 'shout for me'. It is probably to be found in Maurice Baring's marvellous anthology *Have You Anything to Declare?* but although I have turned every page of the book repeatedly the line will not reveal itself. (Found at last. 'Stand in the trench, Achilles, /Flame-capped, and shout for me.' The poet was Patrick Shaw-Stewart). Anyway, having spent so much of yesterday with Matthew Arnold I have now changed my mind and wish I had substituted for the trenches a line from 'The Scholar Gipsy':

> And snatch'd his rudder, and shook out more sail;
> And day and night held on indignantly
> O'er the blue Midland waters with the gale.

That word 'indignantly' does the trick, but the line I should have chosen, I think, is 'And snatch'd his rudder, and shook out more sail'.

One of the great pleasures of the past week was seeing again John Gielgud's gloriously, wickedly funny performance in *Brideshead Revisited*. The Venetian holiday episode is particularly pleasing, largely because the overfamiliar picture postcard views of Venice were scrupulously avoided and one could feel one was there and yet not a tourist. What a city in which to have a little apartment, preferably on the neglected Giudecca. But even the Giudecca is probably being trampled into the water right now.

It is Saturday, 7 February. Got back yesterday lunchtime from a couple of days and nights in London. Jack Nicholson was staying at the Connaught so the entrance to the hotel was besieged by photographers and autograph seekers; rather tiresome for the rest of us. The hotel staff say he, Nicholson, deals with it with charm and patience. How I envy his disposition; my face settles into exasperated grumpiness as soon as I spot the advancing proffered pen (often inky) and ancient photograph to sign. Of course Marlene Dietrich had a point when she was staying in the same hotel in Paris as Richard Burton and Liz Taylor and they complained, in her hearing, about the endless stream of fans swarming round the front door; she turned to them and said, 'My dear Richard, my dear Elizabeth, if you want to escape the crowds don't stay in the same hotel as me.'

On Wednesday afternoon I went to the specialist for a final check-up on the eye which was operated on for a cataract six months ago. All well it appears. But the bad left eye, which had surgery two years ago for some other ailment, now has a little knot in its stitching coming undone and sooner or later that will have to be dealt with. I was unaware of this but was told that as soon as irritation sets in, which it will, he will snip it out. He reassured me this is a very minor job but I don't feel at all brave about it; snips and tweezers around the eyes don't appeal.

In the evening Derek Hill and I dined together. I dislike being painted, drawn or photographed – acute self-consciousness sets in – but the sessions I had with Derek towards the end of last year, when he did an oil of my head, were painless and conversationally entertaining. In any case I was honoured to be painted by him and flattered by the result. He managed to make me look twenty years younger and as if I had just returned from a healthy skiing holiday. The eyes, maybe, are too blue and the nose too neat and straight, and he has been kind about wrinkles, bags and jowliness. He is a fine artist, so I expect he has caught the unguarded me, but that I do not know. His superb mist-strewn Irish landscapes totally convince me so, for the moment, I'm foolishly hoping that I really do look the way he portrays me even if he does make me look rather like Yeltsin. At the end of dinner I discovered he has a passion for Cape gooseberries. The hotel provided an extra helping when the first lot was demolished and then, as we left, kindly presented him with a further supply wrapped up in silver foil.

On Thursday, sandwiched between visiting the Van Eyck exhibition at the National Gallery and Burlington House's masterly 'Art Treasures of England', I went to my dentist for a check-up. In the quiet waiting-room I found Albert Finney, as stolid, robust, warm and genial as ever. We modestly kept our voices fairly low, I hope, but kept up a giggling chatter – mostly about what dear Tom Courtenay's obsession might be for 1998. Albie said Tom's current craze is for computers. We had the year of astronomy a decade ago, followed by the year of ornithology, the golf year, the flute year and the year of climbing plants. Each subject is seized on desperately seriously and results in genuine knowledge. When I mentioned climbing plants I noticed that copies of *Punch*, *Hello!* and the *Geographical Magazine*, which were being gazed at by other patients and held in front of their faces, suddenly became totally still. Not a page was turned. The patients became cardboard cut-outs. Perhaps, after all, we were talking too loudly. Albie volunteered the information that he expected to be filming in Portugal in the summer, and that got me on to the subject of Portugal. I asked him if he knew Wellington's reply when, late in life, he was asked what was the most inane remark he had ever heard. Wellington said, 'During the Peninsular War I heard a Portuguese general address his troops before a battle with the words, "Remember, men, you are Portuguese!"' We both laughed loudly and the magazines covering faces were lowered, rather disapprovingly I thought. One face, now I saw it, looked distinctly Iberian. Oh dear, was I being thought racist? No, not me – and not even Wellington really. On my two visits to Portugal I have found the people kind, helpful and even jolly.

The few Van Eycks (some just attributions) seemed to me poorly presented in a drab room round which a slow-moving crocodile, two to four people thick, made its neck-stretching way. If you were on the outside of the queue you could only see the top half of the pictures and hadn't a remote chance of reading all the information on display. In fact there was much more to read than to look at. I was unable to even glimpse that intelligent, curly little dog at the bottom of *The Arnolfini Marriage* but I did manage to get a reasonable look at *A Man in a Turban*; but they both belong to the National Gallery anyway. What I most wanted to see, *The Annunciation*, on loan from Washington, was obscured not only by the shuffling crowd but by an outsize lady, possibly German, who kept tapping the gloriously coloured wings of the angel with her catalogue while explaining something to her broad companion. The custodian was too busy getting new arrivals into line to notice.

On sale among the art books and pcs were large cardboard masks of Mr Arnolfini in his tall hat and with his nose cut round so you could stick yours through it. I didn't buy one.

At the Royal Academy the 'Art Treasures of England', paintings gathered from the great and small provincial galleries throughout the country, is completely rewarding; I look forward to visiting it again and probably yet again. There is far too much to take in at a single visit. The exhibition was very well attended and yet there was room to move and look without jostling. Most of my time was given up to about eight or a dozen paintings.

The great Stubbs's *Cheetah, Deer and Two Indians* held me for a long time. (The deer looks almost indifferent to its probable fate.) John Crome's *Norwich River*, so placid in its idyllic afternoon sunlight, held me breathlessly still. The backs of the Norwich houses reminded me of houses alongside the canal in Colmar, and Colmar evokes memories of the overwhelming Isenheim altarpiece, painted by Grünewald, in the museum. It is an agonizing crucifixion, with twisted, distorted feet and hands, as far from the sweetness of the Norwich river as you could get. The only comfort in the Grünewald is the caring, fair-haired St John with his remarkably long right arm supporting the Virgin Mary. It was strange to have these images before me when looking at a boat being rowed through such still waters. Next to the Crome are two little, cheerful, sunlit Constables – of Golding Constable's flower garden and kitchen garden. If I could steal anything from the exhibition I think it would be the *Flower Garden*. (A sentence of Abraham Constable's – John's younger brother – came to mind. 'When I look at a mill painted by John I see that it will go *round*.')

The Travelling Companions by Augustus Egg made me laugh. The identically dressed sisters, in their vast silvery skirts, which look like semi-inflated balloons, would totally obstruct anyone else attempting to get into their coach-like railway carriage. Indeed one wonders how they got in themselves. The view outside the window is apparently of the shoreline near Menton, and I am surprised, in my dreadful insular way, to learn that there was a railway along there in 1860. Somehow I have taken it for granted that the steam engine didn't puff its way across the continent until years after there was a vigorous network in this country.

I liked William Rothenstein's self-portrait and was thrilled to see, in the right centre foreground of Ford Madox Brown's *Work*, our beloved Border terrier, Dido, with a collar of wood-shavings.

Also, in the lower left side is a dog similar to our Flora, but too thin and without her beauty. On the whole the picture doesn't please me much; it makes me feel I am being got at in a moralistic way.

Somewhere along the line of the day I managed to buy Ted Hughes's *Tales from Ovid* (and read 'Echo and Narcissus' immediately with intense pleasure while having a haircut; I refrained from looking in the mirror). In the evening Faith Brook and I went to the Aldwych to see *Amy's View*, which she had seen before. The packed audience was astonishingly enthusiastic.

The following morning I had intended to seek out a Chinese emporium in Soho to buy a lot of unfamiliar goodies like fresh ginger, coconut milk, rice noodles and groundnut oil, but I left insufficient time. The Chinese cooking effort (if I ever really get round to it) is a result of watching Ken Hom's enthusiastic expertise on TV and arming myself with his book, *Travels with a Hot Wok*. Merula is almost diabolically thrilled at the idea, knowing that my cooking skills only encompass scrambled eggs, grilled sausages and tinned tomato soup with croûtons. I have no great urge to cook and don't take a great deal of interest in food, but I would genuinely like to take the pressure off M. in the kitchen; also to see if I can chop vegetables as swiftly as Mr Hom. He appears to use a vast cleaver, suitable for decapitating, for the most delicate jobs. One thing is certain – the kitchen will have to be cleared of everything except the pots, pans, bowls, wok and ingredients I shall need.

Many years ago in New York, Alfred Lunt, an actor whom I revered, invited me to dine with him and his wife, Lynn Fontanne, one Sunday evening in their apartment. It was like a most charming but nevertheless royal command. When I arrived Mrs Lunt said, 'Alfred is cooking tonight. It is the staff's evening off. Do go into the kitchen – he loves being watched.' In the kitchen I found Alfred dressed in white cotton and wearing an immensely tall chef's hat. He greeted me with preoccupied gravity. On either side of him stood a pretty Hispanic girl holding a bowl in one of which were mushrooms and in the other herbs. 'Erbs, as the Americans say. How large a staff did they have, I wondered. Alfred took a handful of mushrooms and cast them in a pan on the cooker as if making a brilliant exit line. Then, to top it, sprinkled the herbs and laughed. 'Let's leave it to the girls,' he said, and, taking off his chef's uniform but still wearing the high hat, led me back to the drawing-room. 'All going well?' Lynn asked, and he nodded with satisfaction. That was the end of the cooking; so we sipped our dry martinis and talked theatre. What fascinated me most, and I had difficulty not staring at, was Lynn's reddish-black hair, scraped off her forehead and the sides of her head and screwed up to form a sort of Thai temple on top, about six inches high. It was bound round with beautiful tortoiseshell and heavy gold. I remember nothing of Alfred's dinner.

He was not only a marvellous, tremendously professional actor, but a man of gentle courtesy and understanding; his philosophical courage when his sight began to fail was truly impressive.

Piled on my desk I find personal mail, bills, etc., swamped by the usual glossy unwanted rubbish about which we all complain. It lowers the spirits of every homecoming. 'Congratulations! You have been selected to be on our mailing list!' or 'You, too, could be the proud possessor of a genuine reproduction of Princess Diana's favourite tea-tray. BUY NOW to avoid disappointment. Hurry! Hurry!' Also four identical appeals from Cancer Research; I wince at the money and energy lost by over-insistent charities. But most alarming were two fan letters saying, 'I got your address through the Internet.' It'll be telephone numbers soon. For several weeks I've wondered why so much of my mail has been incorrectly addressed and now it is clear – Internet misinformation.

Enoch Powell has died. He had a most extraordinary voice – high, nasal and whining – which arrested one whenever it was heard. There is no doubt that he was listened to by all and admired by many. In the correspondence columns of the *Daily*

Telegraph I see Sir Edward Heath is being hauled over the coals, as so often, for bluntly speaking his view of Powell. Heath must be beginning to wonder if he is a latter-day St Lawrence, roasting on a grid-iron. 'Turn me over please, that side is done.'

Of course the big stuff at the moment (11 February) is the threat of air-strikes by the USA and the UK against Iraq. Many ladies in high position seem very keen on the idea, as they so often are when war is in the air. They pay lip-service to diplomacy while rattling sabres too big for them to wear. How can, 'Do this or take the ghastly consequences to your children,' be considered an ambassadorial defusion of the situation? Saddam is obviously a horror and a threat to world peace but I suppose he could say to the US and ourselves, with some justification, 'Show me yours and I'll show you mine – my weapons of total destruction, I mean.' Isn't there an islet off the coast of Scotland which cannot be visited because of contamination from anthrax experiments? Or were we misinformed some years ago? Tony Benn made the point tellingly in the House of Commons and on TV a day or two ago but I haven't noticed if the press took it up. I doubt it.

Pickwick is finished and I dropped a happy tear at the end for the sheer goodness and miseries of everyone. I like to think of Mr P. acquiring a smart house in Dulwich where he strolls among admiring neighbours and spends time in the art gallery. And I am relieved to be reminded that the adorable Sam Weller and his pretty wife served Mr P. to the end, and that over the garden gate were often seen two tough little Weller boys.

Loving the book as I do, and admiring its beautiful descriptive prose (something that Trollope couldn't touch), I am aware that the characters are really line-drawings and not full reach-me-down portraits. 'It has been the peculiarity and marvel of his power that he invests his puppets with a charm that has enabled him to dispense with human nature.' So wrote Trollope of Dickens. (Quoted at the annual Trollope Society dinner in 1996.)

Now Updike's *Toward the End of Time* can be started and also, in small doses, *Athene* by Ann Shearer, a gift which arrived this morning and looks fascinating in its Jungian way. Glancing through it I spot references connecting Pallas Athene to various Black Madonnas which have turned up in southern Europe. The first M. and I saw was at Tindari on the north-eastern tip of Sicily. The village and church were crammed with pilgrims; it was, I believe, a feast day to commemorate the effigy being washed up on the shore below, heaven knows how many centuries ago. Inside the church *carabinieri*, crumpled cigarettes dangling from their lips, pushed and pulled people around the altar. The noise, the pressure of the crowd, the vicious elbow work made the Virgin difficult to see, standing (in a sitting position) as it did in a dark corner. I had the impression that it was far from beautiful but undoubtedly disturbing. On the other hand the Black Madonna (marble) in the very baroque abbey church at Einsiedeln, in Switzerland, is highly sophisticated. The only other I know is the reproduction, in a side chapel at Farm Street, of the statue at the foot of which St Ignatius Loyola laid his sword before taking up his mission. And is there one in St Mark's in Venice? Or is that, if so, a painting? Can't remember. I have a sneaking feeling that, whatever it was, the Knights of Malta rescued it from Constantinople.

The weather the last few days has been glorious. Mornings have started very misty; the fat black sheep in the paddock come looming up looking like bison but when the sun has burned all whiteness away everything returns to normality and greenery. At night it has been different in another way.

> But when the fields are still,
> And the tired men and dogs all gone to rest,
> And only the white sheep are sometimes seen
> Cross and recross the strips of moon blanch'd green . . .

Yes, it is a pretty picture out of the living-room but the moonlight emphasizes the hundreds of molehills. Also, it dawns on me that much of what I have taken for grass has become, during the past months, thick moss. If we have a really dry summer we shall find ourselves living in a dustbowl, or at least on a parched sandy strip.

Star Wars – No Peace. Today I received an advertisement from an American magazine for a 'cookie jar' representing Obi-Wan Kenobi (an alias of mine) selling at $275. There are only a thousand for sale, the ad says, and they are all 'hand painted from top to bottom.' It stands 16 inches high. Hurry! Hurry! Not a cent will come to me or from me I am relieved to say.

22 February. Spent two nights in London last week. Lunch with Alan B. (quiet and relaxed); dinner (Indian) with Tom and Isabel Courtenay, a very convivial affair. Tom and I rode our hobby-horses – he on computers and I on Trollope. As they are just off to Bruges for a brief holiday this enabled me to get a foot in another stirrup on another horse, as I know Bruges fairly well. Merula and I had a weekend there before we were married; then there was the film location for Bridget Boland's *The Prisoner*; and three years ago we had a most enjoyable week there, taking Matthew and his wife with us. It is a lovely city but now very different in atmosphere to what it was thirty years ago; then you never saw a smiling face and 'Bruges le Mort' was a well-deserved put-down. The trouble with Bruges is trying to find a restaurant where you can have a simple light meal instead of the rich local dishes which leave you stuffed and breathless.

Another object of my going up to London was to have a look at Agnew's 'Picture of the Month' – a woodland scene, painted about 1830, by William Frederick Witherington, of whom I had never heard. The reproduction of the painting (a large postcard size) which Agnew's had sent gave me great pleasure; the picture itself, oil on panel, is not that much bigger, being 10½ × 14½ inches. It is titled *In Wanstead Park, Essex* and shows seven men digging, very vigorously, what I assume would become a large pond surrounded by trees. In the foreground is a heavily built man carrying a metal urn, possibly containing tea or drinking water. All the brawny navvies except one are wearing hats (no skin cancer of the head in those days) and clean white shirts. The background looks romantic, with dark avenues in a slight summer haze. There is no doubt that I would love to possess it but, to my dismay, commonsense rears its bleak head – the kitchen and back loo need repainting and four large windows must be double-glazed before next winter. So farewell Witherington. And I mustn't even whisper 'Hello!' to a ravishing pen-and-ink Ruskin of a footbridge in Northumberland or let my eye stay too lovingly on a couple of Edward Lears.

There is a new, impressive, vegetable-cum-grocery shop (with a restaurant at the back) in Great Portland Street. Among the shiny avocados, lemons, grapes, spotless carrots, ginger and broccoli heads I spotted bundles of samphire – something I haven't seen for ages or ever eaten. The samphire worked on me like Proust's madeleine.

> How fearful
> And dizzy 'tis to cast one's eyes so low!
> The crows and choughs that wing the midway air
> Show scarce so gross as beetles; half way down
> Hangs one that gathers sampire, dreadful trade! (*King Lear*)

That the plant clings to the chalk cliffs of Dover, or at any rate used to, Shakespeare well knew but is it the same samphire or sampire as found in marshy ground in East Anglia? I walked out into the London traffic carrying a bag of various delicious breads, crème fraîche and coconut milk, my mind revolving on various productions of *King Lear* and the actors who had played Edgar and Gloucester. The late Alan Webb stands out most vividly as Gloucester under Peter Brook's direction thirty years ago and

Robert Harris as Edgar speaking the samphire speech most beautifully in the Granville-Barker production at the Old Vic fairly early in the Second World War. It was the time of the retreat from Dunkerque with the nation biting its nails with anxiety and Gielgud, I remember, who was playing the crazed King, couldn't understand why the audiences were falling off rather sharply; most people, of course, being glued to their radio sets. John's grasp of public events was always rather tenuous. His heart, however, was in the right place. 'I feel so sorry,' he once said, 'for those poor men sitting up there all day. They must be so cold.' He was pointing to the barrage balloons tethered over London.

'A penny for your thoughts,' a taxi-driver said. I had stopped him but then, rather alarmingly, couldn't remember where I wanted to go. Dithering, I thought to myself, with Lear, 'Meantime, we shall express our darker purpose.' Once in the cab I racked my brain for the lines that follow but could only come up with, ''tis our fast intent/To shake all cares and business from our age, . . . while we,/Unburthern'd crawl toward death.' Or at any rate to the traffic-lights which always seem to be set against us, solidly red, while the meter ticks up relentlessly.

Ash Wednesday. The morning Mass and smudging of foreheads was well-attended, the women outnumbering the men by about fifteen to one. We oldies now have an easy time of it so far as fasting is concerned. Perhaps it should be the other way round; it is the young and energetic who need sustenance, while the over-sixties could manage quite well for the day with a boiled egg, a cup of tea and a cheese sandwich. (Vatican kindly note.) At the imposition of ashes I noticed a lady snap up the low brim of her hat and then snap it down again quickly; *she* wasn't going to let the passing world outside the church know that she had an ashen face.

After a scrappy lunch I turned the pages of Ken Hom's *Travels with a Hot Wok* and volunteered to make an attempt to cook dinner. M. jumped at the opportunity to put her feet up and I settled for Mr Hom's Nonya Laska, a vegetarian dish which looked fairly straightforward on the printed page. What's more I had all the ingredients for it, with the exception of coriander. The result was surprisingly good but rather too spicy hot. There was a moment in the preparation when I thought I had scalded my thumb, which got very painful. Having applied an anti–burn cream, which did no good at all, I realized it was neither a scald nor a burn but that when I had been seeding a red chilli one of the fierce little seeds must have got under a thumbnail. In spite of repeated washing of hands and holding under the cold tap it made itself felt for about three hours. It seems I should have scooped out the seeds with a knife, not fingers. We broke out into top-of-the-head sweats when eating Nonya Laska and drank pints of Highland Spring or Badoit.

Now I want to try the recipe for curried celery. A friend is coming to lunch the day after tomorrow who may prove a willing victim; she is, in any case, a brave woman, taking herself off next week to Chernobyl, weighed down with medicines, food and toys for the children of the atomic disaster. How I admire and envy people who have the guts to actually *do* something with their lives. When they are no longer young and yet make these firm decisions it is doubly impressive. No coffee-spoon life for Sarah Badel; and I bet it would never cross her mind that what she is up to is almost foolhardy.

Outside my window there are four goldfinches flicking beautiful colours across a grey afternoon. They are far more heart-warming than Mrs Albright, who is beamed so constantly from Washington on to our anxious, Gulf-conscious TV screens.

13. The Whirligig of Time

The Ides of March have passed and nothing untoward has happened to our quiet lives in Hampshire. Farther afield there are horrors – starvation on every continent, ugliness in Albania and environs, Israeli/Palestinian squabbles, the madness of Northern Ireland, daily murders at the seaside, Madeleine Albright jetting around somewhere, schoolchildren committing suicide, the scandals surrounding the personal life of the President of the United States, paedophile clerics coming to the surface – and so it goes on – but here the daffodils make a fine display and ornamental cherry blossom begins to show. Yesterday morning, standing by our somewhat formal pond, I watched a large lady toad do a steady breaststroke, with vigorous kicks from her hind legs, as she ferried across the water her tiny husband, who clung desperately to her back. He reminded me of the late, much-loved farceur, Robertson Hare, calling out 'Oh, calamity!' whenever his trousers fell. The toads found a submerged brick where she had a little rest and he pretended he couldn't be seen.

Our good neighbour and good friend, Captain Blake Parker (RN rtd), who keeps a very shipshape garden, has been up twice in the last few days, wielding bucket, spade and a mole trap in an effort to rid our ruined ground of the pests. He works speedily and efficiently but it looks to me as if he is setting elephant traps. No luck so far. It is just possible the moles are put off because Japheth, our old Labrador-type, as soon as Blake has withdrawn, visits the spot and contemptuously lifts his leg.

In the past couple of weeks I have had two enjoyable jaunts to the theatre; both by myself, which I prefer unless going to a musical. The first was to see Terence Rattigan's *Cause Célèbre* at the Lyric Theatre, Hammersmith, and the second *Things We Do For Love*, Alan Ayckbourn's new play at the Gielgud. Wandering around before the performance at the Lyric, which has been shifted a short way from its original site and totally redesigned (except for the preserved interior of the auditorium) I stopped to look at some framed old programmes, posters and pieces of information. One particularly caught my eye. 'The first show, attended by Her Royal Highness [sic] Queen Elizabeth II is Shaw's *You Never Can Tell*.' You sure can't. The Queen would take such sloppiness with good humour, I'm sure, but I find the prevailing carelessness in print and speech irksome. Proofreaders used to be reliable; in fact I haven't spotted a single typographical error in any book in my possession printed before 1960. In recent years they have come thick and fast, and my daily newspaper produces, on average, three a day. Habitual grumpiness was about to grip me when a very pretty, smiling usherette approached and said, 'I've seen you on the Parkinson show. You said you liked animals and liked watching them. I thought that was real cute.' Cute? Me? 'Row F,' I said. In the interval she came up to me again. 'I've been watching you. You *are* just like an animal. Fantastic! Are you enjoying the show?' I assured her I was. 'Brilliant!' she said, but I wasn't sure whether it was her comment on the play, my appreciation or her view of life in general.

(Before I forget, the front-of-house staff at the Gielgud were first-class as well – helpful, smiling and smartly uniformed. Things are looking up in theatre-land. And up and up go the prices.)

The first production of *Cause Célèbre*, which I never saw, opened in the winter of 1977 a few weeks before Terry died of leukaemia. On the first night I'm told he sat in a box, physically weak but gratified by the reception he was given. The play was not a success; with hindsight people say that Her Majesty's was too large a theatre for it (many of the scenes are duologues), and by all accounts the production was slow and cumbersome. Such a criticism could not be levelled at the Lyric's current presentation which is really good but almost overreaches itself in its swiftness – a concept of the play that reminds one of film flashbacks, rapid dissolves and abrupt cutting. It provides some fine acting of meaty parts. Amanda Harris is brilliant as Mrs Rattenbury – both attractive and slatternly, humorous, intelligent, wayward and deeply moving. It is a performance which would have thrilled Terry. He would have taken delight also in Neil Stacy as Mrs R's defending counsel – a spot-on performance of wit and humanity. The pleasure of acting in his plays, apart from the fact that they were good stories, was that for the most part the characters were believable and actors could get their teeth into flesh and blood. Perhaps he was not always at his best when his work stepped outside England.

I find it wryly amusing that Rattigan, with *Cause Célèbre* in London and *The Deep Blue Sea* in New York, is filling seats thirty years after he was dismissed contemptuously by the truculent avant-garde, with headquarters at the Royal Court, as being old guard, old hat and sickeningly West End. His sins included being well-mannered, suited in Savile Row, Harrovian-educated and a master of the well-made play. Most champions and detractors are dead now and time has brought in its revenges – and no doubt fortunes and revaluations will revolve yet again.

French without Tears was the first play by Terry which I saw – that was in 1936, at the Criterion – and for some reason I cannot remember I was at the first night and, even more oddly, sitting in the front row of the stalls. I barely knew Terry but I suppose I must have met him at a party and that he extended an invitation. He was always absurdly generous, lavishing gifts on all and sundry with impetuosity. (No one expected *French without Tears*, from rumours we had heard, to be a success and yet within five minutes of curtain-up it was obviously going to be a triumph; it became a landmark in English light comedy.) Years later, on the first night of his *Ross*, in which I played Lawrence of Arabia, he brought two splendid gifts to my dressing-room while I was making up – the Eric Kennington portrait of Abi Ibu El Hussein which was reproduced in *The Seven Pillars of Wisdom*, and a beautifully leather-bound manuscript of the play. When Terry died I gave the Kennington to William Chappell (they had been intimate friends for many years and Billy, who had directed for Terry, had fallen on hard times) and I handed on the manuscript of *Ross* to Simon Ward when he played the part about ten years ago at the Old Vic.

Flare Path, Rattigan's play about the R A F, was a big success in London but didn't set the Hudson on fire in New York. I saw a lot of him at that time as not only was I in and out of N Y, waiting for the completion of the building of my ship, near Boston, but I was released from duty for a few weeks, at the request of the British ambassador (Gilbert Miller, the American producer, having pulled social strings) and invited to play the young flight-lieutenant, which they were having difficulty in casting. A very welcome diversion as far as I was concerned, even if short-lived. We rehearsed for three weeks and, after a week in New Haven, knocked up another three at the Miller Theatre in Manhattan.

Most evenings, after rehearsal, Terry spent going to the theatre and particularly to the ballet; and it was at the latter he suffered an acute *coup de foudre* for a tough young dancer. The young man, in his innocence and straightforward manner, hadn't a clue about the hot desire he had arisen. Terry smuggled him in to one of our rehearsals. He was amazed there was no music, could hardly conceal his boredom but did seem genuinely astonished by our capacity to remember lines. 'Do you say the same words at each performance?' he asked me. 'In much the same way,' I replied, 'as you do the same entrechats.' 'But we have the music,' he said.

Flare Path folded. Terry retired in low spirits to his R A F job of being a rear-gunner. I packed up my seaboots and duffel coat and set off with apprehension to Quincy to commission LC 1 (L) 1 2 4, which smelled of new paint, diesel oil and coir rope – a far cry from the sybaritic life of New York. After some embarrassing sea trials and much minor damage I juddered my way down to Norfolk, Virginia, over to Bermuda and finally zigzagged across the Atlantic to the Mediterranean. At least in the Mediterranean I knew roughly where we were. I doubt if I saw Terry again for about five years, by which time we had both returned to our proper trades and he was flourishing as one of our most important playwrights.

Eighty-four today: that is 30,660 days, mostly wasted. If I had been told when I was eleven, say, that I would live to such an age I think I would have fainted with nausea. Schoolmasters in their thirties already had knobbly knees, revealed by their long, floppy football shorts, and at forty they often had ghastly Adam's apples which not only bobbed up and down in a jokey way but sometimes sprouted single tough hairs. None of these physical attributes of age were desirable, and as for tufts of hair in ears and nostrils, they were not to be mentioned except with horror and youthful contempt.

We came up to Oxford yesterday to give ourselves a little break, a change of view and also to sidestep kindly telephone calls. The last was an unnecessary precaution as there were only four calls in our absence. The Old Parsonage Hotel, where we are staying, is new to us; very pleasant, beautifully clean, has an efficient, cheerful, young staff and is only a six-minute walk from the Ashmolean. Our room (described rather extravagantly as a suite) is on the ground floor at the back of the building and has narrow French windows opening on to a small, gravelled, high-walled garden, which boasts a few shrubs and one or two spindly trees. When the trees are in leaf and the sun shines it must be a cosy place to sit. In any case it is remarkably quiet considering the hotel is sandwiched between two main roads. Church bells clang on the hour but that is a comforting country-like sound and a gentle reminder that we are approaching Easter. Traffic, slightly muffled, can be heard in the rush hours.

The day started chilly and drizzly and for the most part

remained like that. We hired a car to take us to two places we have long wanted to visit – the church of St Mary the Virgin at Swinbrook and the great tithe barn at Great Coxwell; they are each about seventeen miles from Oxford, the first more or less NW and the second SW. We tackled Swinbrook first, a beautiful spot set among gentle, breast-like, green hills, through which a bright little river runs swiftly. In spite of the off-putting weather I thought, 'Here is a place I would like to have lived in.' If I had come across it forty years ago I would have gone to considerable lengths to have got hold of a property.

The church, standing on a grassy knoll, contains a remarkable monument to the Fettiplace family, who were flourishing Tudors and Stuarts. Six gentlemen, with neatly pleated stone skirts peeping out from under their armour, recline on top of each other, resting their elbows on stone cushions. As a monument it manages to be both beautiful and a little funny. It is said that Nancy Mitford is buried in the churchyard but all the headstones looked ancient and tilted, as if struck by a violent wind centuries ago, and it was too cold and damp to make a search.

From Swinbrook it took half an hour to drive south to Great Coxwell. The tithe barn, which now belongs to the National Trust, lies to the side of a narrow country road. It is a knockout. Built by Cistercian monks between 1300 and 1310 it is remarkably well-preserved and cared for. In size it suggests a small cathedral. The exterior, as you would expect, is severe but beautifully proportioned; the inside, with its complicated timber roofing, angled beams and great space is a revelation. The four large doors at the points of the compass stood wide open and the wind buffeted through the building as if alive. There was not a soul in sight. Somehow a glossy modern tractor sheltering at one end seemed reassuring; if it had not been there we might have felt we had entered a time warp. I want to visit it again on a warm summer day when birds are flitting in and out.

Back at Oxford we visited the Ashmolean; surprisingly and inconveniently it closes at 4 p.m. so we only had time to whiffle through the postcards and for M. to gently knock, accidentally, a gigantic Chinese bronze urn which kept up a low hum until we made our exit into the noisy crowd of bored French children, punching each other, smoking, osculating and munching as they straggled down the museum's steps.

In the evening we dined at an attractive-looking restaurant, a sort of greenhouse dripping with ferns and subtropical plants from its glass roof, which hummed like an ocean liner with its air-conditioning. Food was good but our table behaved like a planchette and kept tipping as if it had a message. 'Is there anyone there?' I whispered. 'Give one knock for yes and two for no.' Spookily it all but fell over, scattering wine bottle and water carafe.

Today is Easter Monday, bright and very chilly. Our dear cat, Michaelmas, is in a coma but still faintly breathing. Yesterday he had a series of fits which convulsed his thin frame and we are pretty sure he has gone blind. He came to us as a kitten, a gift from Matthew eleven years ago. The vet saw him on Saturday, gave him an antibiotic injection, and guessed he has either cancer or an infection in his pancreas. A sample of urine was taken and this morning we learn that it is kidney failure and nothing can, or could, be done for him. If he is still alive after lunch we shall have him put down. If he has already died by then we shall bury him in a sunny little spot where dwarf daffodils and grape hyacinths grow. He has been a good, clever cat – adept at opening sliding doors – and his tabby markings were beautiful. The only relief in his passing will be the cessation of gifts of baby rabbits with severed heads.

Outside my study window I see a collared dove sitting, very still, on a branch of the plane tree, which is not yet in leaf. The dove and the tree match each other in their smooth pale way. A greater spotted woodpecker is at the hazelnuts intended for the blue tits and a blackbird is digging his bright yellow beak into the grass and tugging vigorously at what must be a very resistant worm. Michaelmas goes slowly and distressfully out of our lives but nature still provides moments of delight. One searches around for minor comforts.

A week ago someone in Manchester kindly sent me a copy of selected writings from the Mishnah, the Jewish book of oral traditions in law and religious practice; in fact, I suppose, part of the Talmud. Naturally it contains a wealth of fascinating material but a lot of it is too finicky for my comprehension. Because it was Holy Week I looked up, in the Mishnah, the account of the Scapegoat, driven each year out of Jerusalem into the desert, carrying in its lonely self all the sins of the population, symbolized by a scarlet thread tied round its head. At the same time, it appears, another crimson thread was tied to the door of the sanctuary in the Temple. After walking or being driven the three miles to the desert, the goat would eventually die and then, we are told, the thread on the sanctuary door turned white. 'Though your sins be as scarlet, they shall be as white as snow; though they be red like crimson, they shall be as wool.' So Isaiah assures us. The Archbishop of Canterbury was interrupted during his Easter Sunday sermon at the cathedral by gay rights activists climbing into the pulpit alongside him to denounce him and all his orthodox attitudes. The ringleader was led away by police and will be charged with something vague under an ancient and no longer applicable law. It is unlikely that he will receive more than a sympathetic nod and a slap on the wrist. Dr Carey behaved with exemplary calm; on the TV shots we saw of the incident he looked almost welcoming, as if saying, 'And now a few words from our unexpected guest.' He was certainly more polite than some Anglican bishops who are sniping at each other in the press, point-scoring as to whether God exists or not. Bishop Yes, Bishop No and Bishop Maybe are all eager to be quoted and smile flirtatiously at the cameras. It brings to mind – at a remove – a passage in John Updike's novel *Toward the End of Time* which I copied out because it makes me laugh:

Gloria had been an old-style Episcopalian, resenting any prayer book tampering with Cranmer's Prayer-book language and any evangelical or feel-good pollution of the service, such as a homily at morning prayers or the passing of the peace at any service. Perdita had drifted from Unitarianism into Buddhism and settlement-house good works. Both women were religious aristocrats, for whom God was a vulgar poor relation with the additional social disadvantage of not existing.

Of course it is not only the Anglicans who are having trouble, doctrinally or in matters of discipline. My own beloved and revered Holy, Roman, Catholic, Apostolic Church has to side-step, as elegantly as possible, tricky issues and to turn a blind eye when inflated condoms are released during Mass at Westminster Cathedral. We collect more bizarre followers of Christ than most.

Some time ago I attended Mass in a bona fide Catholic church which has a charismatic reputation and my eyes and ears were opening to a new experience. At the commencement a very smartly dressed young man – light-grey, single-breasted suit with razor-sharp creases to his trousers, white shirt, blue tie and highly polished shoes – put aside the electric guitar with which he was entertaining us and grasped a microphone. 'Would anyone wishing to prophesy,' he said, 'please not do so until the end of Mass. Also, unless the prophecy is urgent, it would be appreciated if it was written down on a piece of paper and left in the appropriate basket at the back of the church.' Very sensible, I thought, but what sort of prophecy could be expected? A doom-laden message? News of the Second Coming? or, perhaps, 'Harken to me! I foresee the choirmaster becoming a paedophile. It is Mrs Anstruther who speaks!'

There was a certain amount of arm waving, some clap-happy singing, ecstatic faces wet with joyful tears but, alas, no Toronto Blessing, which I was keen to witness. It was all over the top but more or less acceptable; the only offensive moment was when a fat, unhealthy-looking priest (for whom I prophesied an imminent heart attack) lolled in the pulpit and referred to an internationally well-known and respected actor as 'that git'. I am rather sorry I didn't leave an indignant denunciation in his basket together with my own prophetic warning.

15 April. Today I read in the paper about some very pure, holier-than-thou people (abused, they say, in their childhood, like almost everyone else in the British Isles, if tales are to be credited) who have decided to make a fuss about the Stations of the Cross which Eric Gill started carving for Westminster Cathedral in 1913 and completed in 1918. The objection is because Gill was revealed in a biography a few years ago as having abused practically his whole family. Too bad and too sad, if so; but his work still shines out as a magnificent expression of the human spirit and man's skill with his hands. I wonder if the same objectors would suggest pulling down the ceiling of the Sistine Chapel because of Michelangelo's reputed but unproven homosexuality; or the destruction of dozens of other religious works of art, either in paint or music, because the men who created them may have had sordid incidents in their lives. It is good Catholic doctrine that the unworthiness of the priest doesn't invalidate his celebration of the Mass. Heavens, if that were not so, where would we all be? We most of us say, I think, along with the Centurion, 'Lord I am not worthy that thou shouldst come under my roof,' and hope for the best.

Incidentally the eighth Station of the Cross, in front of which Cardinal Hume is believed to have been seen standing, and so offending the good ladies, depicts the women of Jerusalem lamenting as they watched Christ stumbling his way along the Via Dolorosa. He didn't say to them, 'Thank you for your sympathy; thank you so much'; he said, 'Weep not for me but for yourselves,' – a chilling piece of advice which may have brought them to their senses.

A pair of blackbirds have built themselves a nest in a very precarious position in a cypress tree twenty yards from our patio.

Mrs Spurdle, who gardens for us, discovered the mother firmly sitting on her eggs two days ago. As the whole contraption was being buffeted by the wind and in danger of falling she got some string to bind the branches more tightly together. The bird didn't seem to mind her presence. Yesterday when I took a cautious peek she was still there, bright eyed; and this afternoon both birds were in the nest, cuddled up against the cold. It was a bit of a squash for them. It has been an unthinkable April. The fish lie low in the pond, a barn owl hoots as if taking part in Keats's 'Eve of St Agnes' and only the rabbits and chaffinches don't seem to care. Oh, to get rid of the rabbits. I have just read, in Peter Ackroyd's biography of Thomas More, that in Tudor times it was forbidden to hunt hares if there was snow on the ground – a very sporting attitude; but I would kill rabbits and moles whatever the weather, if only I knew how.

A Monday again; not quite so chilly but grey and melancholic after a sunny start. Disaster has struck the poor blackbirds in the cypress; their nest lies forlornly on the ground. No sign of any eggs so it is possible none had been laid. The destruction was probably done by crows, who have been a great nuisance this spring. Two blackbirds are skimming around quite near the fallen nest, apparently unconcerned. If it is the same pair, searching for another site on which to build, I long to give them some practical advice. A couple who have set up house each year in a tangle of syringa by the front door seem to have no trouble; they look down on me in my study with admirable indifference.

Peter Ackroyd, in his biography, lists words and phrases which he states were first used in written English by Thomas More. These include taunt, shuffle, anticipate, paradox, pretext, obstruction, monosyllable and 'not to see the wood for the trees' and 'out of the frying-pan into the fire'. Without exactly doubting his statement I nevertheless felt I would like to have the list verified, so I spent an enjoyable hour searching through the earliest attributions given in the Oxford Dictionary – enjoyable except for carrying the weight of half a dozen of those vast tomes to my desk – and sure enough, to my delight, the quotes were there and attributed to More. The English language never ceases to amaze me, and its greatest pleasure is in recognizing the modernity of phrases used four hundred years ago. Who would have thought that 'out of the frying-pan into the fire' was in use in 1530?

Word must have got around quickly – 'Have you heard Thomas's latest?' – for his pithy phrasing to have taken such far-reaching and firm root. It is the Americans now, of course, who keep us on our aural toes, so to speak, but the sound-bites come so swiftly and in such quantity that last week's witticism suggests old fogeyism today. 'That's the way the cookie crumbles!' seemed to me the height of sophisticated comment in the early fifties in New York; yet it probably hasn't raised a smile for thirty years. But Thomas More, headless, canonized, carries on regardless of time.

14. Shades of Green

For the blessing of God upon the grass is in shades of Green.
Christopher Smart

We must acknowledge that any skills we may have come from the gods; witness Arachne weaving away under the jealous eye of Minerva and taking all credit to herself. I teased Merula a little as she was working at one of her marvellous stitchwork pictures by reading aloud 'Arachne', in *Tales from Ovid* by Ted Hughes. M. is the most modest person imaginable and she was, I think, a little flummoxed by the poem but she continued plying her needle vigorously and scattering bits of wool. Flora, sitting on the sofa at her side, put out a long, comforting, interfering paw on M.'s arm which, for once, wasn't welcome. Oh, you have to be cautious with artists.

Kipling wrote somewhere, 'When your Daeman is in charge do not try to think consciously. Drift, wait and obey.' Merula's Daeman settles down at her side quite often, I suspect. For my own part I can only recall very few and brief instances in my own professional life when I was 'beside myself'. Certainly once, during a rehearsal of Olivier's *Lear*, in which I played the Fool; there was a sort of click in my brain, or wherever it was, and for a minute I 'took off', knowing for the first time how I might possibly play the part. Or maybe it was a sudden awareness that a pin-drop stillness had descended on the rehearsal room. In any case, if that really happened, the credit must go to Shakespeare and not to any insight on my part. It is, I think, usually in rehearsals, when antennae are feeling around in all directions, that these disturbing but also semi-magical moments occur to actors. On the other hand it was a generous, warm reception on my entrance as Abel Drugger (a very small part in *The Alchemist*) on the first night which provided a spark for me. In *Hitler, the Last Ten Days*, a poor film from a brilliant script, I had an hysterical, screaming speech which I plunged into almost out of control and although I believe I did it well it left me physically drained and wanting to vomit. Something similar happened in the second production in which I played Hamlet (1952) but it wasn't during rehearsal or on a fraught first night but at a matinée in a sparsely filled theatre. Just as I was leaving the stage after encountering the Ghost, having said, 'The time is out of joint. O cursed spite/ That ever I was born to set it right,' I promptly retched into my fur hat; yet I wasn't aware of being 'outside myself' or in any way 'lost to myself'. Presumably I was churned up by some inner experience, something which has sometimes happened to various Hamlets. Perhaps Freud would have had some Oedipean explanation, although I personally had no desire to kill the father I had never known. Of course it would be nice to have been reassured who he was, even at the beginning of a dull matinée.

Ernest Milton, the greatest – but not the most glamorous – Hamlet I ever saw, was sometimes subject to being momentarily possessed by whatever he was playing. He told me, with fear and awe in his voice, that on one occasion, standing before the microphone in a BBC radio production of some historical play, he was so overcome by another identity that he had to struggle for minutes to recover his own persona. It is all a form of madness, I suppose, and those who genuinely experience these things don't attempt to explain it or claim to be in any way special. In my observation it is usually the phoney or inefficient who regale us, in press interviews, with flighty notions or obscure theatrical methods.

Some ten years ago there appeared in a national newspaper an interview with an actor who held forth about what his approach would be to playing in Wilde's *The Importance of Being*

Earnest. ' "My dear Algy," ' he quoted, ' "I thought you were down in Shropshire. How ripping to find you are up instead." ' He went on to ask, 'What is it like to have a friend called Algy? Ask around. Better still look through the phone book and find someone called Algy. Get to know him. Befriend him. Go to Shropshire. Find out why it is so ripping not to be there. The audience haven't paid to see people walking about in clothes saying amusing things, they want *other being*, they want rawness, they want the truth.' His words were harbingers of horrors to come. How much, I wonder, would Oscar Wilde have appreciated 'rawness'?

Red and yellow tulips stand upright in their tangled border in spite of wind and cold but their petals are widely spread and ready to fall. They had a wretched late April and not much comfort in these early days of May. Most of the trees are now in young leaf and the grass, where it has not been overtaken by moss, is a good green. The purple lilac is in flower, showing mournfully against a leaden sky. The bluebells are suddenly adrift in cool patches and along the hedge just outside our bit of land. They make the grass look greener. The sight of them takes me back to bicycling days in my youth when we thoughtlessly dragged them up by the roots, tied them over the handlebars and were surprised, when we got home, that they had wilted for ever and were only fit for the dustbin. And people still do it.

The memorial service for John Wells at St Paul's, Covent Garden, last week was a triumphal and almost jolly affair. A Salvation Army band gave vigour and silvery brightness to the hymns; 'Dear Lord and Father of mankind' and 'The day Thou gavest, Lord, is ended' seemed new minted. The address by the Rt Reverend Lord Runcie was a delight; he boldly introduced himself as 'Runcieballs', the name John and other *Private Eye* contributors had saddled him with when Archbishop of Canterbury. Richard Ingrams's tribute was also fun. I couldn't hear much of what else was said – it is not a good church for acoustics – but Edward Fox, reciting a cricketing poem by A. P. Herbert, scored boundary after boundary.

It was a very high social affair, the pews being packed with the well-heeled from all walks of life, headed by the Prince of Wales. The arts, music, opera, theatre, TV and showbiz were all represented in their higher echelons but not, I think, quite what the autograph seekers were after. Outside the church, as the congregation poured down the steps into the flash-happy cameras, I heard a woollen-hatted little man say to his companion, who was proffering someone an album and a Biro, 'It's no good, dear. There is simply *no one*, but *no one*, here!' One name did ring out, however – 'It is Vernon Dobchef.'

Searching for ideas for a brief holiday I scanned the brochure about the Royal Scot train and its luxurious windings through the Highlands. Being piped aboard is a delight I can cheerfully forgo; and I wouldn't want to wear a dinner-jacket in the evening on a train journey, which the brochure recommends. Of course there might be a chance of an invitation to dine at the engine-driver's table, but I have reached an age when I can resist such lures. All very nice, I dare say, for those who have the dollars. I used to love train journeys but now there appear to be no porters to help with humping luggage and I don't want another hernia, dragging cases from one platform to another with only two minutes to make a connection. So when we go to Cornwall in a week's time, for a short spell at the seaside, we have decided to fly. The journey will take a quarter of the time it would by rail, not be much more expensive and our suitcases will be taken out of our hands.

Now, bang, suddenly, we are into summer weather. Three days of it so far. All trees are a light and feathery green. I celebrated the remarkable change in the look of things by going to the aquatic store near Liss and buying three koi carp; each is just over four inches long, two of them like dazzling newly polished brass and the other silver with blue and black stripes. I have kept an eye on them during the day and they seem to have settled in, if dashing around blowing bubbles and attempting to eat anything too large for them can be called settling in. Also the little bonsai fir tree given me about twelve years ago by Ronald Eyre – who was going through one of his periods of enthusiasm for all things Japanese – has sprung into new life. It has always been a rather weedy plant but now, for the first time I can remember, it is showing fine clusters of bright mauve fir-cones. It has changed from scruffiness to beauty.

Ron Eyre was, in my estimation, the best English theatre director to immediately follow John Dexter, Lindsay Anderson and William Gaskill. He was certainly the most encouraging and illuminating for actors. During the last days of rehearsals for Alan Bennett's *Habeas Corpus* he would scribble schoolmasterly notes to each member of the cast at the end of every run-through. They were so much to the point, imaginative and stylishly written that I regret not having saved them, either for future reference or as an example of what the relationship between actor and director should be. He had a merry eye and could have been a fine comic actor; I did my best to persuade him so but he shyly backed away from the idea. Once a schoolmaster always a schoolmaster. Looking at his little bonsai in its new-found glory I remembered he was colour-blind and he would have seen its mauve cones as drab brown. Cancer ravaged the last years of his life but he was cosseted by loving friends in the West Country, where he died. I always assumed he must be hard up for cash but he left approximately £700,000 – a tidy sum for someone who was not in movies, or on the West End comedy, musical or thriller circuit. But he did have a brush with opera and I suppose that pays well; considering the prices of the seats it certainly should. At his memorial service in St James's Piccadilly, some Buddhist monks hummed interminably and, to my untrained ear, very monotonously indeed. Om-om-om goes a long way. Just as the service was beginning, a handsome girl, dressed smartly in black and followed eagerly by a devilish black dog, barged her way through the congregation (she was stoned out of her mind) screaming 'Fuck off! All of you fuck off!' It was the sort of 'happening' Ron would have loved. Maybe his spirit had directed it.

Today is the late-spring bank holiday. Whatever happened to the Whitsun weekend I can't recall, or why the date was shifted; all part of the secularization of the calendar no doubt. Soon we shall be reattempting the French Revolution's five-day week and the renaming of days. Clintonday, Blairday, Kohlday and even, though unlikely, Hagueday, when all will be required to wear baseball caps back to front – which, of course, many do already.

Our five days in Cornwall were marvellously refreshing. The weather was superb, the Nare Hotel – right on Carne beach in the Roseland peninsula – was just what we wanted: very comfortable, airy, beautifully decorated, lovely views and the food (particularly the fish and Cornish crab) was first-rate. The atmosphere was friendly, the staff mostly young and pleasantly casual. Each day, as the sand appeared in a great stretch from under the ebbing tide, we paddled. I can't have rolled up the bottom of my trousers and sloshed into the shallow sea like that for over twenty years. I had forgotten the feel of ribbed sand on the soles of feet. On two afternoons there was a five o'clock shadow on the sea – five basking sharks lazily parading less than a hundred yards from the shore. One or two small boats put out to quietly circle the sharks and were encircled themselves. They are harmless creatures but their enormous size, which can be up to forty feet long, makes them look alarming. We took a childish thrill in their proximity, staring at their black snouts, dorsal fins and their high, sharp tails moving slowly through the flat blue sea. We felt so childlike that I think if we had had spades we would have set about building sandcastles. The few children about seemed to have no idea how to do such things, their imaginations not progressing beyond an inverted bucket of sand.

An exceptionally nice taxi-driver who drove us one morning to St Mawes and other pretty spots around the coast kept saying, 'Now *this* is a *very* popular place,' whether it was a café, tea garden, a headland view, a pub or a paper shop with revolving garish postcards. He didn't realize that each time he pointed out the 'popularity' two customers were lost. It was quiet and crowdlessness we sought and found. Never a note of muzak inflamed our ears when in Cornwall and only occasionally the sound of a distant car. The air was so breathable we gulped it.

We are home; the weather has broken; we can return to what I believe is referred to as our Pooterish sort of life.

Yesterday, 26 May, a group of veterans, sufferers from the horrors of Japanese prisoner-of-war camps, lined a section of the Mall so that they could turn their backs on Emperor Akihito as he was driven in a closed coach to Buck House. In doing so they turned their backs on the Queen. At the end of the war with Japan the present Emperor was eleven years old and the Queen, then Princess Elizabeth, nineteen. It's a long time ago. If the Queen or President Clinton should accept a state visit to Tokyo I wonder if they would be faced with elderly Japanese turning their backs and holding aloft placards reading 'Remember Hiroshima, 6 August 1945'; 'Remember Nagasaki, 8 August 1945'. When the first atomic bombs were dropped a new era of terrible fear was called into being. But fear is still with us, having changed direction, and worsened, with the knowledge that the world can now be destroyed by germ warfare. Better for the veterans to lower their placards, face front and try to raise some hope for the future.

Presumably it was media pressure that persuaded someone to give us the opening bars of 'Colonel Bogey' on a mouth-organ: it didn't look spontaneous.

And now India and Pakistan are making rival underground mushrooms.

While the Japanese visitors have been lunching in Downing Street I have been trying to find my way round a new mobile telephone which arrived yesterday (a gift, as I understand it, from Vodaphone to replace my old mobile; something to do with possible collapse of computers on 1 January 2000 perhaps). As I only need the machine for emergencies I thought I had better try it out. An emergency immediately made itself felt: a battery sprang from its spring and hit me in the eye. Using my ordinary B T telephone I rang Vodaphone's Customer Service for advice. A sweet-sounding giggly girl assured me all would be working properly within half an hour but she had to know what I had on 'the menu'. (It is impossible for someone of my age, who is blind to instruction manual prose, to keep abreast of the latest jargon). The 'menu', it seems, consists of recalling the names of your friends, individual timers, automatic timers, one-minute timers, something called 'exit to menu' and 'displaying yourself'. Is that the same as exposing yourself? Probably not, but it brought to mind beloved Coral Browne, muffled in furs, skating on a remote section of the Serpentine one winter just after the war. She was executing an elegant figure of eight when a seedy man slid towards her and flashed himself. Coral continued to skim around, calling over her shoulder, 'Put it away at once! You could catch your death of cold!'

The Glorious First of June, 1998; the headlines today are not of victory but of Paul Gascoigne being dropped from the English team for the World Cup and of the Spice Girl called Ginger having withdrawn from the pop group. We thought it must be a publicity stunt to grab front-page space but apparently not. The Afghan earthquake, the southern Sudan famine, the horrors of Sierra Leone, the Indian/Pakistan atomic sabre-rattling, Indonesia, and the alarming financial crisis in Russia, possible civil war in Kosovo, all pale into brief insignificance when put alongside

Gazza's tears and Ginger's enigmatic dark glasses. Well, it's all easier reading than the grim worldwide picture, if that's what we wish to avoid knowing about.

A few days later, after a showery two nights' stay in London, I have decided I must avoid all theatres until the pollen count is way down (although I shall take myself soon to see Eileen Atkins and Michael Gambon in *The Unexpected Man* as it is on for only a limited run). When I went to see Stoppard's *The Real Inspector Hound*, the young woman who sat next to me produced a sopping handkerchief from her bag, gave me a reassuring smile and said, 'It's not a cold, only hay fever.' Then she gave high decibel honks at five-minute intervals. The barrage balloon of a woman directly behind me had a good old-fashioned sneezing fit; I could feel my neck wetted in a disgusting way. As I felt trapped in the stuffiness of the theatre I left in the interval. Sad about that, as I particularly wanted to see the second half of the evening, Shaffer's *Black Comedy*, which I hugely enjoyed when it was first done many years ago. Maggie Smith made a memorable entrance – or rather her long shapely leg did, feeling its way down a staircase in the supposed dark; also Albert Finney was superb, and uncamp, as a falsely butch antiques dealer.

This month has provided much enjoyable reading. At the top of the list I would put Robert Nye's *The Late Mr Shakespeare*. A few years ago I rejoiced in his *Mrs Shakespeare, The Complete Works* but *The Late Mr S.* surpasses that. When I had finished it I felt bereft and sought out a second-hand copy of Nye's novel about Sir Walter Raleigh (Wa'ter Rawley, as Queen Elizabeth pronounced it, mockingly imitating Raleigh's broad Devonian accent, according to Nye). *The Voyage of Destiny*, published in 1982, contains fierce and funny swipes at Francis Bacon and James I but basically it is a sad and moving tale of misadventure.

The oddest book I have read recently has been Trollope's novella, *The Fixed Period*. I must admit I had never heard of it until the admirable Trollope Society produced it as one of their four publications for this year. He wrote it in 1880 but the story takes place on a fictitious island off the coast of New Zealand in 1980 and deals with statutory euthanasia for everyone reaching the age of sixty-seven. His vision of the future (our present) does not include air travel or the internal combustion engine or much of what we take for granted, but there are some remarkable prophecies of small things, such as cricket teams wearing pink or blue instead of the traditional white flannel and batsmen being helmeted and heavily armoured against incredibly fast bowling. It is not, perhaps, 100 per cent satisfactory, nor does it compare favourably with Butler's *Erewhon* but it does raise issues which face us today.

Stacked at my side are three books demanding to be read, Elmore Leonard's new thriller, *Cuba Libre*; *Fools and Jesters in the English Court* by the actor John Southworth; and Ian Wilson's *The Blood and the Shroud* – the shroud of Turin yet again. Inviting as they are they must wait until I have finished the biography of Osbert Sitwell by Philip Ziegler, which has me in thrall.

Edith Sitwell I knew from the early days of the 1939–45 war and she befriended me until not long before her death, but Osbert I met only three times. The first meeting was at a weekend at Renishaw, accompanied by Merula and our three-month old son, whose presence had to be kept secret from Osbert as the sight of a baby made him feel ill. The second time was at the Wigmore Hall when we had a chat after a concert. Edith told me later, and naturally I was very chuffed, that Osbert had commented on how smart I looked in my naval (sub-lieutenant) uniform. 'He knows about these things,' she said, nodding her head approvingly. 'He was in the Guards,' she added with a small, proud smile. The last time I met him was for lunch at Montegufoni, his castle not far from Florence.

M. and I, with our friend Marriott White, were spending a few days in a hotel overlooking the Arno and I got word to Edith that we were in the district – baldly cadging for an invitation really, which promptly arrived. The dreaded Parkinson's disease had started to get hold of Osbert and although he could walk, in a rather shambling way, he would apologize amusingly before making sudden, little tottering dashes to propel himself up a few garden steps. His manners were always exquisite and he was charmingly affable in a slightly distant patrician way.

We sat down to lunch in dappled sunlight under a spreading vine at a large table covered with a beautiful lace cloth. It should have been idyllic but somehow, in spite of Osbert's easiness as a host, the atmosphere was almost grim. Marriott sat at his right, Edith, M. and David Horner (Osbert's intimate friend over many years) at the other end – a silent trio – and I sat at his left. The conversation, if it could be called that, was mostly about the Montegufoni's new wine vats, dusty eighteenth-century parchments to be found in the chapel and the odd behaviour of Harold Acton and other local grandees. I had the impression that so far as Edith was concerned I must have committed some ghastly solecism or *lèse-majesté* but I couldn't think what. When coffee was served Osbert lit a cigarette and it fell from his trembling hand on to the lace tablecloth but Marriott quickly retrieved it and returned it to him. Under his breath he asked, 'Did Edith see that?' 'I think not,' Marriott replied and Osbert relaxed.

As we were leaving Edith hissed in my ear, 'David Horner is a serpent. I can't tell you of his wickedness.' She cast her eyes heavenwards as if she was about to be assumed. Presumably it was in order to shake Horner's hand as we said goodbye but I felt uncomfortable doing so.

To my doctor to discuss slight pain in my left shoulder. It is better than it was some months ago so I'm just to carry on with magic pills for another eight weeks and then review the situation. My blood pressure is 140/85, which he considered good for a man of my age and varied experiences.

Loved a recent TV programme on ravens. Their courtship was adorable. The male approached his intended, fell over sideways in front of her and slid down a slope; picked himself up at the bottom; plodded up to her again; repeated the performance and continued to do so, perhaps a dozen times or until she got the idea and joined in. After that it seems they stay together for the rest of their lives, maybe for another thirty or forty years. In two weeks time Merula and I have our diamond wedding anniversary, so we shall beat the ravens by thirty years or more. We have no intention of falling over and sliding about the place, but who knows when fate may give a shove?

15. The Wide Gap of Time

Last week I spent an afternoon looking at rich jewels but knew I couldn't possibly run to even a one-carat diamond, let alone anything weightier, as a sixtieth-wedding anniversary present for Merula. She wouldn't wear it anyway, however modest; and even if she did it would get lost on that old cardigan with the missing buttons, or dropped down the sink. There was a superb and vast aquamarine I saw, twisted around with chunky gold – the sort of thing with which Edith Sitwell used to clasp together her astrakhan coat and voluminous oriental garments – but I reckoned M. would need two walking sticks to support its weight. I also ruled out, as soon as I was shown the wicked thing, a sort of ankle bracelet with a snake's head of emerald with rubies for eyes. Not to be worn with wellington boots or flashing from scuffed, woolly, tartan bedroom slippers. Fine pieces of Fabergé, at Fabergé prices, were flitted before my eyes, but everything suggested was for a different order of being to my wife.

Then I remembered the catalogue for an exhibition of nineteenth-century French paintings and drawings which is to open shortly at the Hazlitt, Gooden & Fox gallery, and how I had been taken by the illustration of a drawing by Nicolas-Henri Jacob, done in 1810. It is of two children, aged about eight or nine, a brother and sister, looking one straight in the face with penetrating, luminous, sophisticated eyes. I had never heard of Nicolas-Henri Jacob, who, I now learn, was a pupil of David. There is no doubt that he was a master draughtsman, rather in the manner of Ingres. After telephoning the gallery to ask if I could see the picture itself – they were in the midst of hanging

– I taxied to Bury Street, fell in love with it and wrote a cheque. Now it is safely hidden under a pile of sweaters and only to be revealed on the morning of 20 June.

After the extravagance of the drawing I ordered six pots of gardenias from Pulbrook & Gould, which were delivered the following day; fine, waxy, large flowers against rich, shiny leaves. Those I couldn't conceal. They were received with a happy smile. M. obviously thinks the gardenias are the anniversary present, and in a way that is so. Over £100 worth of gardenias look good anyway but they hold a nostalgic sweetness for us. When we were engaged, in the spring of 1938, working together in the theatre, I used to give her a gardenia each Friday night. In those days they were easily obtainable from the old flower women who bunched themselves around Eros in Piccadilly Circus, their wicker baskets crammed with every sort of bloom and buttonhole. Gardenias, I think, cost a shilling each. Merula was always bowled over by their mushroom-like scent. With the war years they became scarce and then unobtainable. Happily they are back with us but to my old and less sensitive nose their scent is less intoxicating than it used to be. That applies to so many flowers and much fruit now; freesias seem to be bred for size and rarely have any smell, while the English peach, that glory of the garden wall, is now usually as tasteless as a cricket ball, and often as hard.

Our sixtieth wedding anniversary was a happy day but too hot. First of all I laid the table indoors, thinking it looked like rain; then, having decided the sun was going to break through, relaid under the vine in the kitchen arbour – where the heat proved really oppressive – so, with Matthew's help, settled again indoors, where some sort of breeze flowed. The Nicolas-Henri Jacob drawing pleased M. no end and all morning she was 'bunched' with glorious bridal tributes. Granddaughter Bethany, nearly aged two, jumped tirelessly around all day with a beaming smile, knowingly saying words like 'car', 'tractor', 'fish' and two or three dozen others which were recognizable even when near misses. There was a gap of twenty-four years between her and her half-sister Sally; I wonder how that will work out for them in the future. Lovingly, I hope.

A week or so ago, there was a revealing and amusing TV programme on the choice of paintings made for their offices or apartments by cabinet ministers, ambassadors and others of high governmental rank. It was significant how many works of beauty were chucked out to make room for the indifferent, cool and aggressively new. The paintings are on loan from a special collection to satisfy ministerial tastes. There was much pretentious talk from some and a few really ugly choices. Visitors to our embassy in Paris must be surprised by seeing an upside-down wine bottle, stuffed with its own label, exhibited on the wall of a grand salon. The People's Choice was very much at variance with chandeliers, tapestries and glittering Empire furnishings. A couple of the lucky recipients spoke of their acquisitions with good sense but one man stood out for his simplicity and genuine appreciation of what had once hung on his walls. You felt he really loved the Bonington and various landscapes with which he had surrounded himself. John Major, no less. Someone else, rather unexpected (could it have been Mr Mandelson? I think not) alerted us when we saw he had chosen two paintings by Merula's brother, the late Michael Salaman. They were whisked by the camera so quickly that we barely had time to recognize them; but it was a nice surprise. The next day M. got back to her easel with renewed enthusiasm.

During the past week I also enjoyed *The Unexpected Man*, by Yasmina Reza at the Duchess Theatre. It was written before her wild success with *Art* and is neither as funny nor gripping, but it provides an hour and a quarter of gentle, intriguing entertainment and dazzling, concentrated acting by Eileen Atkins and Michael Gambon; acting to be treasured, of a kind to make any actor proud to belong to the same profession. The setting had been designed for the steep, claustrophobic, unpleasant pit at the Barbican (where the play was performed for a few weeks before its transfer to the West End) and as far as I could make out no accommodation was made for it moving to a reasonable theatre. The only place from which to view it properly is from the dress circle, where you can look down on the stage and see the rather astonishing pattern of it all; from the stalls you would see less than half of what is on offer. It is all very ingenious and it took me a good ten minutes to realize the actors were walking on a stage totally covered with a sheet of glass, under which you could see a realistic rail track receding diagonally into the distance. A few simple wooden chairs were angled along the line of the track and somehow it never occurred to me that we were not actually tearing along in a continental train.

Eileen has never looked so good (wherever she got that lively golden-red wig, she should cling on to it for the rest of her life) and Gambon has never looked so neat. As for three-quarters of the play they don't speak to each other, and only occasionally take a few furtive glances, confining themselves to long monologues of their passing thoughts, it is magical how they seem to be in contact all the time. It made me realize, without a trace of envy, that I could never have achieved (even if I had the imagination to attempt it) acting of that calibre. I rejoice that I have retired from theatre and films and am no longer tempted to risk making an ass of myself in public. Not so much a case of 'Why should the aged eagle stretch its wings?' as 'If you are an old, featherless, pouter pigeon, stick to the dovecote.'

After the performance I took Eileen to a restaurant which is usually as quiet as a morgue but on this particular night was raucous. It was Ascot week and I surmise each table was occupied by big winners. We changed our position twice, feeling deafened, before spotting a table behind a glass screen, providing virtually another small room. There we happily settled ourselves, a couple of quidnuncs greedily making pigs of ourselves with blinis. I hadn't realized until we got to the restaurant that it was Eileen's birthday.

★

Since the death of poor Michaelmas, birds and rabbits have become much bolder in their approach to the house. We are now besieged on all sides. The latest invasion is from squirrels. From my study window I see three very young squirrels experimenting with their tails. First they curl them over their heads as if they were inflated umbrellas; then they make rhythmic undulating movements with them, like grey waves; then they spread them wide and flat on the ground so they appear to be feathers; and finally, fed up with all that, they just fling them around in the way women did with their silver-fox furs in the thirties.

The World Cup has held me, so far, for four evenings more or less glued to the box and I must admit that there were times when I was aware of my heart thumping. The turns of speed and the deftness of footwork left me goggle-eyed with admiration. But I do wish it was against the rules (surely it used to be?) for players to drag at each other's shirts to impede them. Also the enthusiastic piling up on top of team mates to congratulate, embrace, fondle and ruffle the hair of a goal scorer has now reached a new height of almost orgasmic absurdity. After watching some of these acrobatic, loving scrambles it struck me that actors might be encouraged to attempt the same sort of thing during performances.

After a round of applause, awarded by a simple-minded audience to the actor who had really worked hard for it (assisted of course, albeit negligibly, by the playwright) the actor should clench his fists aggressively, bend his knees and spring round the stage, mouth wide open, screaming and punching the air. This would be the cue for the rest of the cast to tumble him to the ground, sit on his face, derange his wig and generally knock the wind out of him. The audience would be encouraged to renew their applause, clapping their hands above their heads as if at a pop concert. It would be highly enjoyable. Drama critics could have a field day. 'Dame Flora Robson was sat on by the entire cast five times. I predict this will run and run.'

A letter has arrived from the flag lieutenant, Portsmouth – a friendly and informative lady whom I don't know – extending us a kind invitation from the C-in-C to dine on board HMS *Victory* on a date that, unfortunately, we cannot manage. The letter tells me that Nelson died in the *Victory* at the battle of Trafalgar and that we would be seated at a table in his cabin. The letter finishes chummily. 'Yours Aye,' followed by her signature.

It is twelve years since we dined in the *Victory*, on Trafalgar night 1986; a memorable, beautiful and moving occasion, superbly organized by the Navy as always. It was a white-tie and medals affair and we sat down twenty-four to dinner. There was a spectacular pudding called Ships of the Line, which consisted of large cakes, moulded to resemble nineteenth-century men-of-war, which fairly bristled with flaming sparklers and were carried round the table in semi-darkness by ratings in the outfits of 1805. They were followed by a sprightly small band playing fifes, fiddles and an antique drum. Stirring stuff.

The Bishop of Portsmouth, who was sitting next to Merula, whispered to her that he and I were the only two present sporting war-time medals. When that was pointed out to me, admirals, whom I had always revered for their rank, authority and age, suddenly looked as young as policemen.

Apart from the emotionally charged Toast to the Immortal Memory, and the beauty of it all, the evening was memorable for three other things. The Duke and Duchess of York, who were the guests of honour and newly wed, had driven down to Portsmouth separately. She was meant to bring his uniform. Well, she did; but only half of it. However, all was finally well and HRH was fitted out in Admiralty House with the equivalent of the missing bits. I think the Duke found the first half-hour of the evening a bit of a strain.

The second memorable few minutes was when Admiral Stamford read, quite beautifully, a letter from a seaman on the lower deck of the *Royal Sovereign* written immediately after the battle of Trafalgar. He was a country lad called Sam and he wrote to his parents in the West Country as follows:

Our dear Admiral Nelson is killed! I never set eyes on him, for which I am both sorry and glad; for, to be sure, I should like to have seen him – but then, all the men in our ship who have seen him are such soft toads, they have done nothing but blast their eyes and cry, ever since he was killed. God bless you! chaps that fought like the devil, sit down and cry like a wench.

The third happening, for me at any rate, was when M. went up to our recent Prime Minister, Mr (now Lord) Jim Callaghan, whom she had never met, planted a kiss on his cheek and told him she loved him. He accepted her tribute charmingly. It was a side of her nature I hadn't been aware of in nearly fifty years of marriage. And she hadn't been at the ancient rum.

A few nights ago I was watching the men's singles at Wimbledon while M. sat on the sofa, busy at her stitchwork and rarely glancing at the TV set. Then, when there were a couple of double faults in quick succession, she looked up quickly and disapprovingly.

'That boy can't play tennis,' she announced crossly. 'What's his name?'

I replied with satisfaction (and the idea of a quicky divorce crossed my mind), 'Tim Henman.'

'Oh,' she said, and jabbed the needle into her wool. Then, half apologetically, she added, 'I like *him*.' So we plunge on towards another sixty years – or at any rate the millennium.

On the evening of the World Cup match between England and Argentina I had arranged to take a friend to dinner. Before setting out it was noticeable that taxis were extremely thin on the ground; the streets of London were almost empty, the citizens having retired to their pubs or their homes and battened down the hatches. After half an hour I managed to get a cab, but only because I was prepared to go the way the driver wished – he

wanted to be in time for the kick-off. Halfway through our meal
it struck me that my guest and I might have difficulty in getting
to our rather distant beds, so I telephoned the car-hire firm I
have used for forty years or more and who are always most
accommodating. No; they regretted they were totally booked
up. Eventually, when the time came to go, the restaurant rustled
up a cowboy mini-cab driver. He was large, black, full of big
smiles, loud laughter, and surprisingly he knew London as well
as the back of his bejewelled hand. The streets being traffic-free
– almost – he gave us a speedy, hair-raising ride, but he was as
reliable as Stirling Moss at the wheel. Having dropped my friend
and reversed for two hundred yards at 30 m.p.h. he got me back
to my hotel in time for me to watch the last ten minutes of the
game and the heart-stopping, sad shoot-out.

It was Lionel Johnson, I think, who wrote, 'The great artists are
all contemporaries. Progress in art is progress towards simplicity.'
This morning the names of the four finalists for the Turner Prize
at the Tate have been announced. The names, I fear, mean
nothing to me (as yet) but one 'great artist' among them has
certainly achieved simplicity; his offering is elephant dung var-
nished with paint. This is preferable, I think, to the cans of
human faeces, labelled stylishly 'Merde', which were recently
on exhibition in London. The elephant droppings could surely
represent a very cool Britannia on a dining-room wall in some
splendiferous embassy of a lost empire. Elephants being vegetarian, I imagine there would be no unpleasant side-effects.
The tins of 'Merde' were not a British product and must be
championed elsewhere.

In Sri Lanka, during the filming of *The Bridge on the River
Kwai*, I watched an elephant lead a Buddhist procession. He had
a bare electric light-bulb flickering on his forehead, spangles and
flower paintings all over him and carried on his back his mahout
and a cumbersome battery. Immediately behind him marched a
boy of about twelve, with eyes fixed on the elephant's tail. There

followed a bevy of Singhalese dancing girls and a chanting crowd. I asked someone what the boy was doing and was told that if the elephant defecated it was the boy's job to jump immediately on the ball of dung, to make all smooth for the dancers. At the very moment this was explained to me the elephant obliged by releasing a cannonball which thudded to the ground. The boy leapt on it with both feet and the dancers progressed, fancy-free, ankles jingling, wrists and fingers at work, casting wild *oeillades* from side to side as they passed, dry-footed, over a potential Turner Prize palette.

A humid night kept me restlessly awake for an hour or two, ruminating on incidents in the distant past. The legal enforcement preventing the Orange Order from marching through the Nationalist area of Drumcree today came anxiously to mind but I knew I couldn't resolve the ins and outs, rights and wrongs, of that one. I suddenly remembered my mother, when I was about six, dragging me quickly past London pillar-boxes in case they contained revolutionary Irish bombs. (Later she instilled in me the fear of black-hatted, black-cloaked Trotskyite assassins lurking round corners.) It was a few years before I could post a letter without recalling the fear of being blown apart. My mother instilled quite a few silly phobias into my young psyche, including the conviction that rag-'n'-bone men might kidnap me and spirit me away under a heap of old clothes on their donkey-carts as they clattered through the suburban streets, shouting hoarsely their plague-like cry, 'Rag-'n'-bones! Any old rags and bones!'

Flinging aside the duvet, muttering 'A plague on both your houses, for your blinkered obstinacy' and, for good measure, 'The worst thing silly King James did was to lose the Battle of the Boyne', I found my nightshirt was too sweaty to continue wearing. Then, dry and refreshed with clean nightwear, I settled down to happily recalling my twenty-first birthday; that was when I was playing Osric in Gielgud's 1934–5 *Hamlet*. The West

End run had just finished and we were playing a week in the vast theatre at Streatham, just outside London.

Two or three weeks earlier, before we had started the tour, I had held a door open for Frank Vosper (who was playing the King) as he left the stage of the New Theatre and slowly climbed the stairs to his dressing-room. I patiently followed him. He suddenly stopped – probably to catch his breath, as he was a heavy, fleshy man – and said, 'Young man, how old are you?' He had never spoken to me before. I told him I was twenty.

'And when will you be twenty-one?' he asked.

'On 2 April,' I replied.

'And will you be having a party?'

'No,' I said. 'At least I don't think so.'

'So, no one is giving you a party?'

Again I replied, 'No', probably blushing a little.

'That seems a shame,' he went on. '*I* shall give you your twenty-first birthday party. Come and see me in my dressing-room tomorrow, before the performance, and bring me a list of those you would like me to ask.'

He stopped wheezing, said 'Goodnight' and without another word proceeded on his way. I was so astonished I have a horrid idea I barely expressed my thanks.

Frank Vosper was not only quite a star – mostly given to playing charming villains – but also a successful playwright – and the plays were usually thrillers. He was witty and affable and lived, or so I imagined, a fairly hectic social life. He had an attractive but not large house in north London. His sister Margery, who was younger, was a jolly, kind-hearted girl who acted as Frank's hostess when he entertained. Eventually she set up as a theatrical agent and was often to be found around the restaurants and pubs frequented by actors.

When I went to his room on the following evening to hand in my list, which only consisted of four names, he gazed at it uncomprehendingly for a moment.

'That all?' he asked. I nodded. 'I was expecting a lot more

than that. We'll invite John and the company of course and I expect Margery will think up some others. Margery will be in charge.'

And I was dismissed. There never followed any word of confirmation, indeed no word of any sort. By the night of 1 April, one day from the party, I was getting nervous and thought I ought to jog his memory. At the Streatham theatre he had a sort of tent rigged up on the side of the large stage, where he could repair his make-up, change his costume and take a rest without the fatigue of climbing to his proper room. When the curtain fell I went to this tent. There was a gap in the material and I could see him hunched over his dressing-table, a glass of whisky in his right hand, staring at himself in the mirror. He looked sad and rather sinister with his puffy white face, pencil-thin arched eyebrows and shiny red wig. Suddenly he spotted my reflection in the mirror and leapt up with a screech. When he realized it was only me he collapsed back in his chair, clutching his chest. Then he gasped out, 'You mustn't frighten people like that!' I apologized and said I only wanted to know if the party was still on. 'Of course it's on,' he said. 'If I promise something I keep my promise. Now go away.' I left him to his whisky.

The following night was the party, at Frank's house. To me it was a very glamorous affair. Some of the *Hamlet* company were present, including Jessica Tandy, Sam Beazley and Frith Banbury; also Martita Hunt and perhaps three or four leading actors and actresses from other shows, whom I didn't know. Margery Vosper made all go with a swing and Frank was as merry as could be – very different from his lugubrious Claudius. There was a huge birthday cake with twenty-one candles and presents of books, gramophone records, neckties and scarves. I can't remember how I staggered back to my tiny bedsit in Hasker Street (£1 a week) loaded as I was with gifts; perhaps someone treated me to a taxi.

A few months later I met Frank at a small lunch party in Kensington. He took me aside to say, 'I have written a play for you. It's called *Monkey up a Stick*. I hope it may be produced next year. I'll get Margery to send you a copy.' That was the last I heard of it. The play never reached me and I thought it would be too pushy of me to inquire after it. Whether it was ever performed I don't know; if it was, I expect the producer thought, quite rightly, that I was too young and inexperienced to play a leading part.

Before long tragedy struck. Frank fell off a transatlantic liner when returning from the USA and his body was washed ashore in the Channel. There were wild rumours at the time that he had been pushed. It was established, I think, at the inquest that he had got halfway through a porthole (no mean feat, considering his bulk), was probably in his cups and had believed he would land on the promenade deck. But it was a way of no return; night and the sea took him. A kind, funny, sweet-natured and generous man of considerable talent. Time passed, the war came and I suppose that now he is forgotten, except by a very few.

Ah well. 'The strangers all are gone.' The sadness is that so many who were strangers became in time good friends – but eventually had to go.

16. The Clang of Dropped Names

If one is going to drop names with a thud, clang or resounding tinkle, why not start with the Windsors?

The Duchess of Windsor cautiously pushed the pasta and shrimps around her plate with a fork. She turned to me and, lifting a napkin to her mouth, quietly hissed, 'Don't touch it. It's poison.' This was at a small lunch party in Madrid given by a young Portuguese grandee who had befriended me. I had never met the Duchess before; although not captivated by her personality I was hugely impressed by the cut of her mustard-coloured suit and the brilliant, square, yellow diamond which glittered on a lapel. It is, I think, the most beautiful stone I have ever seen. She was polite but had an air of slumming. 'The Dook,' she announced to the six of us at table, 'couldn't come. He allows nothing to interfere with his golf.' I tackled a bit more shrimp, which seemed absolutely wholesome. She flicked an oriental eye at me and said, without a grain of humour, 'You'll regret it.' I hoped our kind and considerate host didn't hear. After that slight reprimand she abandoned me to my fate and, to my relief, gave her attention elsewhere.

A few years ago, at a banquet for film folk at Cannes, I was placed gloriously beside HRH Diana, Princess of Wales. Our starter to the meal was something entirely covered with kiwi fruit. 'The ubiquitous kiwi,' I said, wondering if I had done the wrong thing in speaking first. She turned to me very seriously and, lowering her beautiful head, muttered, 'Don't touch it. It's poison.' Here we go again, I thought, but I was happy to obey her. Conversation wasn't exactly Wildean and after some desperate, brief efforts, we were mercifully distracted by four or five speeches. My heart genuinely went out to her for being saddled with an old bald actor.

Back to the Duchess, this time with the Duke: Paris, 29 November 1966. I had arrived from England that afternoon and arranged to dine with Peter Glenville at Lucas-Carton. Peter told me he had accepted an invitation for both of us to 'drop in for coffee' with the Windsors at some rich house on the Left Bank; 10 p.m. was suggested as a suitable time for us to put in an appearance, so we were there on the dot. (I have no recollection of the name of our hosts but I am sure they had some particular interest in Fauchon, Paris's answer to the food department of Fortnum & Mason). We were informed we were much too early and ushered into an anteroom to wait until dinner was over. After half an hour someone came to say they had started on their pudding and we would be welcome. So into the dining-room we went. There were two round tables with about eight people at each, the Duke presiding at one and the Duchess at the other. To my astonishment the Duke rose when we entered and greeted us most warmly. 'We'll have a talk when we have finished dinner,' he said. 'I'm most anxious to hear your views on Ceylon.' (I had none.) Then he presented me to the Duchess. I bowed and addressed her as Your Royal Highness (well, I thought it expedient) and I noticed that he flushed with pleasure. Peter was taken to the Duke's table and I was squeezed into a place on the Duchess's left. It didn't take me ten seconds to realize she had wined well. She rested her head in her hand and her elbow on the edge of the table. The trouble was the elbow kept slipping off, but she immediately resumed the same position, with the same result. In a steadier moment she explained, perhaps more than once, to the others at the table – 'The Dook is writing a long article for *Life Magazine*. In it he is going to tell us everything that has happened in the world this century. Everything! It'll be great. Too great! The Dook is too great!' The slippery elbow took charge again and she was quiet for a bit. Maybe she took forty winks. With coffee she recovered her composure and elegance.

There was a general rising from the tables and a mingling of guests. The Duke sought me out and started to retail, not unamusingly, his experiences of travelling in the East when he was the young Prince of Wales. While he was talking a flunkey proffered a silver tray with various bottles and glasses. He glanced at the tray and waved it aside.

'Is there something else you would like, sir?' I asked.

'Yes,' he said. 'I'll tell you what I would *really* like. A whisky. In a small glass. I don't like those big things. A *small* glass.'

I excused myself and went in search of whisky, which I quickly found, but locating a small glass proved impossible; plenty of great, chunky, crystal tumblers but nothing remotely small. Another flunkey, to whom I did my best to explain the problem, was decidedly negative. 'So he'll have to settle for what they've got,' I thought; I poured the whisky and returned with it to HRH, who was clearly anxious to get on with his tale about some maharaja. Then his eye fell on the glass. He went scarlet and exploded in what I have heard subsequently referred to as 'The Windsor Rage'.

'I said a *small* glass!' he screamed at me. 'A small glass, a small glass, a small glass! You fool! I told you, a *small* glass. You fool!' With that he turned his back and dashed away to seek comfort from the Duchess, leaving me holding an admittedly large glass with about 2 oz of whisky in the bottom. All conversation had ceased, the hostess, pale as a meringue, descended on me, eyes shocked and blazing. 'What 'as happened?' she demanded. 'What 'ave you said to him?' I tried to explain that she didn't appear to possess any small glasses. She withered me with a look and went to apologize to the Duke for the ill-mannered guest, whom she didn't know anyway.

General chatter slowly began to reassert itself. I sought out Peter, explained what had happened and said that obviously I ought to go. He said we couldn't possibly leave before *they* did; that would be *lèse-majesté*, add insult to injury, etc. 'OK. So I'll have a whisky myself,' I said. In any case the glass was in my hand and I sipped at it for half an hour; after which there was a stir in the room and it became clear that the Windsors were about to depart. They both made their way past me without a glance but when HRH reached the door he turned back, extending his hand. 'I apologize,' he said, 'for my rudeness. I don't know what came over me. I am so sorry.' He gave a charming smile and left. My regard for him increased a hundredfold. It can't have been easy for him.

The World Cup is over but I don't suppose we shall be allowed to forget it, ever. The French win over Brazil in the Final, unexpected as it was, pleased this household. Nothing against the Brazilian team, of course, but they have been champions for so long it is nice to have a change; also France has had a lot of bad luck and yet proved marvelous hosts. We watched with admiration but not with pounding hearts. In any case it was a gratifying distraction from the Orange Order attempt to march at Drumcree, with its attendant horrors (the burning to death of three small Catholic boys elsewhere in the province) and the famine in southern Sudan and shots of the brave limbless victims of landmines.

Thumbing through a glossy magazine at my barber's yesterday I spotted a reproduction of a very old photograph of the ugly, dumpy, New York café society hostess Elsa Maxwell. In 1951, when I was playing in Manhattan with *The Cocktail Party*, Miss Maxwell invited the company to a supper party after the show. We were flattered and taxied off under the guidance of Cathleen Nesbitt, who was a friend of hers, to an unlikely venue which turned out to be a commercial-looking building on, I think, Sixth Avenue. An elevator whisked us up twenty flights where we joined another bevy of somewhat bewildered Maxwell guests.

The party was obviously already in progress as we could hear a woman singing. A wide door was opened by a young man wearing headphones and trailing yards of flex. He put a finger sternly to his lips to hush our chatter. Then a tall, pretty girl beckoned us over coils of heavy cables which squirmed across a linoleum floor and, ducking under TV camera lighting equipment, she shoved us into various sofas and chairs scattered across the vast bleak studio. Maxwell was somewhere in the middle of it all interviewing people. The focus of attention changed and an even taller, prettier girl, wielding a microphone, descended on me as I was sitting primly on my sofa, kissed the top of my balding head – with a knowing wink at the cameras – and belted out 'True to you, darlin', in my fashion' from *Kiss Me Kate*.

None of us, I am sure, in accepting the invitation to supper had anticipated that we were to be stooges in a TV commercial. Actors are always ready for food after a performance and by midnight we were decidedly peckish. But hope reassured our greedy eyes; on the far side of the studio we could see a sumptuous cold meal laid out on a long table covered with a dazzling white cloth. Sides of ham, turkey, chicken, lobsters, salmon and salads looked like a millionaire's picnic. Suddenly Maxwell clapped her little hands, '*À table*, folks!' We made our way across the floor as politely as eagerness would allow. There was a side-table, adjacent to the buffet, holding gleaming plates, sparkling silver and napkins. The cameras zoomed in on Maxwell as she handed me plate, knife and fork.

'Now give that to the lovely lady at your side and' – when I had done so – 'take this yourself. And everyone,' she shouted, 'help yourselves. My, these knives and forks are so pretty.' The lady to whom I had handed the plate approached the feast. I asked her what she would like and she said turkey. As I lifted a fork to pierce the turkey someone bawled 'Cut!' and all the TV lights went out. Not only were we left in dingy semi-darkness but Miss Maxwell had the temerity to shout again, 'Don't touch what's on the table. Your food is in another room.' What we had hoped to eat was all plastic, a mock-up to advertise some company's silverware and bone china. The real food, proffered in a small grotty room, was some sort of rice salad to be eaten off cardboard plates.

'Let's get out of here before worse befalls,' I said to a couple from *The Cocktail Party*. 'There is bound to be a drugstore near by where we can have eggs, sunny-side-up.' We didn't bother with our hostess but just got ourselves out of the building.

Poor Elsa Maxwell: she had a nasty tumble towards the end of her enterprising career. The world understood (through innumerable photographs in the glossies) that she had a close relationship with the Windsors over several years, but then there came a tiff and the swishing aside of skirts. A reconciliation was brought about in mid-Atlantic during very bad weather. The Duchess invited her to a cocktail party in the Windsor stateroom. On arrival Maxwell attempted a deep curtsy, which unfortunately coincided with a roll of the ship. Maxwell tumbled over, clutching at the Windsor legs, which took erratic steps sideways. The cries of 'Wallis!' 'Elsa!' were muffled in the sound of crashing glass.

I have finished Iris Origo's autobiography, *Images and Shadows* (a title which doesn't come trippingly off the tongue), and enjoyed it – particularly the first part – but some of the accounts of farming in Tuscany, although fairly interesting, struck me as more suitable for an agricultural manual than for a good read. And her information about her own writing is depressingly serious. The atmosphere towards the end is somewhat rarefied but made sadly real by the moving account of the tragic death of her eight-year-old son. After such stylish and high-powered sensitivity I feel the need of a change of pace; a good thriller perhaps. How callous that sounds! *Just When We Are Safest* by Reg Gadney has been in the spare bedroom for over a year, unread. That will grab me I am sure.

Here we are on 20 July, enjoying some hot sun at last but with threats of showers. It has been a wretched month, wet, windy and cold. It is odd that during the past few days nearly all our regular birds have deserted us. The tits, which have been like a plague during May, June and the first half of July have suddenly taken their appetites elsewhere and only a couple of finches are around and a solitary blackbird – 'The woosell cock, so black and hue/ With orange-tawny bill' – stands regally on a molehill but there is no sign of his wife; nor of the enchanting wagtails, nor of my sweet robin who lives in the syringa. I find it a little disturbing, this sudden emptiness, as if some distressing message is being withheld. So often I feel that birds are around to keep us informed in some mysterious way, or at least to suggest to our imaginations a larger, unknown world. This is possibly some throwback in my genes to a pagan past, the shade perhaps of a Roman augur in the blood.

If the birds had disappeared ten days ago my superstitious prognostications would have been justified; dear old Japheth, who had just passed his thirteenth birthday, had a stroke at breakfast time and was wretchedly paralysed in his hind legs. The vet came as soon as possible, gave him an injection, prescribed some pills, put him on a strict diet, said he was to have no water but could lap up a saucer of tea with sugar and was to be kept totally quiet. All the time this was going on Flora sat on a banquette, watching with startled eyes and having great fits of trembling. Japheth slept for the rest of the day. Within twenty-four hours he was almost himself again and now no one would guess he had been at death's door. Merula and I had both thought he was a gonner, and even the vet's words of hope sounded hollow in my ears.

Not only have the birds gone but the squirrels also; the latter, for all their prettiness, are a good riddance. (I wouldn't say that if they were red squirrels.) But the tiresome rabbits still abound and 'The blind mole casts/ Copp'd hills towards heaven' – (from somewhere in *Pericles*).

There has been devastation in Papua New Guinea. Two tidal waves, estimated at thirty feet high, dashed themselves into villages scattered along twenty miles of shoreline, leaving three thousand dead. Now there are the inevitable threats of disease and famine. New Zealand and Australia are helping, airlifting food and medical supplies, but there are not enough people to bury the dead.

Tidal waves have always presented an ultimate nightmare in my imagination and I cannot trace the source of this phobia, which shares horror with the green mamba (never seen except in a zoo) and the giant squid (only known from extravagant illustrations to schoolboy yarns). The nightmares of the future, dredged up from memories of TV monsters offered to the children of today, will take some settling down and a strong sedative, I would guess. I have one dream, of rare occurrence, at the beginning of which I am happy and confident but which ends up with me flinging the bedclothes aside in a frenzy. It concerns a series of immense tidal waves on a sunny, almost windless, day in the Thames Estuary.

For some unaccountable reason I am strolling along the riverside with Diana Duff Cooper, who is wearing a wide-brimmed hat and dressed to the ground in a white lacy Edwardian gown and carrying a parasol. She might be in a painting by Tissot. We come across a cluster of elegant rowing skiffs such as one used to be able to hire on the Serpentine. I ask her if she would like me to row her out to sea. The idea seems to amuse her and she accepts. As I hand her into the rear seat and put the ropes for the rudder in her hands she smilingly says, 'I don't think it would be wise to go out as far as that enormous wave which I can see about a mile away.' I turn to have a look, and although somewhat startled by what I saw, I reassure her. 'It's only a tidal wave,' I say, 'which is piling up because it can't reach the shore. Nothing to fear from that.'

The wave seems a hundred feet high, precipitous, white-plumed at the top with broken water, but curiously stationary. I take the oars in a blithe way, do a little show-off feathering, and then pull us out towards the wall of water. When we reach the base of the wave, which is a luminous grey-green in colour, I tell Lady Diana to pull on her right-hand rope to slew us up the side of the wave diagonally. I row like mad and we begin to mount quite easily. When we reach the crest, jumbled about in troubled water but not unduly alarmed, we suddenly see what lies before us and gasp with astonishment – serried ranks of similar vast waves stretching back as far as vision will carry, all waiting to dash for the Thames Estuary, to topple St Paul's and engulf London. There is no wind to speak of but I raise my voice as if in a hurricane and bellow, 'Full astern! Hard to starboard! Where's your life-jacket, for God's sake?'

Now we are planing down the wave as if on a surfboard and the great seas are following us. Diana is still holding on to her parasol but the amazing, blue, steady eyes are taking everything in as we sweep past Greenwich. 'There goes the *Cutty Sark*,' she says. 'A very good whisky.' I turn to look at what is no longer there and when I turn back she has been replaced on the stern seat by three of the cast of David Lean's film of *Great Expectations*: John Mills (who is pretending to be sick), Bernard Miles, clutching a large wooden wheel, and Finlay Currie in a top hat reading Southey's *Life of Nelson*. Some scenes were shot in the Estuary and surrounding marshes.

When the Old Vic sent Larry Olivier's *King Lear* to Paris for a week in 1946 the cast was put up in the railway hotel which has now been transformed into the Museé d'Orsay. My room shuddered and filled with smoke at regular intervals throughout the night. It didn't matter much because of the overriding joy of being in Paris in a liberated France. The Duff Coopers presided over a generous court at the British Embassy and gave a sumptuous supper party for the company. It was at that party I met Diana Cooper for the first time and decided that she must certainly be the most glamorous woman in the world. Every performance at the theatre was totally sold out, and on the first night there was no seat for a distinguished old man who was determined to be present. Larry and the stage management had forgotten to warn the cast that the little humped roof to the *trou du souffleur*, which rises in the middle of the footlights of most French theatres, was to be occupied by a well-known theatrical face. When I made my first entrance as the Fool I quickly spotted an old, handsome, white face surrounded by a halo of white hair – another Lear, in fact – with angry-looking eyes swivelling from side to side of the stage. There was something familiar about the face in that prompter's box but I could make nothing of it. Squatting at Larry's side I said my line, 'Can you make no use of nothing, Nuncle?'

To which he replied, 'Why no, boy; nothing can be made out of nothing.'

And the penny dropped; it was the head of Gordon Craig.

Craig was Ellen Terry's son, had been an actor for a while and then became an artist, writer and pioneering avant-garde scene designer. (The sets were inclined to be severe, awe-inspiring and imaginative – and given to falling down through impracticalities.) The hero-worshipping book he wrote about Henry Irving gives a marvellous insight into a theatrical genius of a previous age. Irving treated him with infinite kindness, like a son. He was born in 1872 and spent the last decades of his life in France, dying in 1966. I feel privileged to have seen him, even if only at my feet.

The next time I met Diana Cooper was about three years later in London, at a vast supper party given by Ann, Lady Rothermere. Numerous round tables, each to hold about six or eight people, were scattered on the sides of a dance floor, at one end of which was a gigantic flower arrangement jutting out of a vase about four feet high. It played its part in the evening. To my astonishment, alarm and delight I was placed at Diana Cooper's right at a table which also held Princess Margaret – probably aged nineteen – Cyril Connolly, Frederick Ashton, Hugh Trevor-Roper, the historian, and a couple of others whom I cannot recall. Diana was looking stunning, as always, but she had had one dry Martini too many, as she readily admitted.

'Can't go out unless I take a little fortification,' she said to me. 'Too nervous. Stage fright. Tonight I fortified myself twice, which was foolish.'

She eyed her fellow diners. 'Who's that little man?' she asked me in a loud whisper.

'Cyril Connolly.'

'I can't bear him,' she said, full voice, and picked up a roll and flung it at him. It was a good shot and struck him on the forehead. Connolly flushed but otherwise didn't react.

The Princess looked amazed. An awkward situation was saved by the arrival at the table of Noël Coward. He stopped to say to HRH, 'I am sorry to read in the evening paper that your mother has the flu. I do hope she gets better soon.'

'Her Majesty the Queen is much better, thank you.'

Coward passed on. Diana D. C. fixed me with those amazing eyes and said, 'Did you hear that? I think I need another drink.' Suddenly she was quite sober.

'When are you coming to Paris?' she asked.

I told her that I was going there the following week.

'Come to lunch at Chantilly on the Sunday. I'll send a car for you. Where are you staying?'

I told her the Bristol.

She settled down to being a hostess. 'Who would you most like to meet? In the world.'

'You again,' I said over-gallantly.

'That is a very boring thing to say.' There was a reprimand in her tone. 'You must always speak the truth; that's the only thing that's funny.'

'It is the truth,' I said. 'You, again.'

'Now you are being tiresome. I shall have to think hard.' With that she fell silent and gave herself up to staring Cyril Connolly out of countenance. A dance band struck up and a few couples rose from their tables but before they reached the floor there was a tremendous crash. Somehow Orson Welles had managed to knock over the great flower arrangement, water sloshed everywhere and any idea of dancing had to be abandoned. There was a little polite booing of Orson and the band gallantly played on as if the Rothermere mansion was the *Titanic* in its final moments. Princess Margaret, as pretty as could be, stood up, discreetly beckoned F. Ashton and disappeared. Cyril Connolly, poor man, nodded goodnights round the table and made his getaway. As for Diana Cooper – I feel for her now – I remember plying her with questions about Max Reinhardt, in whose production of *The Miracle* I had seen her at the Lyceum when I was about thirteen. She talked amusingly and interestingly about the theatre, I know, but I have no recollection of what she said.

A week later, in Paris, I was sure she had probably forgotten her invitation, so taking my courage in my dialling hand, I telephoned Château St-Firman, Chantilly. (The Duff Coopers had left the Embassy in 1947 but continued to occupy St-Firman. He became Viscount Norwich in 1952, four years before his death; but she announced publicly that she did not wish to use the new title.) Yes, I was expected and a car arranged. It was a pleasant sunny day when I arrived at St-Firman and she was standing on the steps of the château, a tall, commanding, beautiful statue wearing a staggering woollen outfit – a wide black hat with slashes of canary yellow and a dress of canary yellow slashed with black.

'I hope I have done all right,' she said. 'I've put you next to Garbo for lunch.' I don't remember who else was there – about eight people – other than Cecil Beaton, who was bitchy about Vivien Leigh and received an indignant rebuke from Lady D., which shut him up for a few minutes.

Indeed I was placed next to Garbo and it was the first time I had met her. (On two occasions, in New York, I had arrived at a house or apartment to be greeted with the words, 'If you had arrived here a few minutes ago you could have met Garbo.' And once, in a cake shop on Madison Avenue, the girl assistant said 'Miss Greta Garbo bought the very same cheesecake only half an hour ago.' So I felt destined to meet her.) Conversation wasn't flowing or easy. Her opening gambit was to ask me if I was an expert on French eighteenth-century furniture. When I replied that I wasn't sure I would be able to recognize a piece of French furniture of any century she switched her serious attention to whoever was on her other side. Laughter and brightness surrounded Lady D. Between courses, before the pudding, she excused herself and reappeared minutes later having changed her wardrobe. It was the same as she had just been wearing but in reverse. This time the hat was yellow with black bits and the dress black with yellow stripes here and there.

During my stay in Paris she asked me to escort her one evening to some minor function at some tatty hall used by a group of young people she had helped and befriended. I think she handed over a cheque to them. The few dozen who were present paid scant attention to her and she and I sat alone at a greasy-topped metal table and had coffee. To her it must have seemed a far cry from the days when people clambered on to table tops in glamorous restaurants just to catch a glimpse of her. She was mostly silent that night and seemed sad. She asked me if I had ever been to Lourdes. I said I hadn't. (I wasn't a Catholic at that time and I doubt if the idea of visiting a mid-nineteenth-century place of pilgrimage attracted me.) She commented that neither had she but one day, motoring past it, she had offered a prayer that she might have a child; a year later her son was born. 'I always mean to go back to say thank you but I don't suppose I shall.'

On half a dozen other occasions I ran in to her, either in Rome or London. The last time was at a dinner when I sat opposite her across a wide table which ruled out any conversation except with one's immediate neighbours. When we rose after coffee I approached her and said, 'We haven't met for a few years; you may not remember me', and I gave my name. She was looking old and very sad, but for a moment the brightness came back in her eyes, and the familiar tone of fun.

'How absurd you are,' she said. 'I always go to see any play you are in.' Then she took my hand, held it against her bosom for quite a while and gazed into space. Finally she said, 'I'm so tired of life. So many friends have left me behind. And frankly, I am very very bored. Sit for a while and talk to me.'

I sat for a while but could think of nothing to say which might interest her. Someone came up to pay his respects – something she was used to – and I kissed her goodnight and left.

17. The Return of the Birds

Five days ago an old friend, whom I first knew when we were both about nineteen, died peacefully in his Sussex village. I have always felt close to him but had not seen him since his wife died four years ago. He became a wheelchair case and things were difficult. A week before I heard of his death all birds suddenly disappeared from the garden, except for a bedraggled crow and an unpleasant magpie. At the time I thought it odd, wondering what could have frightened them away, or whether I was to read into their absence, superstitiously, some portent. The funeral, which I shall attend, is tomorrow and as soon as I was told that the birds began to reappear. First to arrive was the spotted woodpecker; only the robin, who keeps an inquisitive eye on me, and the wagtail couple who dance so joyously, have not yet reappeared.

Last night Jill Balcon and Anne Kaufman Schneider came with me to the Chichester Festival Theatre production of David Hare's *Racing Demon*. Merula felt as if a heavy cold was coming on so decided to stay at home. It was an enjoyable outing. I had seen the play when it was first done at the National ten years ago. Then I sat among a heap of elderly clerics adjusting their whistling hearing-aids; this time I was a retired thespian, fiddling with my own instrument among an assortment of concentrated blue-rinsed coiffures. It remains good theatre, in spite of the time gap and the intensifying problems of the C of E and its synods, but I did find two or three scenes rather long and self-indulgent. The acting was first-class and my old friend Mark Kingston gave a beautifully judged performance as the priest blackmailed by a Sunday scandal sheet: clear as a bell, simplicity itself and never a gesture too large or a tone anything but true. Leaving the theatre, jammed in with the slowly moving audience, I kept my ears pricked and my hearing-aid well-balanced. I had the impression that the citizens of the Cathedral City of Chichester had been interested – indeed had quite liked the play – but pursed their lips at some of the implications of clerical life.

Today, in the light drizzle, I went to my friend's funeral; a good turnout in a small country church but there were things which puzzled me. There were two hymns but nothing that you could call a prayer – not even, it strikes me now, the Lord's Prayer – but perhaps I am wrong. I get things wrong very easily these days. There *was* a reading of the opening verses of St John's gospel, I know, because that hit home to me unexpectedly. I well remember the two of us, when serving in the RNVR and temporarily based in Inveraray, in Argyllshire, entering the very High Episcopalian little church on the outskirts of the town one afternoon and finding it deserted. A Bible stood on the brass lectern. 'Read something aloud,' he said. I declined. 'Oh, go on. Read the beginning of St John; it's my favourite passage.' So boldly I went up to the chancel and read 'In the beginning was the Word, and the Word was with God, and the Word was God,' and the following dozen verses. We walked out of the church and strolled silently for half an hour along the shore of Loch Fyne. Our conversations were frequently of religion and he had an inquiring, often original, philosophical turn of mind. Neither of us, I am sure, thought we were very bright but we laughed a lot, were easy with each other and admitted our ignorance. His name was John Rotton.

Yesterday's funeral was an ecological affair; the body was not in a coffin, as we understand the word, but in a cardboard box. At the first sight of it I was disconcerted and thought of 'Cash on delivery' or a Christmas hamper from a London store, but finally decided it was typical of his humility.

My will must be altered so that when the time comes to bury me as much wood as possible may be saved; I have always disliked those veneered, brass-handled, satin-lined receptacles for the dead. No hymns for me, by special request, but I would like a splash of holy water, a whiff of incense and the voice of Victoria de los Angeles to lull me on my way.

A few hours after my return from John Rotton's funeral there was a telephone call to tell me that Beryl Daniels, a close friend for over sixty-six years, had died that morning. Oddly, it had been she who had introduced me to Rotton. She was the daughter of the headmaster at my school in Eastbourne and, like several other boys in their late teens, I had fallen in love with her, in spite of her being seven years older. She was warm-hearted, laughed easily, was sympathetic, and a superb listener when the subject was serious. When I last spoke to her – about three weeks ago – I was amazed at how clear and appealing her voice had remained in spite of serious illness.

It was Beryl who, through friends in the advertising world, managed to find me a job as a copywriter when I left school. Her letters, short but not abruptly short, reassuring and wise, reached me about once a fortnight in reply to my weekly sixteen-page outpourings, which she must have dreaded the sight of as they thumped down on the breakfast table. She had very meagre savings but whenever she turned up in London she managed to find an hour in which to give me tea or, on a couple of occasions, to pay for upper circle seats (a luxury compared with my habitual perch in the gallery) at some Shaftesbury Avenue theatre. The theatre had obsessed my imagination since about the age of fourteen, or even a few years earlier, and whatever she may have really thought, she always expressed confidence in my future. Her greatest, most endearing quality, was a genuine interest in everyone she knew; not just family and friends but even in those who rarely and briefly crossed her life.

The world at large was probably unaware of these two friends of mine, but I am sure their goodness made ripples far beyond their own particular circles; they themselves would be astonished if they could know the range of their influence.

★

The 'tough' language of thriller writers strikes me as very old hat and no longer wearily acceptable. Who do they think they are kidding? The last two I picked up each had the word 'shit' on the first page and no doubt there were other four-letter spellings to follow. If this is meant to grab the attention it failed totally with me; I decided I just couldn't be bothered to continue. So I had another stab at *The Wings of a Dove* – which people keep assuring me is marvellous – but a few pages of Henry James left me dizzy, confused and breathless with the length of his sentences. There is a lot of James I have greatly enjoyed but this cold and damp August leaves me unreceptive to him. With relief I heaved off a bookshelf the weight of *The Last Chronicle of Barset* and within a few minutes found myself responding happily, for the third time, to living, vivid characters and finding new depths in them. My only grumble is that the admirable Trollope Society didn't print four or five of the longer books – including *The Last Chronicle* – in a two-volume edition.

Today I ordered flowers by telephone from a classy London florist.

'I would like to have some flowers sent to an address in Chelsea.'

'Lovely!' the assistant said. 'What sort?'

'Perhaps some sweet peas, if they are still available.'

'Wonderful! How much would you like to spend?'

'Not more than £40,' I said.

'Brilliant!'

After that I called a London bookshop.

'Would you please send a copy of Iris Origo's *Images and Shadows* to an address in Chelsea?'

'Super!' the lady assistant said. 'What name?'

'Mrs Kaufman Schneider.'

'Fabulous!' she said.

'Well, that's wonderful of you,' said I, and gave the address. As I put down the telephone I couldn't help speculating that almost all exchanges of words have become meaningless, friendly rubbish; and hardly ever the sight or sound of a surname. 'Please call Geraldine, 0171 . . . for further information.' 'Desmond is away on holiday but I will put your letter on his desk as soon as he returns. Yours ever, Heather.' Who the hell is Desmond and what is Heather? Neither is known to me.

There are great, resonant lines in *Tamburlaine* and superb visual images (it is a play with which I am not at all familiar) but now and then it descends, or so it seems to me on a current reading, to something akin to 'The most lamentable comedy and most cruel death of Pyramus and Thisbe' in the *Dream*. Here's a little something from *Tamburlaine* for an actress to try to deal with:

> *(Bajazeth brains himself against a cage; enter Zabina)*
> What do mine eyes behold? My husband dead?
> His skull all riven in twain, his brains dasht out?
> The brains of Bajazeth, my Lord and Sovereign?
> O Bajazeth, O Turk, O Emperor.
> Hell, death, Tamburlaine, Hell. Make ready my coach, my chair,
> my jewels. I come, I come, I come.
> *(She runs against the cage and brains herself)*

Even Mrs Siddons would have had trouble with that; Maggie Smith, of course, would have an hysterically funny field day with it. It strikes me as a possibility that Shakespeare had it in mind when he has Master Flute, appearing in drag as Thisbe, discover the dead Pyramus:

> Asleep, my love?
> What, dead, my dove!
> O Pyramus, arise!
> Speak, speak! Quite dumb? . . .
> Come, trusty sword,

Come, blade, my breast imbrue!
And farewell, friends;
Thus Thisbe ends:
Adieu, adieu, adieu!

It amazes me that there are people who think Marlowe wrote
Shakespeare's plays, although there is every likelihood that Shakespeare either deliberately plagiarized an image now and then or
that a line of Marlowe's, when first heard or seen, had struck so
deeply into his soul that he imagined it his own. Marlowe's
stagecraft is crude or non-existent when compared to Shakespeare's know-how. And is there a character in Marlowe which
makes one smile, let alone laugh outright? – I must cease to ride
this hobby-horse and give my attention to *The Simpsons*, to
which I'm getting addicted. Also I should bear in mind a line
the hero, Dennis, says in E. Waugh's *The Loved One*: 'In the
dying world I come from quotation is a national vice.'

Before leaving for the 1958 film festival in Mexico City, to
which I had been induced to go by the Foreign Office, I received
a script of *The Loved One* with the suggestion that I should play
the lead. It was a marvellous script, in which the great director
Buñuel had had a hand. Shortly after arriving in Mexico Buñuel
sent me a note inviting himself to coffee at my hotel the following
morning. He arrived at noon, full of amiability and chuckles.
He kept removing his glacé-mint-type spectacles to wipe tears
of laughter from his eyes.

'I am a very happy man today,' he said. 'I have just been to
the screening of my last movie, for the critics. It is good I think.
They all congratulated me. How did you like the music, I asked.
Mm – mm – wonderful, they said. The music was truly *wonderful*,
they said.'

He took off his glasses again and mopped his eyes. 'I promise
you there is not one note of music in the movie.'

Then we got down to discussing *The Loved One*. All his ideas
were simple, true to the novel and yet sometimes daringly odd.

He told me he didn't wish to use wax models for the cadavers in the mortuary scenes or funeral parlour but blocks of wood roughly hewn into human shape. We got on well and I was thrilled at the prospect of working with him. He explained he would be unable to start for at least another four months, which didn't worry me, although it should have done. What happened I don't know; presumably something to do with the film rights. Whatever it was, we were beaten to the post by Tony Richardson, who directed a quite different, heavy-handed script, an unwitty version as far removed from the factual, debunking spirit of Waugh as a flying saucer.

It is mid-August and the few days of hot sun have broken, followed by strong, cold winds and a touch of rain. Spent a day and night in London to see my doctor, have my left shoulder X-rayed and to dine with the Sinclair-Stevensons at Cecconi's. My shoulder has been playing me up for almost a year; the X-rays apparently reveal that it is arthritic. So before long, I suppose, I shall have to have a beastly cortisone injection; and then I shall be able to toss the caber or indulge in some other performance-enhanced sport. During the past two weeks I have found it painful lifting a fork to my mouth with my left hand so I have reversed my eating habits and taken to the American way, which I find much more sensible and stylish; it also has the added benefit of slowing me up. Merula and I are inclined to be gobblers so this may bring us, me at least, more politely into line with guests.

We have finally made a holiday decision, which is a relief, as I have spent hours during the past month riffling through a variety of guidebooks, dismissing a dozen ideas from Istanbul to Barcelona, from the remoter parts of Norway to the Azores. We have settled on eight days in the Camargue in late September and have booked ourselves into the Mas de la Fouque, about three miles NW of Les Saintes-Maries-de-la-Mer. It is thirty years since the only time I glimpsed the Camargue, driving across the south of France from the Atlantic coast. It was blisteringly hot and, dizzied by the road, which shimmered like a mirage, and the powder-blue haziness of the lagoons, I dozed off. It all looked very flat – 'very flat, Norfolk' – but there was a suggestion of magic about it which has often made me want to return. Perhaps it was just the knowledge that all those famous white horses must be around somewhere, and pink flamingos would be delicately treading through shallow water, shrimping backwards with those oddly curved beaks; or the fanciful legends concerning the little town of Les Saintes-Maries, which has been a place of pilgrimage for fifteen hundred years. Twice a year, in April and October, gypsies come there from all over the world. Our visit will be too early for the autumnal festivities but surely we shall be able to see the boat (without sail or rudder) in which St Mary Magdalene, St Martha, Lazarus and other sainted characters were miraculously whisked from the Palestinian shore to Provence. (The late Jini Fiennes, mother of the actors, gives a vivid and enchanting account of it in her very enjoyable book, *On Pilgrimage*.)

Oh, I hope that in my excitement at the prospect before us I'm not building up something which is bound to be a disappointment. That has happened before.

At the beginning of this week we had Michael Mayne (lately of Westminster Abbey) and his wife Alison for dinner and to spend the night. Our neighbours the Parkers joined us for the evening and, it being reasonably warm, we were able to eat out under the vine in the kitchen arbour. With stubby, long-lasting candles glowing steadily in their clever glass and copper containers it all looked very pretty as dusk fell and when darkness surrounded us it was magical. The candles lit the underside of faces, like the footlights of yesteryear, and gilded the vine leaves; in fact all looked bosky and quite as good as Tuscany. Everyone seemed relaxed and chatty; conversation slipped easily along, from the frivolous to the Clinton scandal; from the charm and intelligence of Chelsea Clinton, vouched for by the Maynes, to the charisma of Diana P of W when embracing AIDS patients; from Anglican priestesses (not championed by the Parkers) to recommended books, theatre offerings and the merits or otherwise of contemporary poets. Merula provided smoked salmon, curried chicken (after Vincent Sardi's New York recipe) and raspberries mixed with very robust blueberries. It all seemed just about right and was well washed down with Cloudy Bay from New Zealand and a rough red from the Rhône. The dogs behaved perfectly and didn't demand too much attention. When we went to bed M. and I voted it the most enjoyable evening we had had for a long time. Never mind the guests, say I, so long as the hosts have had a good time.

The following evening was rather different. We took ourselves to Chichester to see *Chimes at Midnight* – the Orson Welles reduction of Shakespeare's two parts of the *Henry IV* plays. Two into one won't go. Simon Callow, as Falstaff, was a touch on the loud side but his delivery of the 'Honour' speech – 'Honour pricks me on. Yea, but how if honour prick me off when I come on? Can honour set to a leg? No, or an arm? No . . .' – was brilliant and his native wit shone through. Our friend Keith Baxter was admirable as the King – finely spoken, handsome, and he took the stage with regal authority. Two drama critics I had read said Baxter's speaking was 'Gielgudry' (by which, I suppose, they were trying to be pejorative; though why the greatest speaker of Shakespeare in our time should be held up as an example not to be followed I can't imagine. The Gielgud of sixty years ago – not seen or heard by current critics I imagine – could be hair-raising.) In any case Keith Baxter was very much his own man. He provided the only true gravitas of the evening.

I never saw the Welles film of *Chimes at Midnight* which everyone says is brilliant, but I cannot believe this theatrical version ever stood up firmly on its splayed feet. How could it? The world's greatest dramatist shaped his glorious play into two parts; what Shakespeare kept asunder let no man have the effrontery to join together in truncated form.

On the way home, being driven through the quiet night-time Sussex roads, my mind flickered on and off about acting and the quality of actors. My spirits were raised and flattened every few minutes. Words spoken by Theseus, after witnessing Pyramus and Thisbe in the *Dream*, stole into my memory. 'The best in this line are but shadows; and the worst are no worse, if imagination amend them.' Ah, well – often true no doubt; but that would leave it all to the perception of the spectator, like beauty being in the eye of the beholder. And yet surely the stuff of greatness sometimes, if rarely, asserts itself when, by a trick of nature, the poet speaks wiser than he knows and the player reaches above his own imagination.

Such silliness has overtaken me with age (it has never been far out of sight) that I don't know how I dare to express an opinion about anything, even in an area in which it might be supposed I had some sort of knowledge. I have none. When it comes down to it I fear I am reduced to saying, 'I know what I like,' and leaving it at that. What I *do not* like is the pretence of some to be actors at all. Returning from the theatre the other evening my mind eventually settled down to a pudding of chaos.

Barbellion, in his *Journal of a Disappointed Man* (1919), which I used to dip into quite a lot when I was about twenty, quotes Nietzsche as saying, 'You must carry a chaos inside you to give birth to a dancing star.' Barbellion's diary entry after he had read that sentence was, 'Internal chaos I have, but no dancing star. Dancing stars are the consolation of genius.' I like the word 'consolation' there, as so many of us think that the state of being a genius must be a happy one. Yet Barbellion was a truly great naturalist in the making and a star might well have danced for him, given half the chance. He was quite a funny man, but predominantly despondent, while stretching out to make a great name for himself. Constant ill health finally defeated him at the age of thirty, when he died. At the age of thirteen or fourteen, articles he had written on insects and his observations of nature were accepted by learned journals.

Every actor, I imagine, has had hopes of giving birth to a dancing star, imagining he could hear in his youthful ear thunderous applause as the curtain falls. Maybe a handful in this century have totally fulfilled their dream; they are the ones who have instinctively, and successfully, fished and chosen well in the maelstrom of their souls.

To the young generation I can only say, if asked, as Auden's Prospero does in his leave-taking of Ariel – 'then brave spirit,/ Ages to you of song and daring, and to me/ Briefly Milan, then earth.' It seems a fair-enough parting. Personally I have only one great regret – that I never *dared* enough. If at all. But no way. Not at all.

I am quite happy waiting for more birds to reappear, as they surely will. A crow is circling the house, like the raven returning to the Ark each evening until the waters had tumbled away and the dry land appeared. It was the dove, of course, which brought reassurance to all on board when it came back with an olive leaf in its beak. We could do with a bushel of olive leaves scattered around the world now, in this terrorist and cruise missile horror of late August.

18. Bon Appétit

The waiter's gestures were so extravagant and his accent so aggressively French, of the *'Allo! 'Allo!* variety, that I surmised he was probably born and bred in Southend. He managed to kick the leg of my chair a dozen times; and his chum the 'sommelier' rested his exhausted arm on my shoulder while I ran an alarmed eye down 'La Carte des Vins' (it was very much that kind of evening) counting the cost. It was certainly not going to be an occasion – I can't imagine such an event for anyone, however thick their wallet – for Bordeaux at £1,000 a throw. But the waiter was enthusiastic and, sure enough, he brought one of my guests a piece of cod stuffed into what looked like a Swiss roll; she had ordered calves' liver. The food, I have to say, was very good but over-decorated. Each minimalist portion was arranged to maximum effect as if by Matisse.

'You would like to take ze café in ze bar?' I told him we were comfortable where we were apart from the chair-kicking. He looked disappointed. The restaurant was doing good noisy business but there were two or three empty tables and I suppose they had hopes that mine would be free before it was time for last orders. The three of us – Mark and Marigold Kingston and I – had sat where we were for just under two hours, which seemed to me not unreasonable for a meal costing £210. Much time had been wasted with acknowledging the endless wishes of '*Bon appétit*' before each course and nodding to the countless inquiries – always interrupting a conversation – as to whether everything was to our satisfaction.

On leaving, a charming chorus of hat-check girls said 'Have a good day' as we groped our way out to the dark. The doorman, in Stygian black and wearing a curtailed top hat, looked remarkably like Ralph Fiennes playing an undertaker. He kindly offered to find us a taxi but I declined, fearing he might summon up a hearse.

My beloved Connaught Hotel, where I have spent so many nights during the past forty years and still use as my London base every week or so, has relaxed its rules in order to attract a more 'with-it' and easy-going clientele, and to encourage ever larger groups of businessmen. Gentlemen are now permitted to lunch tieless. This is a pity, I think, as there are remarkably few places left where you dare to smarten up a little for some small celebration, and a table without ties, except out of doors or in some jolly trattoria or taverna, creates a somewhat naff atmosphere. Briefcases are clicked open or shut and the ubiquitous mobile telephones advance like an army of Triffids – and who, I wonder, is impressed? During the sixties, particularly in Hollywood, it was considered smart to have a telephone plugged in to your table so that you could be seen and heard to be doing your tremendously important business. In the sophisticated dark of the Polo Lounge at the Beverly Hills Hotel, where the Hollywood élite sipped their Gibsons or Daiquiris, or rattled the ice cubes in their beakers of Jack Daniels, it was hard to make out faces, but if telephones were being plugged in to various tables you got the message – some film agent or just-glimmering rising star was seeking attention.

A memory game has seized the press (not for the first time) – 'Where were you when you heard of the fatal accident to Princess Di and her Dodi?' This is a follow on from 'Where were you when President Kennedy was assassinated?' I would add where were you on 3 September 1939 when Britain and France declared war on Germany? If you had been born. And add to that 6 August 1945, when the atomic bomb was dropped on Hiroshima and a new horror enfolded a frightened, war-weary world.

On the morning when Chamberlain ('Peace in our time') announced, gravely, that we were at war with Germany Merula and I were at her parents' house in Surrey. Everyone was clustered around the radio. The garden looked beautiful in warm sunshine but a chill struck all our hearts. High in the bright blue sky a tiny single-prop plane was flying north. That was the start of wartime rumours. It was piloted, people speculated, by the Duke of Windsor, or by some important Nazi defector come to sue for peace or half a dozen other absurdities. I can't believe that any of us on that September day could have envisaged that Europe – with the exception of Switzerland, Sweden, Spain and Portugal – would be blacked out for six years. If we had known I wonder if our courage, after the initial shock, would have been so high.

The news of Kennedy's death reached me in short, indecisive, incredible scraps of hearsay while I was rehearsing a play about Dylan Thomas in a disused theatre in New York. The assassination was confirmed shortly before we were due to break for lunch. We were all stunned and it was agreed that work should stop for the day and that the management would telephone each of us when it was considered suitable to resume. New York was in full mourning within an hour; most shop-windows were draped in black, a vast number of large photographs of the President appeared all over the place and the city, usually so siren-ridden and traffic-bound, seemed almost hushed. People walked the streets in a daze, making for their apartments, radios and TV sets. There seemed nothing else to do.

When the atomic bomb was dropped on Hiroshima on 6 August 1945 (and another on Nagasaki two days later) I was stationed at Southampton without a ship, sitting in a stuffy little office facing an empty desk. Now and then a few American naval personnel could be heard bawling down the echoing passage, 'All Limeys are chicken shit'; there wasn't much love lost between our services. (My own antipathy towards them was solely based on the little, pencil-thin, Adolphe Menjou – twenties film actor – moustaches many of their officers sported.) Merula and I had rented rooms in a house near Fawley, belonging to the mother of the painter Richard Eurich. The atmosphere there was very Quakerish. Neither of us, to our shame, can recall how we first heard of the bomb but M. remembers us sitting on a grassy bank overlooking Southampton Water watching a distant, joyful firework display. If we had had enough imagination to appreciate the poisonous threat which had been released on the world we might have rejoiced more soberly. When it did dawn on me what it all signified I am sure my reaction was simply one of personal relief – 'Now, surely, they can't send me to the Far East.' After two and a half years away from England the possibility of another long stint deprived of home, wife and small son was a nightmare.

If I had to state in a court of law how, when and where I heard the news of the death of the Princess of Wales I would swear I was sitting in my study at nine o'clock on that Sunday morning listening to the radio news. My diary for 31 August 1997 shows me to be wrong. I was indeed at my desk and Merula, who had been out early walking the dogs, came into the room, agitated, to say she had just encountered neighbours who had given her the news. 'It's the end of the monarchy,' they had said in great distress. Well, the world has continued on its elliptical course, the year has completed itself, the Prince of Wales and the young princes have stood firm and smiling, whatever their feelings, and no one, I hope, would attempt to fault the Queen. It is, I regret, no longer an age of hat-wearing but hats should be doffed in the right direction.

Private thoughts and expressions of public grief don't always coincide. Trollope has something to say about that in *The Last Chronicles*. The irascible yet endearing Archdeacon Grantly says, on hearing of the death of the bishop's wife, the unspeakable Mrs Proudie – 'The proverb of De mortuis is founded on humbug. Humbug out of doors is necessary. It would not be good for you and me to go into the High Street just now and say what we think about Mrs Proudie; but I don't suppose that kind of thing need be kept up in here, between you and me . . . You may as well give me my tea.'

For several years my two favourite fish in the pond have been a couple of blue orfe. They were handsome, swift, spotted bright blue along their backs, and they always swam side by side and often broke water seeking food. This morning I found one of them floating on its side, feebly flapping. For the last few weeks I have been anxious about its sluggish behaviour and lack of interest. I decided it would be kind to put it out of its last agony so I took the fish from the water and gave it a sharp *coup de grâce*. It was about fourteen inches long and I was amazed at the brilliant silver of its flanks. Its companion hasn't been seen for twenty-four hours but the water is rather cloudy and possibly it may be hiding under a lily-pad. The little deaths in nature sometimes disturb me more than that of humans. The thought that we can neither comfort, explain nor help in any way seems so pitiful. And yet how the hell could one comfort a fish? My blue orfe might swivel an eye and say, 'If you are so concerned, why have you eaten so many trout, halibut or Dover soles?'

Merula has put on my desk a little, dark brown, earthenware pot containing a clutch of pale mauve petunias. Their deep red, complicated veins look like a medical diagram of human lungs. Our lungs, if stretched out, would cover an area the size of a tennis-court; or so I am told. A large rectangle of fragile petunias would be a great deal more attractive.

Yesterday, in London, I browsed in the paperback department of Hatchard's bookshop, selecting slim volumes I might like to take on holiday to the Camargue. I came away with Mauriac's *The Knot of Vipers* (forty years since I have read any Mauriac), Evelyn Waugh's *Put Out More Flags* – not read for a long time – and *Trust Me*, a collection of John Updike's short stories. Waiting for me at home I knew there was W. G. Sebald's *The Rings of Saturn*, which has received tremendous praise. It is a curiously produced book, not inviting to handle, and the photographic reproductions of forlorn east-coast beaches and dreary hotels look as if snapped by a very old box Brownie. After reading a few pages my impatience began to rise; then I spotted a parody of it in last week's *Private Eye* and the rings of Saturn were quite flattened for me.

'Ah, never mind,' I thought, 'I will have another attempt at *The Wings of a Dove*.' So I sat down to read the first pages and nearly passed out with exhaustion; over and over I had to return to interminable sentences to try to fathom – not so much what he might be getting at under the surface, which was rarefied to a degree – but just to grasp the plain story line. So the wings of the dove were plucked and replaced on their high shelf, and there they will settle until some distant day when I may feel strong enough to blow the dust off them again. A Shakespeare will be taken, for safety's sake, and, if by chance a well-recommended one turns up, a thriller. Merula is deep in *Captain Corelli's Mandolin*, so she is taken care of – until we are on our way to the airport when she is likely to announce, 'I finished *Captain Corelli* last night and I have nothing to read.' She will have to make a choice from the usual lurid fare on offer to the travelling public.

Mornings have been wasted in recent days by spending far too much time poring over newspaper accounts of Clinton, Starr and That Woman. It is all very sordid and, after the first few minutes of prurient reading, basically uninteresting; also there is nothing we on this side of the Atlantic can do about it. My only anxiety is about the rockets dropped on the alleged chemical war factory in the Sudan, but that was an action approved by the majority of Americans; it also received plaudits from our Mr Blair and our Mr Hague – but not from everyone in Europe – and the President, the US Commander-in-Chief, is not being questioned about that. My hunch is that he will see out his term of office.

The grand climacteric passed me by twenty-one years ago and I thumb through Montaigne in the hope of seizing on, and remembering, shreds of wisdom. Yesterday I found this: 'As I grow older I dare a little more, for custom apparently concedes to old age a greater licence to chatter more indiscreetly about myself' (M. A. Screech translation). But I *don't* dare a little more; I'm just careless of what I say and before whom, and even if I tread cautiously it is not without frequent, unexpected stumbles.

Today the white horses of the Camargue have their behinds facing the strong chilly east wind. We arrived at Montpellier airport yesterday afternoon and drove for fifty minutes through a grey-green, lagoon-striped countryside to our pleasant-looking, ranch-like hotel a couple of miles from the little seaside town of Les Saintes-Maries-de-la-Mer. Our vast bedroom (with sitting area) is charmingly decorated but decidedly odd. Two double beds stand on a raised area at one end with a sharp step down on one side and a short steep ramp on the other. There is a smart jacuzzi bath in one corner of the room (with neither door nor curtain). That also goes for a shower-room, about 7 × 7 ft, halfway along one wall. In fact the only privacy is to be found in the loo. Even the glittering twin wash-basins are in a sort of open-ended passage, well exposed to anyone with a voyeuristic appetite. Two sides of the room consist of sliding glass panels which give on to a patio. The 'ponds', a stretch of water perhaps fifty yards wide, twists around some uninviting-looking grass and clusters of grey-green shrubs.

We were entranced, as dusk fell, to see swimming and fishing outside our room what we took to be otters but which we were later informed were *ragondins*, a species of beaver with long rat-like tails. They have a fine turn of speed and the effect of two of them chasing each other on the surface suggests an appearance of the Loch Ness Monster. Their upper lips, from nose to mouth, are extremely deep, giving them the look of the old-time film star George Arliss or the late Harold Macmillan. They are a bonus. The only flamingos we have seen so far were groups primly wading and scooping up water on the wetlands we passed on our drive from Montpellier.

Returning to our room after dinner I spotted a baby grass-snake coiled up on the floor. It was very small, greyish with a yellow band and a few dark spots. Snakes are not my favourite members of creation so I picked him up – he looked harmless enough – and released him on the patio. Then I had a good search around to make sure there were no siblings or mum or dad or poisonous relatives.

Our dinner was good but I managed to knock over a bottle of red wine. The staff didn't turn a hair and poured the marvellous local salt over the stain. My clumsiness was caused, I think, by suddenly hearing raised American voices at a far table informing each other about the most recent Monica Lewinsky revelations. Oh, dear – you would expect to be spared Lewinsky in a remote district of southern France.

My meagre schoolboy French deserted me this morning when I was trying to explain to the manager that a lamp in our room wasn't working and I suspected it to be a dead bulb. On reflection I realize that what I came out with, translated, was, 'I fear the dead octopus isn't marching.'

We went to Aigues-Mortes for a little exploration and lunch in a dingy bistro where the food wasn't bad. The town is rectangular, encased in fine walls with spectacular ramparts, and is set out on a square grid, as if it were a medieval Manhattan. It was from Aigues-Mortes that St Louis set off on the Seventh Crusade, joining up with a thousand ships. When booking for the crusade your Middle Ages Thomas Cook insisted you take your own fresh water butt and a long box which could serve as your trunk, bed and, if necessary, coffin. Now the sea has withdrawn from the little town but there are a few pleasure craft on the canal, and not far off are the Midi salt-marshes which provide the saltiest table salt I have ever tasted. (The people who put it in small plastic bags, and charge the earth, say it is scooped off the surface of the sea; they go in for some pretty colourful, lyrical prose in its praise. It's good anyway.) The church, Notre-Dame-de-Sables, struck us as being fine, in a simple way, with lovely arches and a timber roof. The only jarring feature was the crude Matisse- or Picasso-like windows, which seemed to depict yellow boiled sweets on a greenish transparency or pink ones on baby-blue. I love Matisse but I wish he hadn't influenced ecclesiastical decoration so vigorously. And that goes for Cocteau as well.

The main square, la Place St-Louis, is quite small and entirely surrounded by cafés and tourist gift shops, but in the centre, sheltered by tall plane trees, is a large black nineteenth-century statue of the crusading saint. Rain began to patter down just as a contingent of very old French people arrived, sweetly helping each other over the road and up steps, and being carefully minded by middle-aged women with kindly smiling faces. It was the most gently happy old people's outing I have ever seen; there were probably thirty of them and their bus must have been outside the town walls, as traffic is greatly restricted and the place is almost car free. Merula and I were having a coffee, sitting under the awning of an empty café as the rain increased but nothing deterred the old folk or their happiness. As two of them reached the somewhat indifferent statue they bowed and I heard one of them say, 'Thank you, St Louis.' It was touching and a far remove from the indifference of Londoners as they stroll past the Cenotaph, which in the old days – well, say forty years ago – always meant raising your hat or, if hatless, at least giving a thought to the war dead.

Today is Saturday, 26 September. We had arranged to go to the ornithological park, quite close by, this morning but the heavens unleashed themselves, the wind is violent and the surrounding waters look troubled, so we have confined ourselves to the hotel until after lunch. It has given me time to finish Jennifer Johnston's odd but gripping book *Two Moons*. If the weather is still awful we shall taxi to St-Gilles to look at the famous façade of the church. (Merula once did a picture of St Gilles saving a fawn from the arrow of a huntsman so she will be content to see his tomb.) In the meantime I have rescued a beady-eyed lizard which was seeking shelter in our room.

Later, we made it to the bird park under a gloomy sky but the rain held off, which was our only consolation. Apart from the pleasure of watching flamingos close to – and being startled at how red their wings are when spread for flight – and encountering a couple of friendly storks, their beaks clattering with pleasure (their eyes are, I think, the jolliest of all bird eyes), it proved a rather drab place extending for many scruffy acres. Looking at the flamingos we were struck by how small their actual bodies are, not much larger than a decent chicken, with long twisting neck and those absurdly jointed legs as thin as coathangers. If stretched out from beak to toe I imagine they would resemble an eight-foot snake which had swallowed a Christmas pudding.

After half an hour of ornithology we moved on to St-Gilles. The church was so dark we couldn't see a thing but tickets for the crypt proved very worthwhile. The subterranean architecture is magnificent and complicated, steep steps leading up and down all over the place. The saint's tomb, surrounded by pale blue votive lights, is in a sunken area at one end of the crypt, all very well cared for and cherished.

Outside the fine façade of the church, on a wide stretch of level stone, a tall youth exercised his not very great skill on a skateboard, keeping up a constant clatter as he crashed into steps, abandoned impossible tricks or, on occasion, just flung the board away. It was the only sound, and a very irritating one, in an otherwise tranquil spot.

Today is Sunday and we have just returned from mass at the extraordinary fortified church at Les Saintes-Maries-de-la-Mer. There the crypt is given over to the gypsy saint, St Sarah, who is alleged to have accompanied the two St Marys on their perilous sea trip in a small open boat from Palestine and to have beached on this shore. She is presented in her effigy as a dark brown young woman. Great candles burn around the stone sarcophagus where her remains are laid and the heat is oppressive. The walls of the church proper have large framed displays of votive paintings of various local events in the nineteenth century – a man recovered by the saint's intercession from a nasty road accident with his white horses; people fleeing from a terrific storm which appears to hurl down boulders from the sky; many an *accouchement* and several sea rescues.

Twice in the past I have seen extreme beauty in a face: today I can add a third, possibly even more striking than the first two. The first was during a visit to Annecy in 1949. Merula, Matthew then aged nine, and I followed instructions and pulled the chain which rang an old, distant bell somewhere inside the grey stone nunnery close to the basilica of St François de Sales. M. and I hoped to see the famous room of the Visitation where St F. de S. and St Jeanne de Chantal meditated. The front door, after much unchaining, was opened by a nun probably aged sixty. She had an aristocratic bearing, charm and the breathtaking beauty of a well-lived-in face. When we had explained that we were not Catholics but had an interest in St François she beckoned us into the passageway and then opened a door to a fairly small room. The atmosphere was charged with a sort of positive stillness. We must have stood just inside the room for almost a minute before realizing it was full of people; what we had at first taken for furniture were the backs of nuns kneeling. We stepped outside again quietly and were rewarded by a beautiful wise smile and an inclination of the head. No word was spoken. The main door was re-locked and I could hear the chains being readjusted.

On Christmas Eve, during the filming of *The Bridge on the River Kwai* in Sri Lanka, we went to midnight mass at a convent chapel near Colombo, where we were greeted by a young nun – Australian I think – who was even more beautiful than Audrey Hepburn, whom she resembled.

And now, this morning, a third personality whom I expect to remember until all memories are beyond recall.

We arrived at the church, a sort of small fortress, about ten minutes before the service started, and after visiting the crypt chose a pew about five rows back from the chancel. There were not many people to start with and they were nearly all elderly or old. Then this large figure came in and sat in front of us at the end of an empty row. The first thing that caught my eye was a pair of enormous, well-worn but carefully polished black lace-up boots. Then came wide black trousers, spotlessly clean, of some coarse material. Above the trousers there was a loose tank-top made of black wool, and then came the head, with dark hair scraped fiercely back and twisted into a tiny knot at the nape of the broad neck. For a moment I couldn't see the face. A seaman? Or a gypsy? As tough as they come whatever the calling or origins; that was for sure. Then the face turned, as if looking for someone, and it showed a fine aquiline nose and thick black eyebrows. The skin was very fine and although inclined to be pale the cheeks were weathered to a biscuit colour. With something of a shock I realized I couldn't be certain if I was looking at a man or a woman.

It was the most handsome face I have ever seen, like the marble bust of some unknown Roman emperor. An angelic smile of total ravishment swept across her as she greeted two women friends who joined her. I spotted a moonstone or pale opal, in a rather tarnished silver setting, on the little finger of her right hand. Something made me think it was probably her most treasured possession. The hands were large, workmanlike and yet delicate. One hand looked as if bruised but it may have been only a shadow. The massive figure and broad shoulders suggested masculinity and yet, in her stillness, a sweet femininity began to appear. She sat straight-backed and with total concentration.

One of her companions began to fidget as if unwell and then got up to leave the church. The woman in black waited a bit before going to her assistance but when she did it was with a calm air and unhurried. She took the woman outside and returned unobtrusively a few minutes later, only giving a reassuring smile to those around her. The smile, which we witnessed perhaps half a dozen times, was like a shaft of summer light; nothing saccharine or even polite – just something straight from the heart. Difficult to assess her age, probably mid-fifties.

Outside in the little *place* which flanks the church, I watched her carry a fairly substantial chair – one of those that Van Gogh painted so often – as if it was a bunch of feathers and take it to the door of a neat house. As she reached the door it was opened by an old welcoming nun, and the chair and the woman in black were swallowed up in the little convent. Maybe this is all madness on my part but the sight of that woman left such a deep impression I want to see her again.

That was all yesterday, Sunday. This afternoon we have been back to Les Saintes-Maries-de-la-Mer to revisit the church and have a look around. The extraordinary woman was sitting alone on a bench with her back to the church wall. She was very busy trying to remove some unnoticeable stain from a leg of her trousers. She tackled it almost angrily and she looked a little glum. I was trying to summon up courage to speak to her – perhaps to inquire about the remarkable and strange black head of a beautiful girl which we had just seen in the crypt – when she got up, perhaps to avoid my staring at her, took out a bunch of keys and let herself in to the nunnery. I wouldn't have offended her for worlds, but I fear I may have done so with my curiosity. Apart from wanting information about the black head I wanted, even more, to see her smile again. It was not to be.

We have been unable to find out anything so far about the black head. (It would be better to refer to it as a mask, I think, as being encased in a shiny glass or plastic dome it is very difficult to make out its dimensions.) Apparently it was dug up from deep down in a well shaft in 1975. The face is life-size, with great almond-shaped eyes of some dark glittering substance, probably made from a semiprecious stone, and it has the appearance of those alien faces so frequently depicted in sci-fi films. It is undoubtedly pagan, even if there are extravagant claims made for it. It stands at the side of the stone sarcophagus which contains the relics of St Sarah. The heat of the crypt from the flaring of innumerable votive candles was oppressive and once out in the windy fresh air we sought out a café to have a *citron pressé*; over £2 each.

After the refreshment we had a look at the dazzling choppy sea and the long sandy beach where there were couples here and there walking their dogs or sheltering from the wind behind tufts of grass or little bushes.

Back at the hotel we gazed at a superb sunset over the straggle of water outside our room and two white horses browsing on the far side. Before leaving home an old friend, knowing we were coming to this horse-filled part of the world, sent me a copy of Edwin Muir's poem 'The Horses'. Here are a few lines from it which I have taken into my heart:

> And then, that evening
> Late in summer the strange horses come.
> > . . . yet they waited,
> Stubborn and shy, as if they had been sent
> By an old command to find our whereabouts
> And that long-lost archaic companionship.

The few hours we spent in Arles were hot and sunny. The Théâtre Antique was prepared for a concert, the vast stage sheeted with thin plywood, and consequently the atmosphere was disappointing. As we arrived at the great Roman arena, where the bullfights are held, the gates were closed in our faces. The quick glimpse we had of the inside was not very impressive but the grey-white walls and arcades of the exterior are magnificent. The town, complicated in its streets and *places*, its jumble of attractive houses with sun-bleached blue-, green- and grey-slatted shutters had great appeal and looks prosperous and bustling. We even saw a man with a younger version of our Dido on a lead. I asked him about her. He proudly said, 'Two years old and already a wife.'

We lunched marvellously well on the narrow second-floor balcony of Le Vaccarès in the Place du Forum – juicy pieces of fresh cold lobster in a light garlic sauce followed by tender lamb cutlets, with small boiled potatoes, and then an orange crême brulée. Le Vaccarès goes to the top of the class as far as I am concerned – courteous, prompt, unobtrusive service and no one got entangled with the legs of our chairs.

After admiring the beautiful plane trees which line the Allée des Sarcophages, and deciding everywhere looked too far to walk after a substantial lunch, we made our usual foray on the revolving postcard stands and then returned to Les Saintes-Maries.

The last day of our holiday was hot. In the afternoon we went to the bullring in Les S.-M. to watch the local team of twelve young men, smartly dressed in white T-shirts and trousers, go through their brilliant attempts to remove strings stretched between the horns of the bulls. It was very exciting and although there were moments when we worried for the safety of various contestants this was nothing resembling a blood sport. At the end of each round the bull, slightly puffed, trotted back to his quarters looking satisfied. The first bull which appeared was young, on the small side, glossy and frisky. He was going to take no nonsense from the impertinent young men so, having scattered them and forced them to leap from the arena, he charged the barrier, jumped it (I suppose it was about five feet high) and pursued them around the inside of the enclosure. The team worked beautifully together and after some brilliant acrobatics they tricked him back into the ring. There was a happy, enthusiastic atmosphere, the sun beat down and we reluctantly left after watching four bulls do their stuff. The concrete tiers were hard on old behinds, even with jackets spread under them.

And so we finally say adieu, have a good day, etc., etc., to the Camargue – and the the horses, flamingos and jolly bulls.

19. A Glimpse of the Eumenides

Loneliness is something I imagine very few people are prepared to admit to, but since our return from France I am very aware of it. Perhaps the very flatness of the Camargue, with its meandering shallow waters, crept into my soul and spawned a form of acedia.

On getting home I thought I would be interested to reread *Coriolanus*, largely because my eye caught a notice of what sounds like an intriguing current production. In 1948 I appeared with the Old Vic Company under E. Martin Browne's direction at the New Theatre, playing the loyal old patrician Menenius. To my consternation I find I have no recollection of saying a single line, and yet there are lines in abundance and I must have sweated them into my brain. Everything Menenius says looks remote and totally unfamiliar. John Clements was Coriolanus, Harry Andrews Aufidius and Peter Copley and Mark Dignam the trade-unionist Tribunes; which is about all I can remember – except for wearing chopines on my feet, to give me extra height, which caused me to trip on innumerable steps on the set. Also I know I took particular care with my make-up, of which I was rather proud, copying an old Roman portrait. This blank in my memory caused me so much anxiety that I telephoned Peter Copley just to verify that he and Harry Andrews were in the play, and almost to be reassured that it was done at all.

It was necessary for me to go to London last week for a day and a night but I could find no one to play with. Friends I particularly wanted to see were unavailable – the Sinclair-Stevensons and Drue Heinz off to New York, Keith Baxter not yet back from wrestling with Hurricane George in Florida, Mark Kingston still wowing them in Toronto, Eileen Atkins trudging the cliffs of Cornwall and everyone else I tried – at very short notice – otherwise engaged. Finally I decided I would go to see the film *Elizabeth*, but when I got to Leicester Square I found a long, slow queue in a cold wind; so I returned to the hotel, had a light dinner and settled down in my room to flicking through the TV channels until, weary of that, I polished off the remainder of the unrecognizable *Coriolanus*. It meant lunch, dinner and the following lunch taken alone and discontentedly; a situation which, should it continue, could drive me to drink. Just to keep some sort of control I think it would be wise to go on the wagon for a few days.

It is rare for me to have intense melancholy bouts. At first I put the blame for this on the flatness of the Carmargue but that wasn't altogether fair as we had some enjoyable and interesting days on our holiday. Finally I laid the blame on the strong shoulders of my beloved two-year-old granddaughter Bethany. Matthew brought her down for breakfast and to spend an hour or two in the country shortly after our return from France. She was as bright and happy as could be, looked enchanting, was smartly dressed in a black wool pullover and baggy blue trousers and wore an enviable yellow hat. She stomped around the place keeping up a prattle of separate words, being charming to the dogs and generally lovable. Then suddenly she turned to stormy tears, shrieks, ugly anger and being disgusting with her food. Her face became dark and suffused, the usually bright merry eyes looked alien and hostile. Never having seen this side of her before I was appalled and distressed. 'She is just overtired,' people said, but after she had gone my mind was clouded by fears for the future; which was absurd, as no doubt the tantrum was similar to that experienced by thousands of two-year-olds every day. It was the violence that haunted me. Not long ago there was a production of Eliot's *The Family Reunion* in which the Eumenides were presented as children. There may be something in that.

For me there are two salves to apply when I feel spiritually bruised – listening to a Haydn symphony or sonata (his clear common sense always penetrates) and seeking out something in Montaigne's essays. This morning, in spite of the promise of a bright cloudless day, I woke curmudgeonly and disapproving of the world and most of its inhabitants. Montaigne pulled me up sharply. 'What we call wisdom is the moroseness of our humours and our distaste of things as they are now . . . Age sets more wrinkles on our minds than on our faces.' I don't care about the facial blemishes but the wriggly, acid convolutions of the brain must be smoothed away somehow. Two or three days in a Benedictine monastery might do the trick.

The big ornamental cherry tree planted forty-four years ago outside one end of the living-room has been felled. For the past three years it has looked drab, its glorious white blossom diminishing wretchedly each spring and the time had come for it to go. A sad wrench but as a result the house is remarkably lighter. We lost twenty-seven trees during the hurricane a decade ago and have taken down another six in the intervening years. We made the initial mistake of the amateur of planting too close together and thoughtlessly. Now it costs hundreds of pounds to have it all roughly tidied up. It is nearly mid-October and all trees are still remarkably green: I had half hoped to show off a newly discovered word – flavescent – but that will have to wait for another couple of weeks or a sharp frost. In the meantime there is a fine splash of crimson across the north side of the house where the Virginia creeper has changed to autumn colouring.

A thousand miles from the parish pump we are told that some sort of agreement has been all but finalized between Nato and the Serbs over Kosovo. It never seemed to me (from reading newspapers or watching TV) that Nato had all that many sabres to rattle, in spite of half a dozen vast US bombers landing in this country and our own display of a handful of fighters. (Not exactly 'four or five most vile and ragged foils, Right ill-disposed in brawl ridiculous' I admit, but surely not enough to subdue a large well-equipped army). Of course there are a couple of aircraft-carriers in the Adriatic, representing gunboat diplomacy, but if anything unfortunate happened to them things could look dicey. Why, oh why, do we always think force is the answer? 'I have a bigger missile than you so I have moral right on my side and you are a war criminal.' I would like to know if what is called diplomacy has always been as aggressive as it is today. *Chambers Dictionary* defines diplomacy as 'the art of negotiation, esp in relations between states; tact in management of persons concerned in any affair'. Now the Serbs are claiming a sort of victory and so does our foreign secretary for Nato. The only people who are left exactly where they were a few weeks ago are the Kosovo Albanians, frightened, ill-fed, hiding in ramshackle bivouacs on the mountains as winter closes in. God knows what the solution could be but I cannot believe it lies in a couple of thousand foreign ramblers wandering the countryside inquiring if all is well.

On BBC Radio 4 News this morning the admirable Mr John Humphrys interviewed Mr Robin Cook about the whole Balkans situation. No doubt there may have been certain points cleared up ('clear' has been the wildly overworked word used by politicians for about five years, and we still haven't got rid of 'look' – introduced by Mrs Thatcher – as the first word of any remark) but basically what we heard was, 'Yes, John – No John no – You see John – Tony made it clear John – Listen John – Look John – You're wrong John,' ad nauseam. It was a patsy Christian name appeal. At least Humphrys kept up the formal dignity of referring to Mr Cook as Foreign Secretary. Unlike the Channel 4 TV presenter last night (*not* Jon Snow of the bright neckties but a saturnine young man) who gave no one their title or rank and assumed the manner of an inquisitor, interrupting, waving his arms and being just ill-mannered. If he had been interviewing the Queen I imagine he would have addressed her abruptly as 'Elizabeth Windsor'.

Today there is a news item to warm the heart. After so many years of accounts of ill-temper or sleaze or cheating in the sporting world there is the noble story of Mark Taylor, Australia's cricket captain. Batting against Pakistan yesterday he scored 334, which equals Don Bradman's record Test Match score against England in 1930, and Taylor refused to go beyond that point, which he could have done easily, so as not to outshine Bradman. That, it seems to me, deserves an Australian knighthood. Is there any hope that such reticence in triumph could be emulated all round the cricketing and football fields, the golf-links and tennis-courts?

The brightness and buoyancy of the day (light-heartedness largely due to Mr Mark Taylor's action) were slightly marred by the irritation of reading in the *Sunday Telegraph* a snippet by a lady journalist writing of a forthcoming production at the National Theatre of *Antony and Cleopatra*. She says that the director 'has cut one of Shakespeare's flabbier works to bring it in under four hours.' Oh dear, oh dear! That makes it sound like the successful landing of a marlin or some monster of the deep. I would guess the average playing time of *A. and C.*, if the actors are not too self-indulgent, to be little over three and a half hours even when including the lady's 'flabbier' bits. But then I haven't noticed the flab. It is a speedy play of mostly short scenes and hardly a minute goes by which isn't shot through by some memorable line or remarkable image. No one is obliged to admire a truly superb play but a lack of awareness, a failure of appreciation and a blindness to great dramatic poetry should be kept under wraps and not flaunted. Prick up your ears, madam. Leaving aside the indisputably great and well-known set pieces the minor lines constantly give pleasure; picking at random from a barrelful you find the following:

> The time of universal peace is near . . .

> Swallows have built
> In Cleopatra's sails their nests . . .

> Tell him he wears the rose
> Of youth upon him . . .

> Like to the time o' the year between the extremes
> Of hot and cold, he was not sad nor merry . . .

> The star is fall'n.
> And time is at his period . . .

All, and a hundred more, worth keeping an ear open for.

> Unarm, Eros, the long day's task is done,
> And we must sleep.

But not, I hope, in the theatre, in spite of the example set by one or two notorious drama critics. Probably their sleeping doesn't greatly matter, for as they slump in their privileged seats they have already arranged for their vigilant wives to take notes for them, even under the indignant noses of the actors.

The Eumenides terrify because they force you to face up to the truth about yourself and they drag your misdeeds and doubtful motives not only before your own appalled eyes but hold them up to contemptuous public gaze.

It was Disraeli, I think, who said, 'Something unpleasant is coming when men are anxious to speak the truth.' That, I find, is one of the traps of age. Some of my contemporaries have been, during the past decade, unexpectedly and often brutally frank. (Forget the very chubby taxi-driver who unwittingly risks halving his tip by informing you that you have put on weight, and questions if you are still employable, because that is par for the course.) I remember thinking, when I reached seventy, 'Ah, now I can say exactly what I feel about everything, personalities, books, plays, performances, art or food, and no one will take offence. All I have kept bottled up for years can come tumbling out and every indiscretion or beastly remark will be forgiven me.' Not so. Far from it. There is a foolhardiness in the old which makes the tactlessness of the young look very circumspect. I fear the misjudgements of age, particularly in regard to my own recent profession.

How often as a young actor I blushed to see some ancient and at one time respected mummer think he was being funny on the stage when he was, in fact, unbelievably abysmal. That is a truth I take every evasive action not to face; and then I sense the Eumenides taking a step closer to me and I don't like the experience.

Recently I was complaining, volubly, about all the outward and visible signs of the malaise in our country when Merula put down her wool work and announced that everything unacceptable in western culture stems from the aggressiveness of Donald Duck. Maybe, but Donald Duck has been squawking around for more than sixty years I would guess, and I don't think M. has thought it through. But she is inclined to take a more sanguine view of things than I do; the Eumenides pass her by. The low clouds and intermittent rain of the last few days have produced darker early evenings than usual; tomorrow we lose summer time so I think we shall draw the curtains at about 18.30 to shut out the disturbing world. That is a silly thought because, of course, the disturbances are within.

General Pinochet, ex-dictator of Chile, is on one of his visits here; this time to have an operation at the London Clinic. This is going to cause a good old rumpus. How wise the French were to deny him entry to France. We, having permitted him to come here on previous occasions without let or hindrance, now appear to be playing some unpleasant game of 'Come into my parlour, said the spider to the fly.' I can see no decent reason why he shouldn't be sent back to his own country, where he enjoys immunity from prosecution. Let the Chileans remove the stitches. His reputation is grim but probably no worse than that of half a dozen 'strong men' throughout the world. There seems to be a lot of prevarication in grand circles – 'Oh, it's purely a legal matter and has no political overtones' – which is rubbish on stilts. It is not the niceties of the law that people demonstrate about, either in London, Santiago or Madrid.

War, bloody revolutions, military coups and assassinations all seem to lead to tribunals in which the victor calls the moral tune. Is there a coin which doesn't have two sides? Prior to the invasion of Sicily in 1943 I listened to a senior army officer of great charm, elegance and gentlemanliness address his junior officers: 'Tell your Jocks we don't want any prisoners. When Gerry comes running with his hands in the air crying *"Kamerad! Kamerad!"* tell your chaps to stick in the bayonet and finish him off.'

As Fluellen says in *Henry V*, ''Tis expressly against the law of arms.' I feel much the same about the bedside arrest of a ghastly old man who had been welcomed here by the high and mighty.

This morning when I woke, at about seven o'clock, the world was dim grey and very still. Not a leaf stirred, there was no sound of traffic from the A3, no sight of the South Downs, the tops of nearby trees were shrouded in mist. It had been a tiresome night as poor old Japheth, who is feeling a bit rheumatic and has slightly cut a forepaw, got me out of bed four times with his barking in the kitchen. On two occasions I found him stretched uncomfortably across Flora's squashy basket and Flora curled up luxuriously on Japheth's cushion under the table. Each time I persuaded them back to their rightful places. The third time he called me down he was just standing, asking to go into the living-room, and this I refused, crossly. The fourth summons was to tell me, shamefacedly, that he had done a job in a corner of the kitchen. I hadn't the heart to rebuke him as he was so apologetic.

Thoroughly awake after that I thought I would read another chapter of *Skin Tight* by Carl Hiaasen, a good gruesome thriller with very funny bits. That was an absurd thing to do as I kept at it for an hour before forcing myself to switch off the light.

Disturbed I suppose by Hiaasen's horrors I sat up abruptly in bed on this gloomy morning saying to myself, 'You have only another seven hundred days to live.'

A quick rough reckoning gave me until November 2000. Not bad, I thought, so long as I can sort out a few things before then and grasp the intricacies of changing over next week to banking with Coutts; bearing in mind that I can't take the modest amount concerned with me. Several important-looking dark red leather files and folders have arrived, all embossed in gilt, and I haven't an idea what I am supposed to do with them. Among other childish things I must admit to my bank manager is the fact that I don't know what a giro is. I must ask for an explanation. So far as I am concerned a giro was always a fast spinning, nicely engineered, metal top. Later it had something to do with a ship's compass; but banking, no. Perhaps seven hundred days won't be enough.

'Death was sent by God to Abraham. Abraham said, "I understand your meaning but I will not follow you yet." Then Death was silent, and answered him not a word.'

And now the rain pelts down; there is bad flooding in the West Country with winds gusting up to 80 m.p.h. The clocks go back an hour in the early morning tomorrow. I shall greet the day by taking a leaf out of Father Abram's book and tell the Eumenides to shift their arses away from here.

20. Mummers on the Road

Strolling Players
A troupe of strolling players are we,
Not stars like L. B. Mayer's are we,
But just a simple band
Who roam about the land
Dispensing fol-de-rol frivolity.
Mere folk who give distractions are we,
No Theatre Guild attraction are we,
But just a crazy group
That never ceases to troop
Around the map of Little Italy.

We open in Venice,
We next play Verona,
Then on to Cremona.
Our next jump is Parma,
That dopey, mopey menace,
Then Mantua, then Padua,
Then we open again, where? . . .
In Venice.

      Cole Porter, *Kiss Me Kate*

In the Pierpont Morgan Library in New York there is a small drawing by Rembrandt entitled *Two Mummers on Horseback*. It is executed in brown ink and red and yellow chalk. The actors are a little past their middle years; one has a vast moustache with a long Vandyke beard, no doubt the height of fashion, and there is an arrogance in the way he sits on his horse, his right hand on

205

his hip, the elbow jutting forward. He wears a giant ruff and on his head a very tall, bulky-looking copin hat which sprouts a few feathers and long spiky quills. You wonder if it is a loaf of bread or his laundry concealed up there. He is a heavy-set man, rather snub-nosed. His companion, close at his side, is leaner, with a fine straight nose, a dapper white moustache and an ingrained expression of disapproval. He has no ruff but a large white collar; on his head there is a dark flat cap with a single dipping feather. Somehow you know they are actors and you can guess at the sort of loud-voiced performances they gave, quite arresting and yet a bit lazy with repetition.

They look remarkably like two elderly actors I knew when I was young; very decent, very kind, but there were times you wished to avoid their company to seek out younger blood. One was inclined to recount, endlessly, his former triumphs, producing tattered, greasy press clippings from a wallet splitting at the seams to confirm his fairly modest achievements. The other, leaner one, would put him down with a wry remark hissed through a crooked smile. They were companions rather than good friends, cemented in their hate of the juvenile lead and almost anyone whose name was above theirs on the theatre bills.

The heavier one, when in the mood, was inclined to thump the bar in any public house and call out in a rich voice, 'We are *the* people and when *we* die *talent* dies *with* us! Two pints of bitter please.' He was a widower and after a few drinks could get embarrassingly maudlin.

'Poor little Meg,' he would say. 'She was a lovely artiste. You should have seen her in *The Immortal Hour*. Only a small part, but outstanding. But *outstanding!* She was forced to give up after she broke her leg and went stone deaf in the same year.' He never disclosed how she died. The white-moustached one was often silent, always observant through his hawk-like eyes, and was a great reader. He was well versed in Victorian literature but had no time for any writer after Kipling; when he mentioned Kipling in his reedy voice, he always glared as if he were an irate colonel expecting his orders to be challenged by some whipper-snapper subaltern. An uneasy man, not without flashes of charm, but probably lonely. He should have been a school-master and maybe that was his first vocation, as it has been for so many actors. He was unmarried, as they say in the classier obituaries. He kept a little notebook in which he wrote down, very neatly, the addresses of good 'theatrical digs' in all the major touring cities. One or two were firmly crossed out. 'If you go to Manchester,' he would inform me, 'it's best to stay in Acker Street. They are used to our little ways there. At all costs avoid Mrs Brough of Caledonian Crescent. She is a harridan and a cheat. Charges two shillings for a bath – and a rusty explosive geyser at that – when everyone knows the going rate is a shilling.'

The two Rembrandt mummers, riding from somewhere to somewhere in the Netherlands, could easily be on the lookout for suitable digs on their tour. Put them back some years and it would be possible to imagine them on their way to Elsinore to try their luck with the young Danish prince who recently lost his father. After all, the prince had seen them and their company years ago in an old Greek piece and had been quite enthusiastic.

'It might be a good idea, before reaching Denmark, to sort through the old scripts and refresh our memories of certain passages. What was the play called?'

' "Caviar to the General".'

'No, no, too fanciful.'

' "Rosencrantz and Guildenstern go to 't?" '

'No, no, you are hundreds of years out. And it is "Guildenstern and Rosencrantz go to 't," – not the other way round.'

'Rosencrantz and Guildenstern sounds better.'

'Have it your own way. As you like it. What you will.'

Then, triumphantly, ' "The Mouse Trap!" '

Just two actors lightly bickering on a journey. After a while they will fall silent while each skips through the lines in his head for the next performance, have a moment of panic as a word evades him, then happily think of a variation on a reading. No pedantic, university-trained, upstart director from Wittenberg to interfere with his native imagination or knowledge of his craft – he will be his own man and not someone's marionette. But he will gratefully raise his feathered hat to the poet who penned the words.

During school holidays, in my early teens, I would head as soon as possible for the local theatre to see what was on offer and what was expected shortly. Often there would be a sticker across the theatre bills saying, 'Your Last Chance to see Bromley Challoner in *When Knights were Bold*' or 'Final Appearance' of Matheson Lang (in *The Wandering Jew*) or 'Bransby Williams presents Characters from Dickens For the Last Time'. Once, on a wet, blustery, winter's day, probably in about 1927, I saw an old poster, much defaced and torn by wind and weather, which advertised Fred Terry and Julia Neilson in *The Scarlet Pimpernel*. 'Coming shortly. By popular demand,' it said at the top; but flapping across it was a sticker which just read bleakly, 'Cancelled'. The poster must have been there for a year or two before they died. Phyllis Neilson-Terry, their daughter, whom I saw perform many times, was frequently announced as giving her final performance, but I saw her again years later as a very buxom Oberon in *A Midsummer Night's Dream* in Regent's Park, and years after that in Graham Greene's play *The Living Room*. The Positively Final Performance gimmick was simply an effort to sell a few seats, but eventually it ceased to pay dividends; the public probably became aware that it wasn't strictly true, just a ruse to enlarge a bank balance or pay off debts.

Looking at those old posters, increasingly ousted by cinema advertisements, was a forlorn experience on a winter afternoon. Young as I was I think I realized, even then, that an actor's life was very transient. Names topping the billboards become meaningless all too soon and now have no echo.

... These our actors,
As I foretold you, were all spirits, and
Are melted into air, into thin air.

If we can imagine some performances of distant times – stretching back maybe a couple of thousand years – it is through the good offices of great writers or perceptive drama critics or brilliant diarists. Two or three years ago I gave a short question-and-answer talk to a group of about thirty theatre students and it dawned on me within a few minutes, to my great sadness and disgust, that they had never heard of any actor who was dead and weren't even vaguely interested in who or what had gone on before their own young lives. Olivier, yes – there is an auditorium named after him – and Gielgud, but anyone else – forget it.

Perhaps the fact that an actor's life is so ephemeral is what makes it enjoyable. (Nice work if you can get it.) In old age one may think, as I often do, 'Oh, it has all been a load of rubbish'; but I can't remember ever talking to a proper actor – at any rate in his prime – who didn't rejoice in belonging to a profession that could boast Roscius, Burbage, Betterton, Garrick and Irving and latter-day saints in the theatrical firmament.

One of the leading actors of the twenties and thirties whom I sometimes saw on tour was Godfrey Tearle. He was stalwart-looking, forthright, had a strong stage presence and a well-shaped head with rather grizzled hair. His superb voice somehow reminded me of very dark Christmas pudding with a dollop of brandy butter. He had the reputation of being a keen womanizer. He was also very kind and considerate. His was the first *Hamlet* I saw; that was at the Haymarket in 1931. It was a gloomy affair set in drab curtains and dressed stiffly in what were meant to be stylized tenth-century costumes. They say that the first *Hamlet* you see is the one that leaves the greatest impression and that you love it for the rest of your life. That wasn't my experience with Godfrey's. (A bit cheeky of me to call him by his Christian name as I only met him once, for a few minutes, but he made me a most generous offer in 1951 which I feel justifies it.) That year saw my disastrous *Hamlet* at the New Theatre – I had played the part previously at the Old Vic in 1938 – and four days before we opened Walter Fitzgerald, who was playing the King, slipped a disc. He was in agony and it was doubtful if he would be able to appear. News of this got around and Godfrey telephoned me to say that if Fitzgerald couldn't make it he would be willing to take over; he knew the lines backwards and would be prepared to rehearse all night if necessary. It proved unnecessary to accept his kindness because poor Walter struggled on, encased in plaster and suffering horribly.

Godfrey, when appearing in large-scale productions of Shakespeare, always managed to find small parts or crowd work for his innumerable relatives on the fringes of the theatre. On one occasion, during a performance of *Henry V*, his voice rang through the auditorium as he embarked on 'Once more into the breach, dear friends, once more . . .'; the chain-mailed crowd in front of him made suitable, or unsuitable, noises. Tearle thundered on – 'I see you stand like greyhounds in the slips, Straining upon the start. Uncle! Your helmet's crooked!'

The last time I saw him was as Antony to Edith Evans's Cleopatra at the Piccadilly Theatre. What might have been his greatest achievement was handicapped by Edith's age and lack of sexual allure. It was not a successful production, as was prophesied by one of the extras at the dress rehearsal. He was a huge black man, dressed as an Egyptian eunuch, who had insisted on sitting in the stalls to watch the performance and no one could budge him. When the curtain fell he turned to everyone there and said, 'Mr Tearle and that old lady are sure goin' to lose a lotta money.' And he sure was right. Godfrey Tearle was knighted in 1953, which I hope compensated him for what he may have felt was, in some ways, a disappointing career.

Sir Frank Benson, Sybil Thorndike, Ruth Draper, Fay Compton, Gertrude Lawrence and a host of others paraded before my admiring eyes; I couldn't get to the theatre often enough; it became obsessional. If I were to gauge lasting influences on my subsequent professional life I would head the list with John Gielgud (hero-worshipped), Edith Evans, Ernest Milton and, perhaps surprisingly, Beatrice Lillie. Also there were directors like Tyrone Guthrie and Michel St-Denis.

Bea Lillie was a small-scale clown of genius. By small-scale I mean she was at her best in an intimate theatre; her neat features and sophisticated personality could get swallowed up in a large auditorium. The tiny gesture, the wicked shrug, the quick double-take, the wry smile and the totally false seriousness all required proximity. She did appear in some big revues and held her own conspicuously but was never at her best in them.

She was born in Toronto towards the end of the last century but spent most of her life in England. Her early ambition was to be a serious singer but the impresario André Charlot spotted her and quickly recognized her unique, almost surreal, sense of comedy. She made her name under his guidance, as to some extent did Gertie Lawrence, who was Bea's understudy at that time. The material she used was often not much above common-place camp but she made it flower, in her absurdity, into something almost poetic and totally memorable. Her precision and witty, unexpected timing took my breath away when I first saw her.

One of her acts, perhaps my favourite, she created shortly after she had been on holiday in Japan and had watched very closely a tea ceremony. In her version it lasted about seven minutes and not a word was spoken until the end. There was no one else on stage and no props other than a low, lacquered table. She was dressed in a flowery kimono and wore a tall black shiny wig through which were stuck two long, white knitting needles. On her entrance she crouched on the floor to slide open an imaginary screen. Every movement was sedate and yet humble; there was not a whiff of humour – it was almost as if it was a lecture for an anthropological society. When the tea was finally poured –

all mimed – into a tiny cup, she removed a knitting needle from her wig, vigorously stirred the tea with it and returned it to the wig with a confident, piercing gesture. She took the imaginary cup in her hands, had a sip and allowed herself a small smile of approval. She bowed to the audience and said, 'Mazawattee.' The whole episode had the intensity of a No play in Kyoto.

When I first knew her she was fundamentally sad; she was widowed a few years before the 1939–45 war and her only son had been killed serving with the Navy in 1942. She kept up a brittle brightness in company but she never recovered from the loss of her boy and she began to drink unwisely; but not in the theatre. My first meeting with her was in north Africa, where she was on tour with Vivien Leigh and Michael Wilding in an ENSA tour of sketches and songs. Her husband had been a baronet, Sir Robert Peel, but she took her title very lightly. In Paris, but not I think in her cups, she would answer the telephone at her hotel with, 'C'est Lady Parle qui Peel.'

A few years after first meeting her I crossed the Atlantic, from New York to Southampton, in the *Queen Elizabeth* and found that she and her friend John Philips, with whom she had been associated for some time, were also aboard. We arranged to meet up for the evening of our second day out. Bea wanted to dance; dancing is not my strongest point. She wore her usual red fez perched on the back of her head and a slinky black dress. For some reason all the girls on the dance floor were in pale blue or mauve silk frocks. The weather was rough and the great ship, for all its stabilizing equipment, gave the occasional lurch. Bea rejoiced in the resulting roll and would take advantage of it to gently collide with one or other of the young dancers. She would apologize to the couple, somehow indicating it was my fault, and then eye the girl's dress.

'My-oh-my,' she would say admiringly, 'you got that at Macy's! Now, didn't you?'

'Yes,' the poor girl would say, half flattered, half embarrassed. Then turning back to me Bea would say, in a loud stage whisper,

'I knew I had seen it before; in the shop window. Dozens of them.'

Then off we would slide again on the same mission. She must have manoeuvred this silliness about four times before she decided she needed another drink. We returned to John Philips, sitting patiently at his table, large whiskies at the ready. I invited them to join me for lunch the following day in the Veranda Grill.

They didn't turn up. I waited for three quarters of an hour before telephoning their state-room. No reply. So I had my lunch, feeling rather cross and then, the weather having improved, decided to take a brisk healthy walk around the sun-deck. The sun shone, the wind was a bit fierce and the sea was a dark blue with a thousand white horses riding the waves. The long row of reclining chairs was empty except for a couple about midships: Miss Lillie and Mr Philips, of course. She was wearing a mink coat over a two-piece bathing costume, her head was wrapped in a turban and she wore huge very dark glasses. He was in a thick white sweater, flannel trousers and also wore dark glasses. They had obviously entirely forgotten about the lunch date and, seeing that the deck was cluttered with innumerable empty Pimm's glasses, I was rather relieved. 'Get you, taking the air!' Bea said in a rather slurred way. 'Come and sit down.'

We had a little meaningless conversation for a few minutes before an elderly American couple hove in to view. They approached us with severe looks, both peering through rimless spectacles. They were on the frail side, cocooned in thick grey cardigans and carrying rugs and books. They stood looking at us for a moment before the man approached Bea.

'Pardon me, ma'am, but you are sitting in our chairs.'

Bea and Philips looked fore and aft, up and down the empty deck.

'You mean you want us to move?' she asked.

'If you please, ma'am.'

'There are plenty of other deck-chairs, as you can see,' put in Philips.

'Yessir, but these are the chairs we booked and paid for, Nos. 39 and 40.'

'Okey-dokey,' said Bea, very slowly extricating herself with handbag, camera and binoculars and, stepping cautiously through the empty Pimm's glasses, she walked to the ship's rail. She gazed at the sea long enough for the American couple to get comfortably, triumphantly settled and then turned to face them. She took the binoculars and looked at them steadily through the wrong end.

'I spy with my little eye, two teeny weeny assholes.'

Philips and I pleaded with her to come away but she pushed us aside.

'No, sirree. I'm goin' to settle with these two old anuses.'

The Americans made an elaborate show of tucking in their rugs, opening their books and pretending to read. Bea unwrapped her mink coat and slapped her bare midriff. 'Just look at that,' she said. 'You'll never get a brown tummy like mine all smothered in those woollies. Off with them! Off with them!'

She ran to the side of the poor woman, seized her by the cardigan and tried to pull it over her head. Spectacles and book went flying. Pimm's glasses rolled on the deck and the husband jumped up and down shouting 'Steward! Steward!' Philips and I manoeuvred Bea back to the ship's rail but the light of murder was in her eye.

'You just get that steward,' she said. 'He's a good friend of mine. He's called Eric. Whenever we meet we always have sex, whatever the weather.'

The little man took some ineffectual steps, backwards and forwards, shouting, 'This is an outrage. I am going to make a complaint to the Captain.'

'Yes, Arnold; get the Captain,' the old lady moaned, fumbling for her specs. Bea drew herself up haughtily. 'Yes, sir, you speak to the Captain; you just do it and I'll tell you what'll happen. The Captain of this ship is my intimate friend. I've slept with the Captain of this ship every time I've crossed the ocean. Maybe forty times. When he hears about your silly meanness over seats 39 and 40, I'll tell you what he's going to do. He's goin' to tie a rope round your middles, sir and ma'am and have you thrown overboard and keelhauled. That's the way we do things on this ship. Yours sincerely, Lady Peel.'

With that she stomped away, laughing. Picking up her bits and pieces, making apologetic gestures to the Americans, muttering something about her feeling unwell, I followed as quickly as I could.

For all that I cannot imagine her, in her right mind, ever being cruel or even bitchy.

The last time I saw her was at a party in someone's New York apartment. She was sitting alone, small and waif-like, in the corner of a sofa. It was sad that no one was paying court so I crossed the room and asked if I might sit beside her.

'You know something?' she said. 'Since I gave up the liquor – oh, a year ago, five hundred years ago – I have become the world's prize bore. I'm just not worth speaking to. Forget me.'

I held her hand for a moment but she withdrew it.

'Forget me,' she repeated.

I sat next to her for perhaps ten minutes but she wouldn't speak. She just sat, small, straight-backed, sometimes putting up a hand to make sure her little red fez was straight or perhaps to reassure herself that it was still there. It had been very much her professional badge. There was nothing to do but leave her. And, my God, I needed a drink.

Rembrandt's touring actors went by horse and probably sometimes by foot. Actors have to get around somehow. In Florence, in February 1939, which the Old Vic Company took in its stride in a tour down Italy from Milan to Naples, I went to the theatre on the Sunday night of our arrival to see what it looked like. It was a pretty white and gilded building. As I arrived at the stage door I was surprised to find an Italian company, about eight in all, just leaving, having packed up after a Sunday matinée. Their scenery (waxed paper), costumes and props were strapped on to bicycles which they themselves then mounted and pedalled away. To where, I wonder? Shortly after the war they could be singing, from *Kiss Me Kate*, 'We open in Venice, we next play Verona. Then on to Cremona . . . Then Mantua, then Padua . . . and Venice.' (God bless Cole Porter.) The sight of young, impoverished actors, facing up to the hardship of being unwanted (I assume) itinerant players I found moving and disturbing. Many of the Old Vic Company, including myself, had very little money – my salary was £20 a week; it had been £12 a week at the home base in London – but we were taken care of and housed pretty well on our tour. I doubt if we could have matched the determined enthusiasm of those Italians.

Touring was very much part of an actor's life in England in pre-war days. Great London terminals like Euston and King's Cross stations were hives of theatrical activity on Sunday mornings, with stars and all ranks seeking their trains to Leeds, Newcastle, Manchester and points north. Whole carriages would be labelled 'Reserved for Hamlet and Company', or 'The Student Prince, change at Crewe', or perhaps just two compartments marked, 'Private. The Ghost Train. To Darlington only.' At Crewe, or various junctions where changes had to be made, the platforms would be milling with actors who knew each other going in opposite directions. Much waving and cries of 'coo'ee!'. Those were the days when men wore trilby hats so there was a lot of hat doffing to leading ladies, and young men in Oxford bags unclamped their straight, shiny Dunhill pipes from their firm white teeth to call out hearty cheerios. There would be shouts of 'Darling! Fancy seeing you here. I had heard you had become a cinema usherette,' or some such badinage. The tiresome, pejorative word 'luvvies' had not yet been invented but 'darling' could carry a variety of intonations. My own use of 'darling' has been confined, I think, to a term of exasperation. Then there came the guard's whistle, swift clambering back on board, shrieks of steam from the engine's pistons, mushroom clouds of smoke and soot; then with deep grunts the trains would majestically pull away with their thespian loads. After some gossip and exchanging of newspapers the company would settle down to reading their Edgar Wallaces, Agatha Christies or Compton Mackenzies. Most would take a nap; one or two anxious actors would rummage for their scripts and silently mouth their lines.

Imagining what touring must have been like in the heyday years of the century I am reminded of a touching story Claude Rains told me about himself at the age of fifteen. I never saw Rains on the stage, to my great regret, but I revered him as an actor and liked him enormously as a man. We first met during the filming of *Lawrence of Arabia* and dined together a few times. One evening I asked him about Beerbohm Tree, for whom I knew he had worked, and he told me, with great amusement, a story against himself about a momentous event in his life.

Claude came from an impoverished Cockney background; his mother took in washing and, in an effort to make ends meet, he got himself a job as a call-boy at His Majesty's Theatre, then under Tree's direction. He was only paid a pittance (but probably picked up worthwhile tips from the actors) and it occurred to him that there was quarter of an hour at each performance when the entire company was on the stage; Friday night was pay night for everyone and it was on Fridays that he took to augmenting his wages. While the actors were giving their all downstairs he would slip in to each dressing-room and rummage around for some small silver change and the odd sovereign. After a month or two the actors began to comment to each other about missing money; the management was informed and one Friday the police were called in. They marked the cash and waited at the stage door as the cast and staff left the theatre. Claude was told to empty his pockets and there were the marked coins. No charges were brought and none of the actors wanted him sacked. He was told to report to Tree in his office the following morning.

When Tree asked him why he had 'embarked on a life of crime' he boldly replied that he wasn't paid enough to keep himself in food let alone to help his mother. Then Tree said, 'What do you want to be when you grow up?'

'An actor, sir,' he replied.

'An actor? Good God! But you have a vile Cockney accent and you are almost a midget; you must be mad to think you could be an actor. Now get out of my office. Apologize to everyone you have so wickedly robbed and come and see me here at eleven o'clock next Wednesday.'

So he left the great man's office, relieved that he hadn't been sacked and wasn't on his way to prison. He kept his appointment for the following week punctually. After knocking at the door he entered the room cautiously.

Tree was sitting at his desk, which was empty except for a large piece of pink blotting-paper.

'Who are you? What do you want?' he barked.

'Rains, Mr Tree.' (This was some years before Tree was knighted.) 'You said you wanted to see me.'

'About what?'

'About me wanting to be an actor.'

'I must be as mad as you. Don't waste my time. Run along.'

Claude, in a state of dejection, reached for the door when he was peremptorily called back.

'I almost forgot,' Tree said. He slid his hand under the blotting paper and brought out a cheque for £30. 'This,' he said, 'is not for you, but for Mr Edmonds.' (I can't recall the correct name.) 'You are to hand it to him, with my compliments, and ask him to give you voice lessons. You must ask him to get rid of your horrible, horrible accent. In a month's time, if I notice signs of improvement, I shall make you my personal prompter. You will cease to be a call-boy. You will conceal yourself behind trees or rocks or furniture on the stage and if I dry up you will prompt me in correct, understandable, gentlemanly English. You will receive £2 a week in addition to whatever you are paid now. Listen carefully, Rains. You are uneducated but you are not stupid. From now on I shall undertake your literary education.

I shall tell you every few weeks what books to read and question you about them when you have done so. We'll start off with *David Copperfield*. When we go on tour you will always have a good book with you and I shall expect to see you reading it on the train.'

Claude told me that Tree was as good as his word and that he would walk along the train corridors until he spotted, through the glass, a small figure with his nose buried in Dickens or Thackeray.

Claude Rains, apart from eventually becoming a Hollywood film star of distinction, was an actor greatly admired for his beautiful voice and incisive diction. His light-fingered boyhood combined with Beerbohm Tree's perception and generosity made him the artist and man he was.

He died in 1965.

Oh, if only I could get that damn refrain 'We open in Venice' out of my head! It intrudes on shaving, shoe-shining, stamp-licking, mixing a Martini and getting ready for bed.

21. Where is the Life That Late I Led?

Where is the life that late I led?
Where is it now? Totally dead.
Cole Porter, lyric from *Kiss Me Kate*

The first job that came my way in the theatre was on my twentieth birthday, while I was still a drama student. It was a terrific birthday present even if the pay was only twelve shillings a week. The play was *Libel*, which opened at the old King's Theatre, Hammersmith, and then transferred to the Playhouse, where my status as a walk-on was upped to under-studying two lines and my salary increased to £1 a week. Out of the salary had to come some make-up – sticks of Leichner's No. 5 and 9 greasepaint, a black pencil liner and a crimson-lake ditto, a stick of carmine, a tin of face-powder and some cocoa butter with which to remove it all. I can't believe I grudged a precious penny on such a lovely outlay. My last performance was at the Comedy Theatre on 30 May 1989, in an American play called *A Walk in the Woods*. It was a two-hander, with Ed Herrmann, with whom I became great friends, and I playing USA and USSR diplomats. When the curtain finally fell I remember turning to Ed and saying, 'That's the last performance I shall give on any stage'; to which he replied, 'Balls!' or something like that. But I knew in my bones it was true and that made me sad; not because it was my positively final appearance, but because it hadn't been something of greater distinction. Sandwiched between 2 April 1934 and 30 May 1989 I played seventy-seven parts in the theatre, fifty-five in films, fourteen on TV, and during the Second World War put up the pretence of being a naval officer and a gentleman. I have no intention of listing the roles I played.

The life of the theatre always suited my inclinations more than filming but an element of success in films enabled me to provide for wife, son and my mother in a moderately comfortable way. After a very impoverished period in my young manhood this was important to me. Hunger and shoes worn down to their uppers leave a harsh mark and suspicion of the future, and a determination that the experience will not be repeated. Providence has been exceptionally kind and so have many friends, most of whom are now dead. When I look back – which is something I don't often do – I think it was loneliness in youth, rather than shortages, which probably distressed me most. Even now, with a lifetime's experience behind me, I sometimes wonder, when I invite someone to a meal, whether I am bribing them in some way – 'put up with my boringness, silliness, deafness and long-drawn-out monologues for an hour and you shall have foie gras and a glass of Sauternes wherever you go.'

Getting to the theatre on the early side, usually at about seven o'clock, changing into a dressing-gown, applying make-up, having a chat for a few minutes with the other actors and then, quite unconsciously, beginning to assume another personality which would stay with me (but mostly tucked inside) until curtain down, was all I required of life. I thought it bliss. On the other hand, to find myself at early breakfast time in the make-up chair in a film studio, while someone painted my face; knowing that the scene I was about to act was under-rehearsed or had not been rehearsed at all; that I wasn't much more than a marionette restricted by marks on the floor, and that I was likely to be required to contort myself for the sake of a camera, was as confining to the spirit as the theatre was liberating. Naturally there were films or sections of films which I greatly enjoyed doing. And I always had huge admiration for the painstaking work of camera operators, chippies, best boys and gaffers, to many of whom I became attached; particularly when they confided something of their home lives. But so many of the actors encountered in films were here today and gone tomorrow, literally.

It is mid-November. Last Monday and Tuesday I spent agreeably in London. On the Monday afternoon I went to the Fine Arts Gallery in New Bond Street to see an exhibition of pottery by Patricia Low, recommended by Michael and Henrietta Gough whose judgment in such things I always respect. The pottery was quite large, very classical in shape, usually white and quite beautifully decorated with paintings of animals and birds. If it hadn't been already sold I would have been tempted to lay out good money for a white jar with a gaggle of very spirited Indian runner ducks scampering all round it. In the evening the Goughs joined me for dinner at Lindsay House in Romilly Street, Soho.

Lindsay House is a fairly new restaurant on the London scene. In the thirties and forties it went by a different name and was owned by two genial brothers who waited at table, while their elderly mother did most of the cooking. It was not expensive and late at night usually had a clientele of actors and musicians who were beginning to unwind. One night I joined Jack Hawkins, Jessica Tandy and George Devine for supper; at the next table sat Hermione Gingold. An air-raid warning sounded and we all groaned. A moment later all the lights went out and we were in total darkness. Then there came the whistling of a bomb which sounded if it was directed straight at us. We all did what we knew was the drill – we threw ourselves under the table and covered our heads with our hands. The whistling stopped with a thud which shook the building but there was no explosion. A minute or two passed in breathless silence, which was finally broken by Hermione Gingold's voice. She just made one announcement from under her table – 'Now I look at my best.' A moment later the lights came on again, we regained our chairs, dusted ourselves down and rather noisily, indeed hysterically, ordered more drinks, trebles all round this time. Jack, I imagine, was paying.

On the Tuesday the Profumos had invited me to see the film *Primary Colours* so we arranged to have a light meal at the Connaught before the showing. That was all very agreeable but I thought Valerie looked rather tired. Jack was fascinating about visiting Hiroshima shortly after the bomb had devastated it and was particularly interesting about the impossible lives the kamikaze pilots were forced to lead after the Japanese surrender. (I never knew, for instance, that once they had undertaken to be kamikazes they had to attend their own funeral ceremony and were from then on officially dead, with no status; their wives could remarry.)

Primary Colors I thought interesting and well acted – particularly by Travolta and the always appealing Adrian Lester – but too wordy and sometimes confusing. Emma Thompson was excellent, as always; she would take the first prize in any face-slapping competition. Jack seemed indifferent to the film and Valerie nodded off once or twice. They drove me back to my hotel and I kissed her goodnight. It struck me she might be quite anxious to get to bed so I didn't offer a nightcap. In the morning she telephoned, leaving a message, but I had already left for home.

Merula and I were shocked and deeply saddened to hear that she had died in the early hours of Friday morning, three days later.

Valerie had been one of England's top film stars in the forties and fifties; that was before she had made an almost unexpected success in the musical *The King and I* at Drury Lane. Apart from the great asset of her beauty she was always elegant, precise and exquisitely mannered. She was also a woman of moral and physical courage, a demon behind the wheel of a fast car and the proud holder of a pilot's certificate. Her interests, apart from charitable work for sufferers from Down's syndrome and other charities, included painting. She painted herself (she received advice from Matthew Smith; I once mistook an oil by her as being by him) and had a collection of work by Orovida Pissarro, which was somehow surprising.

In younger days she suggested a certain aloofness in her bearing, which I later attributed to shyness, but in fact she was warm-hearted, loving and full of good humour. We were together in the films of *Great Expectations, Kind Hearts and Coronets* and *The Card*. It was during the making of *The Card* that I got to know her. There was a brief scene in which we lay tumbled together in an overturned pony trap and had a pile of vegetables emptied on us. She never flinched but laughed a lot, and if there was the thinnest layer of ice between us before (which I doubt) it was certainly broken then.

During the past two years she had a wretched time, undergoing long operations in an attempt to rectify a malfunctioning, painful shoulder. She made light of it and somehow seemed indestructible. Her beauty remained with her as the years advanced and I am told she looked remarkable in death. At the very last she was smiling.

During the past few weeks I haven't found much to satisfy me in the books I have picked up, and even less pleasure on TV, where it has been cookery, cookery nightly or nineteenth-century bonnets ad nauseam. A noble exception, in both book form and television, has been David Attenborough's magnificent *The Life of Birds.* Also, welcome every time they appear, John Bird and John Fortune who, for my taste, are quite the best act on TV. Why can't I find their names listed in the press or on the screen? They provide a brilliant, inane, and sane five minutes sandwiched between Rory (who else?) Bremner's faces, voices and frenzies.

Last night's showing of *The Life of Birds* contained marvellously funny and astonishing footage of a black heron turning its wings in to a sort of umbrella, or the vast *faldetta* worn by Maltese ladies, underneath which it could peer into the water for small fish without dazzling itself in the sunlight. The cunning and ingenuity of birds takes my breath away and leaves me smiling like a gormless fool.

Of books, *Captain Corelli's Mandolin* eventually defeated me (it was a big success with Merula) but I whistled happily enough through the absurdities of P. G. Wodehouse's *Thank you, Jeeves*. Patrick O'Brian is a favourite of mine but somehow he didn't grab me with *The Hundred Days*. Maybe it is just because I'm going through a hard-to-grab phase. *The Journals* of Woodrow Wyatt were rather nasty, I thought, but I admit to having enjoyed some of the bitchiness. All the racing stuff bored me and as soon as I saw the word tote coming up I flicked over a couple of pages, hoping for better things. Robert Nye's *Falstaff* (I loved his *The Late Mr Shakespeare* and *The Voyage of 'The Destiny'*) I thought too Rabelaisian. Hilary Spurling's biography of Matisse awaits me, but, dear, oh dear, it looks bulky and very detailed.

Yesterday I settled for rereading Boswell, starting halfway through, at the year 1772, when Johnson was sixty-three. Some of the letters Boswell quotes are ponderous and slow things up, but there is so much wit, kindness and John Bullish commonsense that one's heart is constantly warmed. Except when it comes to Johnson on corporal punishment, when he is quoted in conversation about his firm conviction that complete submission of the young must be beaten in to them: a chilling idea, like breaking the spirit of horses or forcing wild animals in circuses to cowering obedience. I read that Johnson piece last night and today, shifting some books, opened Montaigne's *Essays* at a paragraph on 'Affections of fathers for their children'. It was probably written about a hundred and ninety years before Johnson's statements. Montaigne says, 'I have never seen caning achieve anything except making souls more cowardly or maliciously stubborn.'

Two hundred years forward from Montaigne's writing to Johnson's conversation there is no great moral advance discernible; and then two hundred years back from ourselves to Johnson and we find the following statement on a subject with which we are familiar:

I remember being present when he showed himself to be so corrupted, or at least something so different from what I think right, as to maintain that a member of parliament should go along with his party, right or wrong . . . It is maintaining that you may lie to the public; for you lie when you call that right which you think wrong, or the reverse.

Today the sky is low and leaden, the trees look sullen, there is hardly any wind but it is penetratingly cold. It is not yet three o'clock in the afternoon but lights are needed. Somehow it makes me recollect winter afternoons seventy odd years ago at my prep school, when we set off, two by two, in loose crocodile form on obligatory walks, scuffling through the fallen leaves in residential roads which wound through Southbourne or Bournemouth, or out to sniff the steel-cold sea at Hengistbury Head. What on earth did we chatter to each other about, I wonder? We were too young and ignorant to whisper about sex; most boys probably talked of sport, of the merits of various motor cars (particularly if their fathers were affluent) and some of what was still required to complete their cigarette-card collections. Cricketers were highly prized, followed I think by steam-engines and jungle animals. The information on the back of the cards was inestimable. Small boys must have pushed their parents ruthlessly to great heights of smoking to obtain more cards. One topic which did crop up from time to time, and was discussed with a mixture of interest and dread, was the preference for which public schools we would like to go to, from the little we had heard, and if we were successful at our Common Entrance Examination. Most parents had put down their children's names at a very early age for the usual clutch of admired schools, such as Marlborough, Shrewsbury or Repton. I had been told that I was to go to Fettes – the school at which our future Prime Minister was to be a distinguished pupil. Somehow it never happened for me; lack of funds, I imagine. I wasn't distressed at missing a remote Scottish education, however admirable. The realities of life for the future were mapped out by a solicitor whom I only glimpsed twice in my life. So much for guardianship.

The drenched, blue-raincoated crocodile slithered on, collars turned up, shoulders hunched and school caps beginning to pucker or shrink. Bare knees went from white to pink to mauve.

Back at school it would be a noisy tea before a lesson, prep and time which could be our own. On winter evenings there would be much ragging, sitting around on radiators while a few got on with their hobbies. One serious boy spent a whole term making a beautiful model destroyer from wood; he was so obsessed with it that we called him 'Admiral' and mockingly saluted whenever he passed. He should have gone on to be eventually a high-ranking naval officer but I believe he ended up as a solicitor in a market town. For my own part I gave my time to a very collapsible cardboard model theatre, for which I had designed a variety of baronial halls, dungeons, drawing-rooms and 'a glade in a forest'. With the help of two or three pocket torches highly dramatic effects could be achieved in one of the smaller, darkened schoolrooms. Little cut-out paper or cardboard figures, attached to pieces of wire, were eased on and off stage from the wings or sometimes dangled from up top. Needless to say I did all the voices for the quite incredible dialogue. Usually I managed to collect an audience of about three or four, suitably spellbound. Even if there was no audience I still carried on, but perhaps in low heart. (A foretaste of *Under the Sycamore Tree* at Aberdeen or *The Witch of Edmonton* one Christmas Eve at the Old Vic.) My tiny audience was shocked to the core, I remember (Bea Lillie's 'We are rotten to the core, Maud' floats in to my mind), one evening when I made my very svelte, white-evening-gowned heroine say 'Damn!' when she saw her wicked uncle peer through the French windows of the superior drawing-room set. Damn was a taboo word of such horror that, if heard by authority, it could bring down awful wrath and dire punishment. It was a four-letter word of its period but not used as frequently or meaninglessly as the current four-letter words on T V, film or in print. How these idiotic plays and the ridiculous dialogue came into my mind I don't know – it was years before the arrival of 'talkies' so the cinema wasn't to blame – and yet, looking back, I must have known, however unconsciously, that the theatre was to be my life.

The only time I asked the headmaster of my prep school if I could be in an end-of-term play (they were always farces and often quite funny) he dismissed my request curtly with, 'You'll never make an actor.' If dumbfounded at the time, as I expect I was, in retrospect I believe I turned it to a useful warning, because it put in my soul a little grain of iron determination. I was to encounter the same sort of dismissal even after I had won a scholarship to a drama school and carried away the annual prize after having been there only seven months. 'Get off the fucking stage, you're not a fucking actor,' was shouted at me by the director (not a name to conjure with) when I auditioned for a small part in *Antony and Cleopatra* at the Old Vic.

It is assumed by most people, I think, that actors must be, of necessity, loud-voiced exhibitionists with no interest beyond their own applause. I haven't found this to be generally so. In fact most actors of my acquaintance are rather retiring folk who are only socially happy when with their fellows.

The dark glasses for conspicuous anonymity are a Hollywood invention.

A few nights ago, leaving a London hotel where film stars often stay, I was astonished by the nice, chummy taxi-driver, who sort of recognized my face, when he said, 'I'll leave the lights on in the back of the cab; I expect that's what you like.' I had a picture of myself, brightly illuminated, waving from side to side in a traffic jam, with bewildered passers-by asking each other, 'Who's the dotty old party all lit up?'

'Put out the light,' I said, 'and then put out the light.'

'Whatever you say, guv.'

22. Exit Pursued by a Bear

Exit pursued by a bear. *The Winter's Tale*, III, iii. The end of November: a constant drip from a dark sky, birds are sheltering here and there thinking night has returned at mid-morning and the dogs gaze out of the windows with forlorn expressions, their tails hanging limp. The gurgling in the gutters is maddening.

> The day frowns more and more;
> . . . I never saw
> The heavens so dim by day.

The Winter's Tale again. The Globe Theatre, in some printed matter, reprimanded me for having referred to '*A* [sic] Winter's Tale'. Ask any actor – not an academic – which of two plays he is in and he will reply 'A Winter's Tale' or 'The Dream' (meaning of course, *A Midsummer Night's Dream*). They also put me right over my tentative suggestion that, situated as it was, Shakespeare's theatre could easily have had access to a real bear, seeing bear-baiting was so local and so popular.

Now I come to remember it, the most disturbing image of the bear I have seen was in Ronald Eyre's production at the Barbican. A vast black shadow of a bear filled the back of the stage; it was more than a bear – a bug-bear, a nightmare, the jaws of hell. In that same production Leontes was played by Patrick Stewart, easily the finest performance of the part I have ever seen. *There* was a man who had actually stepped in to the jaws of the hell of jealousy. The moment the first evil thought crossed his mind his pale face was suffused with the weak sickly smile I have sometimes seen used by the jealous to disguise, as they hope, their illness. We all deny being jealous. (Peter Brook told me that when he was directing the play, several years ago, he said to John Gielgud during a rehearsal, 'John, Leontes is riddled with jealousy and I don't get any feeling of jealousy from you.' John replied, 'I don't know what it means. I've never been jealous in my life.' After a pause he added, 'But I admit I did burst in to tears when Larry Olivier got such good notices for his *Hamlet.*') I rack my brains for traces of my own jealousies and I can find none. Here, perhaps, I should pause and reconsider my whole life. Yes, when I was about twenty-two, I felt put out when a very small part, for which I was sure I was suited, went to a perfectly nice young actor who, in my arrogance, I considered talentless.

The ugly farce of the Pinochet case continues but we are promised that the Home Secretary will make up his mind one way or the other (assuming he hasn't already done so) within ten days. I find it all very disturbing and somehow un-English. Eight judges have expressed simple, categorical opinions on whether Pinochet should be extradited to Spain for crimes committed under his dictatorship in Chile. Three judges in the law courts said he should be sent home. Of the five Law Lords who, a little later, heard the appeal against the first decision, two held up the original judgment and three were for overturning it. So, basically, it means five judges were for returning the sick old man to Chile and three for flying him off to Spain, a country which has only re-enjoyed democracy for the last twenty-five years after a Fascist dictatorship of thirty-five years. Where is democracy heading in our own beloved land? There is, I fear, a whiff of Mussolini in the air. Straighten the waving arm, flatten the fingers, make it all more rigid and before we know where we are we shall be goose-stepping while pretending it is only a morris dance.

I returned yesterday from a rather unsatisfactory couple of days in London. Drue Heinz joined me for lunch at the Russian restaurant, Kaspia, which was very pleasant but unfortunately

Alan B., who should have been with us, was feeling unwell and called off at the last moment. In the evening I decided I wanted to see De Filippo's play *Filumena*, but when I got to the theatre there was such a noisy, squealing, elbowing crowd in the foyer that I fled, my nerves completely jangled. Noise distresses me more and more in spite of my increasing deafness. I walked a mile and a half back to the hotel, had a sandwich and beer in the quiet of my bedroom, watched some indifferent TV and then settled down happily to the latest volume of James Lees-Milne's diaries.

The following morning I went to the Tate Gallery hoping to see the Sargent exhibition. Red arrows pointed the way, through caverns measureless to man, past hooting children inserting fists into the holes in Henry Moore's great reclining figures; finally arrived at the right door, my Senior Citizen money in my hand. 'You must get your ticket outside,' said the perfectly polite gallery attendant. To walk those hundreds of yards of slippery floor four times (up and back and up and back) was more than I was prepared to suffer, so I gave up. On the way to the exit I stopped for a few minutes to admire a Barbara Hepworth, a sort of Bath bun in creamy marble. That had a couple of holes in it as well. After looking around furtively to make sure I wasn't seen I ran a hand round one of the holes. It was a rather pleasant sensation, like popping your tongue into a Polo mint.

From the Tate I went to see Mu Richardson at her little house off Eaton Square, hoping for a coffee. I had telephoned earlier so I knew I was expected. Unfortunately Mu had lost the keys to the front door. After ten minutes of grimacing at each other through a slit of glass we both gave up. She showed me, with a despairing shrug, a tray of porcelain eggs – presumably to demonstrate the key wasn't among them. She called out that she would telephone the police but that she knew it would be mid-afternoon before they would come. So then to the Albery Theatre to collect tickets for *Britannicus*, handed through the box-office grille by a sweetly smiling girl who had disfigured herself with a large silver stud jammed into her chin. At first glance I thought, 'I wonder if she realizes she needs a hand-kerchief.'

Then to a shop where, for twenty years, I have bought my supply of long-lasting candles and their clever copper containers. A very charming and would-be helpful assistant told me, with regret, that they had discontinued the line. 'There is no demand for them.' Except from me, it appears. How often, in recent years, have I heard that said of something really good and useful.

It was a busy day. Luckless with candles I went to the V & A to see the Grinling Gibbons exhibition. Glorious workmanship but somehow uncomfortable when not in its proper setting. Also, I have to admit, I am a bit nauseated by his endless entanglement of dead animals and birds. Nature should be depicted living, not dead.

Eileen Atkins and I met at the theatre and I tripped nastily at the bottom (uneven) step into the stalls and went hurtling, knees bent in a Groucho Marx run as if in pursuit of Mrs Hackenabush, and finally grabbed at a mink coat a lady had rashly thrown over our seats. Much breathlessness, together with irritation at a theatre I love and outrage at the price of the programmes. Then I settled down to be a bit bored by Racine. Eileen enjoyed herself on the whole and Sam Beazley, who was two rows behind us, was full of enthusiasm. It must be superb in French, from the way people talk, but Racine in translation means nothing to me; in fact I would rather hear it in sonorous, incomprehensible French alexandrines and make brave attempts at the meaning. When it comes down to it I know that Molière and Feydeau are the only French playwrights I can thoroughly relish. *Britannicus* was well done but I spent quite a lot of time watching the tropical fish in two great tanks on one side of the stage. I must have missed the point; that is if they were ever referred to, which I doubt. Eileen asked me how I thought the fish spent their time when not on stage. Quick as a flash of a fin, 'At Sheekeys,' I said. Sheekeys fish restaurant has just been refurbished and is not twenty yards from the Albery stage door. Barbara Jefford appeared from time to time, impressively, and as her hair-do suggested Agatha Christie's Miss Marples I had hopes she might solve the fish-tank mystery for me; but no, she had other things on her mind.

The Albery, which to me is always in my heart as the New Theatre (Sir Bronson Albery, who was the licensee, also ruled Wyndhams and the Criterion) was famous for being immaculately kept and beautifully managed. To the best of my recollection I have appeared there a dozen times, from my first part (Osric in Gielgud's 1934 *Hamlet*) and other very subsidiary characters, to finally swanning around playing the lead; so it has always felt more like home to me than any other theatre.

Before I was a professional actor I would sometimes walk through the courtyard formed by the backs of the New and Wyndhams theatres, particularly when I guessed the scene-dock to the New was likely to be open, with sets for the next show being lowered to the dark flooring of the stage. There was a certain fusty smell of canvas, size and freshly sawn wood which I found intoxicating. The gluey smell of size I find nauseating and usually too pervasive, but in those heady days it was almost a perfume.

Sam Beazley, Eileen and I stood chatting for a few moments outside the theatre after seeing *Britannicus*. Sam's eyes were screwed up and nearly closed, in a way he has when cogitating, but I am sure I know what was going through his head. We had shared a dressing-room – was it No. 11 or No. 14? – in that same theatre sixty-four years ago and long forgotten things were resurrecting themselves for each of us. We both read *The Turn of the Screw* at the same time, I remember, and scared ourselves silly with masks, made by Motley, which we carried before our faces in the 'Mouse Trap' scene in *Hamlet*. Mine suggested the evil Quilp. We used to clatter noisily down the stone stairway until we reached the imperative SILENCE painted in great letters over the heavy door which led to the stage. From there on it was groping in semi-darkness until we strode, not with much confidence, into the blinding lights. On stage Gielgud's thrilling voice was throbbing away or he was quietly mouthing other actors' lines while they were speaking. I realize now that Sam and I were not much more important than the *Britannicus* tropical fish.

Looking up at the dressing-room windows of the Albery I see in my mind's eye and hear one or two things from long ago. I see, for instance, the vast woolly costume which George Devine wore when he played the bear in André Obey's *Noah* hanging out of a window to dry after hot summer matinées. (The whiff of this inside the building was carried on the lightest wind.) And I hear the clicking of swords, or rather, foils, not from the stage but from the topmost corridor where two or three of us who had nothing much to do practised fencing. For a short time I became an enthusiastic swordsman and took lessons in épée once a week from the very French and excitable Captain Felix Gravé and later from the more solid Gabriel Toyne, who was a much sought-after arranger of fights. Gravé charged, quite rightly, for attendance at his Kensington salon but Toyne gave his services free to the young. Eventually the dressing-rooms below complained of our racket and mock shouts of '*touché*' and we were obliged to put up our bright swords and rusty foils.

Then there was the middle-aged small-part actor in *Romeo and Juliet* in whom the whole company took an anxious interest after he informed some of us that he had been rigidly costive for ten days. When John G. heard of this he cast a very fearful eye at the poor man when he made his next entrance. It was, of course, an exit he was really seeking. To my shame I used to speculate what horrors might happen if movement came on his late night, corridor-less, train back to Croydon. Oh, there wasn't much we didn't know about each other. For all our foibles, problems and gossip I think we were mostly fond of each other.

It was oddly disturbing to stand outside in the cold for such a brief time and be confronted with all that and much more.

★

The word retirement doesn't appeal but states a fact I faced up to about three years ago. It is indecent to shuffle on in one's eighties, hoping for the sympathy of a sentimental audience, knowing one's capacity to learn is as full of holes as a dented colander and one's energy has been used up before the curtain rises or the camera turns. I have seen too many old and gifted actors cause acute embarrassment and twice I have witnessed them wet themselves from fear, once on the stage and once when filming. To see an old man, once admired as a fine comic actor, standing, shaking with nerves as his trousers darkened and he flooded the floor, is one of the most painful sights I have ever witnessed. 'Christ!' said the famous film director, to get a laugh, and then, showing no pity or concern, walked away with contempt. I am not going to risk any of that. My compulsion for the limelight is not all that strong; besides, pride played a part in my decision to retire – I don't wish to be seen as I am now when I know there was something better on offer thirty years ago. A sticker could be pasted across a poster of my life, 'Cancelled, through circumstances outside his control,' and I wouldn't object.

Unless something very untoward happens to us all I have enough (just about) in the bank to live out my days fairly comfortably and leave a drib or a drab to my family; I see no reason to fret unnecessarily. My life has been enjoyable and basically content; the rewards I have received, both professionally and privately, have been undeserved and surprising. If, God forbid, I am struck gravely ill in my last days, I pray I won't have the effrontery to complain; after such largesse having been poured on me for decades that would be outrageously ungrateful. An unhappy childhood and adolescence? Yes, it could be judged as such, except that I think the young accept their own lives as the norm. If I have one regret (leaving aside a thousand failings as a person, husband, father, grandfather, great-grandfather and friend – and my lazy, slapdash, selfish attitude as an actor) it would be that I didn't take the decision to become a Catholic in my early twenties. That would have sorted out a lot of my life and sweetened it.

In 1945 I was given by an Anglican priest a copy of Dom Cuthbert Butler's *Western Mysticism*. Butler had been an abbot of Downside. Whether I read it all I can't remember but I certainly dipped around in it, as I was interested in such things. Yesterday I came across it again and decided it might make good Advent reading at bedtime; so blowing off the dust I took it to my room. In his chapter on St Augustine I find marked a footnote, a quotation from the fourteenth-century hermit and mystic Richard Rolle: 'I wot not in what manner, I felt in me the noise of song, and received the most liking heavenly melody which dwelt with me in my mind.' He must have thought it the singing of angels or the music of the spheres and that somehow, in actual bodily experience, he had brushed against the Godhead, so to speak. Such elevated joy is certainly not for me in this world, and probably not in the next, but I love knowing it exists for some. I have never detected any of these holy men in fabrication.

Last night on TV there was another one of David Attenborough's marvellous programmes from his *The Life of Birds* series. It seemed to me that the music of the spheres had inspired the courtship dance of the western grebe. A couple of them were shown joyfully and solemnly water-skiing side by side somewhere in America. They literally ran on the water, confronted each other, dived and ran again in perfect harmony. It was the most beautiful display I have ever seen. Almost as moving, in a very static way, was footage of a male and female albatross sitting closely side by side and gently preening each other with their huge formidable beaks. The gentleness shown by great strength is always wilting. Those albatrosses had seen a thing or two, no doubt, and heard heavenly choirs perhaps as they glided for thousands of miles across the southern oceans. They looked loving and wise. The anguish of Coleridge's Ancient Mariner for having killed one struck me with a renewed horror.

That, and a light-hearted feeling of music in the air, completed my day. The music that whirled in my head was not the angelic sort but the endlessly repeated rhythm of Cole Porter's 'We open in Venice'.

When I finally switched off the bedside light I found my thoughts were not of a great mystical experience but of how I had managed to make such rubbish of Delia Smith's instructions on how to poach an egg. Heaven knows I patiently watched tiny bubbles forming on the bottom of the pan, and was prepared to whisk it off the heat at the first sign of boiling, and I treated the eggs with cautious respect, but the result was a wishy-washy nonsense that had to be tipped into the dogs' bowls. It was much the same with Merula's attempt at D. S.'s toad-in-the-hole and something else which was unrecognizable as well as inedible. No blame is being ladled on to Delia Smith; we just need her sunny kitchen, those lovely working surfaces and all those gleaming pots and pans. Perhaps, too, we would do better with a stove which wasn't encrusted with yesterday's spillings. Years ago she taught me, in one of her books, how to boil an egg, for which I am eternally grateful; though I must say I still hold my breath when I give it the first smack with a spoon – is it going to be too runny or even hard-boiled?

One good thing about making a hash of cooking dinner is that you go to bed on a light stomach. What dreams may come – ah, that is a different matter and must give us pause.

In a book of casual reminiscences called *Blessings in Disguise*, published thirteen years ago, I quoted the last three lines of *Love's Labour Lost* and the effect they had on me as spoken by that extraordinary actor, Ernest Milton.

> The words of Mercury
> Are harsh after the songs of Apollo.
> You, that way: we, this way.

They are my favourite lines about being an actor. I went on from that quote to add, 'The small hairs on the back of my head stirred: he had put a great gulf between audience and players; a gulf which would widen as the curtain fell, the lights went out and the auditorium and stage would be empty even of ghosts.'

Tonight I feel that gulf, almost palpably. In the darkness I can only point out to you −

THE NEAREST AVAILABLE EXIT

Index

Index